WOMEN AND LABOUR MARKET POVERTY

by Morley Gunderson
and Leon Muszynski
with Jennifer Keck

June 1990

Canadian Advisory Council on the Status of Women

Prepared for the
Canadian Advisory Council on the Status of Women
P.O. Box 1541, Station B
Ottawa, Ontario
K1P 5R5

This book was commissioned by the CACSW. This document expresses the views of the authors and does not necessarily represent the official policy of the CACSW.

Available free of charge from the
Canadian Advisory Council on the Status of Women
by quoting No. 90-E-164
(The Council reserves the right to limit quantities)

Canadian Cataloguing in Publication Data

Gunderson, Morley, 1945-

Women and labour market poverty

Issued also in French under title: Vivre ou survivre?
Includes bibliographical references.
ISBN 0-662-17366-X
DSS cat. no. LW31-32/1990E

1. Poor women — Canada. 2. Women — Employment — Canada. 3. Women — Canada — Economic conditions. 4. Poverty. I. Muszynski, Leon. II. Keck, Jennifer, 1954- . III. Canadian Advisory Council on the Status of Women.

HC120.P6G86 1990 339.4'6'0971 C90-098624-7

TABLE OF CONTENTS

LIST OF TABLES

LIST OF FIGURES

ACKNOWLEDGEMENTS

Special appreciation is owed to our interviewees across Canada who gave their time and effort to this study. They were honest and open, and the information they provided was very useful to us as well as making the work more interesting and real. Jennifer Keck, who travelled across Canada and conducted all the interviews, also organized the interview material and prepared the profiles for use throughout the book. We would like to express our appreciation to Ken Battle of the National Council of Welfare for his generous support in kind and in spirit. We would also like to thank Prem Khosla and Bill Bradley of Health and Welfare Canada for technical assistance. Several anonymous reviewers provided very useful and constructive comments on the first draft of the manuscript. Pat Parisi-Smith assisted in the word processing under very strenuous deadlines. Finally, we would also like to thank the staff of the Canadian Advisory Council on the Status of Women as well as the Council's Economic Development Committee for their continued interest and support.

Morley Gunderson
Leon Muszynski

Introduction

Most people in Canada believe that anyone who is willing to work can earn a decent living. Having a job is equated with living well; not having a job is equated with being poor. The reality is not so simple. In fact, 1.3 million people in this country work either part-time or full-time in the labour market and are poor. Of this group (often termed "the working poor"), 383,000 people work full-time for the entire year and are still poor.

In Canada, having a job is better than not having a job, but it is no guarantee of an adequate income. Many jobs simply do not pay enough to keep families, or even individuals, out of poverty — even if they work full-time throughout the year. The increasing number of part-time and seasonal jobs in the labour market as well as continued high unemployment have made it difficult for many people in this country to earn an adequate annual income from employment.

Women are more likely to be poor than are men. Much of women's poverty is linked to the labour market; because they experience low wages and unstable employment, their incomes are lower than men's. But women's poverty is also associated with numerous other factors, especially their unpaid domestic and child-care work as mothers and wives.

It is now well known that women experience discrimination in pay and job opportunities and are segregated in low-paying occupations and industries. Research on women's inequality in the labour market has been critically important in developing strategies to alleviate discrimination and inequality in employment, even if the policies adopted have not had much impact to date.

This book examines the problem of working poverty in Canada with a special focus on women. Women's poverty is a complex problem, with many causes and solutions. Although we have a significant understanding of the nature of poverty in Canada, including women's poverty, we do not yet have a clear idea of the relationship between women's poverty and women's labour market experience. Nor do we have a comprehensive policy plan aimed at solving the problem of poverty among women participating in the labour market. This book is an attempt to fill that void.

The five chapters in Part One constitute the theoretical, descriptive, and analytical sections. Policy solutions to women's poverty in the labour market are examined in Part Two (chapters six and seven), the Summary and Conclusion, and Authors' Proposals For Action: An Agenda For Reform.

Included throughout the text are quotations from interviews with working poor women from across Canada. The interviews were conducted as part of the study and provided useful qualitative data, the human face, in addition to the statistical treatment of the problem. Appendix 1 includes a brief description of the method used in selecting and conducting the interviews.

PART ONE: THEORY, DESCRIPTION, AND ANALYSIS

Chapter 1: Women and Poverty

WOMEN AND POVERTY IN CANADA

There were 2.8 million poor adults in Canada in 1986, representing 13.9% of the adult population.[1] The probability of being poor if you are a woman is much higher than if you are a man, evidenced by the fact that women make up 51.1% of the adult population but they constitute 58.7% of the poor.[2] Looked at another way, 16% of women are poor and 11.7% of men are poor (Table 1.1).

TABLE 1.1: Poverty by Sex, Canada, 1986

Category	Both Sexes		Female		Male	
	N (000s)	%	N (000s)	%	N (000s)	%
Adult population	19,807		10,113		9,695	
Distribution by sex		100.0		51.1		48.9
All poor	2,758		1,619		1,139	
Distribution by sex		100.0		58.7		41.3
Incidence (% of pop.)		13.9		16.0		11.7

Source: Tabulations by Analytical Services, Health and Welfare Canada on Statistics Canada, Survey of Consumer Finances, Public Use Micro-data Tape: Incomes of Individuals, 1986.

These figures represent people in Canada who are economically deprived — people who don't have enough to live on. Poor people are more likely to suffer from a range of problems: inadequate housing, poor health, inadequate nutrition, and the inability to enjoy the benefits of living in an affluent society. The existence of poverty amidst plenty should be considered an embarrassment for a society that has the means to provide a fairer distribution of its abundant resources.

Although the percentage of the total population living in poverty decreased from 14.6% in 1971 to 13.9% in 1986, the actual number of poor people increased by 63.2% (Table 1.2). Over this period the number of women living in poverty increased by 110.3% while the number of men living in poverty increased by only 23.8%. All of the increase in women's poverty, relative to men's poverty, occurred in the 1970s. In 1971 women made up 45.6% of those in poverty; by 1981 they had become 60.3% of the poor. From 1981 to 1986 the proportion of those in poverty who were women declined slightly to 58.7%.

TABLE 1.2: Poverty by Sex, Canada, Selected Years, 1971-1986

	1971		1977		1981		1984		1986		Increase
	(000s)	%	(000s)	%	(000s)	%	(000s)	%	(000s)	%	1971-86
Both sexes											
All poor	1,690		2,180		2,611		3,086		2,758		63.2%
Incidence		14.6		15.1		14.1		16.1		13.9	
Women											
All poor	770		1,160		1,574		1,810		1,619		110.3%
Incidence		16.9		18.0		16.6		18.4		16.0	
Distribution (% of all poor)		45.6		53.2		60.3		58.7		58.7	
Men											
All poor	920		1,030		1,037		1,276		1,139		23.8%
Incidence		13.3		12.9		11.4		13.6		11.7	
Distribution (% of all poor)		54.4		46.8		39.7		41.3		41.3	

Note: 1971 data uses 1969 LICO (low income cut-offs) base; 1977 to 1986 data uses 1978 LICO base. Numbers may not add up due to rounding.

Source: Tabulations by Analytical Services, Health and Welfare Canada and Statistics Canada on Statistics Canada, Survey of Consumer Finances, Public Use Micro-data Tape: Incomes of Individuals.

Women have always had a higher likelihood of being poor than have men; in 1971, 16.9% of women were poor compared to 13.3% of men (Figure 1.1). But the phenomenal rise in the relative importance of women's poverty in the 1970s signalled an important change in the social status of women. This phenomenon has been referred to as the feminization of poverty (Figure 1.2).

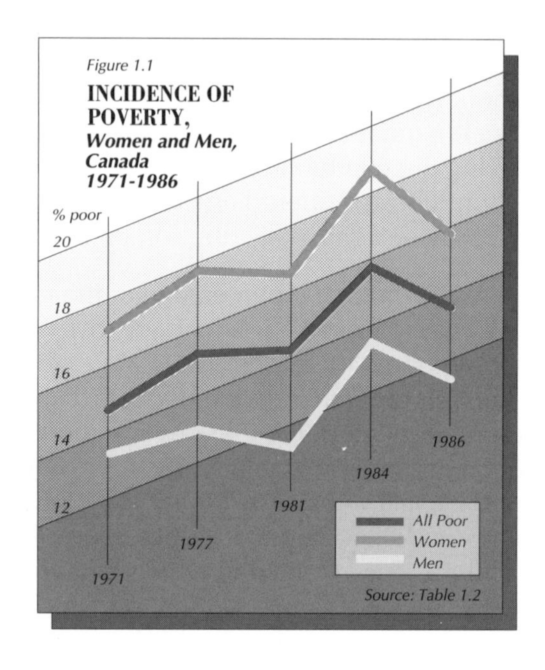

The term "feminization of poverty" was first used by Diana Pearce in 1978 to describe a basic contradiction that was emerging in the United States (and Canada) over the 1970s.[3] Women were entering the labour force in increasing numbers, they were the supposed beneficiaries of affirmative action policies and strategies, and they were making significant inroads in the professions. Yet the number of women in poverty was also increasing, and at a much greater rate than for men.

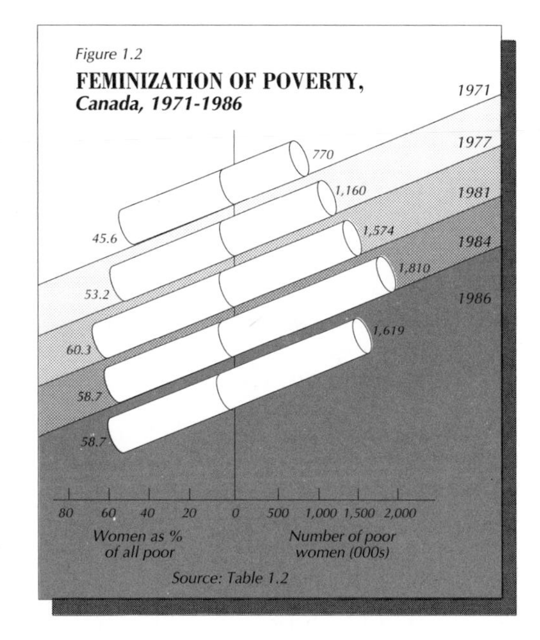

Analysts of the feminization of poverty have emphasized that the causes of women's poverty differ in many ways from the causes of men's poverty. The poverty of individual men most often can be linked directly to the labour market, through inadequate wages for certain jobs or through the lack of employment. In contrast, the poverty of women is more complex. It is related to dynamics in the labour market such as the inadequate wages generally received by **women as a group**[4] and their systemic lack of access to well-paid employment.[5]

> " *. . . you get a little depressed when you can't do some things like have coffee with a friend . . . invite people over . . . or buy fruit for the kids . . . especially when both of you are working full-time and can't afford nothing . . .*
>
> *Married retail clerk, Saskatchewan* "

But women's poverty also springs from the complex interplay of factors such as divorce and separation and their unique roles as mothers, homemakers, caregivers, and nurturers. These social factors place limitations on the paid work that women have been offered or permitted to do, and they are one explanation given for the discriminatory practices of employers. This study focuses primarily on women, poverty, and the labour market. But any study of women and poverty must begin with an understanding of women's roles in society and how these roles shape their experience in the labour market.

THE CONCEPT AND MEASUREMENT OF POVERTY

> *. . . No one has much money in the community where I come from . . . I guess you would call us poor . . . but I never felt that way on the reserve . . . I came into the city to get a job . . . but I feel poverty here . . . things are more expensive . . .*
>
> *Aboriginal single mother, social service worker, Saskatchewan*

Before we begin, it is useful to define poverty — the central concept used in this study — and to discuss some of the limitations of this concept for understanding the economic deprivation of women. For most people, poverty connotes low incomes and extreme hardship. Few would deny that someone without enough money to purchase the basic necessities of food, shelter, and clothing is poor. But what are the basics required in our society, and how much is adequate? Are telephones, televisions, and vacations basic necessities? Requirements also vary with location, type of work, and family structure. Food costs, for example, may be very different for people in rural areas if they can produce and process a large part of their own food requirements. Similarly, because of shared housing costs — a substantial component of anyone's budget — two people sharing the same household usually will not require as much income as two people living alone.

> *. . . right now we are going without fruit and we all love fruit . . . we go buy groceries and you think, well, I guess we really don't need this or that and just leave it for now . . . each month it seems like we are 'leaving' more and more . . . even with both of us working . . .*
>
> *Married retail clerk, Saskatchewan*

There is a large degree of subjectivity inherent in the everyday use of the concept of poverty. For example, although some people with few resources consider themselves poor, other people similarly situated do not consider themselves poor even though their incomes fall below widely used standards. As well, some people feel their everyday hardship would not be considered poverty by many people who have it much easier. As a result, social scientists have developed methods of measuring economic hardship. The most commonly accepted method is to specify a level of income[6] required by a person or a family in order to live adequately in a given place. If income falls below this level, the person or family would be considered poor. This is called a low income cut-off or poverty line.

We have adopted the most commonly used standard for measuring poverty in Canada, Statistics Canada's low income cut-offs (LICOs), 1978 base,[7] sometimes referred to as the "official poverty line"[8] (see Appendix 2). LICOs vary by family size and by population size of area of residence and are adjusted annually to reflect the change in the consumer price index. The LICOs for 1986, the year of analysis for this study, are listed in Table 1.3.

TABLE 1.3: Poverty Lines/Low Income Cut-offs, Canada, 1986

	Population Size of Area of Residence				
Family Size	500,000 and Over	100,000-499,999	30,000-99,999	Less Than 30,000	Rural
1 person	$10,651	$10,116	$ 9,490	$ 8,774	$ 7,877
2 persons	14,053	13,339	12,445	11,546	10,295
3 persons	18,799	17,815	16,650	15,488	13,785
4 persons	21,663	20,588	19,246	17,903	15,936
5 persons	25,243	23,902	22,290	20,768	18,531
6 persons	27,571	26,049	24,349	22,647	20,231
7 persons	30,347	28,735	26,856	24,975	22,290

Source: Statistics Canada, *Income Distributions by Size in Canada, 1986* (Ottawa: 1987), p. 34.

The Statistics Canada LICOs were chosen as the study's poverty definition for several reasons. First, because the Statistics Canada standard is the most widely used poverty standard in Canada, its credibility is well established. Second, it falls roughly in the middle range compared to other poverty lines.[9] Finally, the particular survey micro-data tapes that we favoured for our analysis already had the 1978 base LICO coded as a standard variable. As with most other studies, we use the terms low income cut-offs and poverty lines synonymously.

PROBLEMS WITH POVERTY LINES

> “ *. . . one thing about welfare . . . we might be poorer now than before my husband left . . . but at least I know that there is money coming in regularly . . . and I don't have to worry about him spending it all after work . . .*
>
> *Divorced mother with two children,*
> *works part-time and collects social assistance,*
> *Nova Scotia* ”

Poverty lines are not perfect indicators of economic deprivation. For example, Statistics Canada's LICOs are based on family income requirements. The family, for purposes of poverty analysis, is defined as an economic family.[10] All family-based measures of economic deprivation assume economic equality within the family,[11] i.e., it is assumed that each individual's income in the economic family is pooled with the income of other family members and that all family members have equal access to total family income. It is also assumed that the consumption of goods bought with family income is equal by all family members. These assumptions are largely unverified.[12]

Although little research has been carried out on the income status of individuals within families, some research indicates that we cannot assume that the distribution of income and consumption within families is always equal. Evidence from Britain and Australia indicates that women who live in families where the total income may be adequate are individually deprived because they do not control family resources or have adequate personal spending money.[13] Unfortunately, the available Canadian survey data do not identify cases where family members are living in poverty as individuals even though they are part of an economic family with adequate overall income. Nor is there consensus on the need to develop an income standard for individuals within families as well as for the family unit. We acknowledge that, in using the conventional family-based concept of poverty, it appears as though we assume implicitly that women in non-poor families are not economically deprived. This is an assumption we do not necessarily hold; we acknowledge that the concept of poverty used here undoubtedly hides individual poverty within the family. The difficult problem of measuring intra-family income distribution merits additional research.

Another problem with LICOs is that they are expressed in terms of **annual** income requirements. This does not take into account monthly fluctuations in income. Individuals or families could have severe income problems in one or more months of the year, despite a total annual income above the poverty line. Monthly fluctuations in income were identified in our interviews as an important aspect of the experience of hardship; poverty standards based on annual income do not identify this reality.

WOMEN AND ECONOMIC INDEPENDENCE

Traditionally, women's work roles in the domestic or informal economy were related to childrearing, housekeeping, caring for sick and elderly family members, and community activities. This work has been carried out with little recognition and no financial reward. Estimates of the financial contribution of current household production to the Canadian economy range from 32% to 59% of the Gross National Product.[14] The economic value of women's household work is also addressed in a portion of the scholarly feminist literature on women's domestic labour.[15] Traditionally, men worked for wages in the formal economy; women as wives often had no paid work and were dependent on husbands for financial support. This dependency relationship has changed significantly over the past several decades.

Women have entered the formal economy in unprecedented numbers in the past fifty years. In 1931, 19.7% of all women in Canada were participating[16] in the labour market; the rate increased to 29.5% in 1961, 51.7% in 1981, and 55.1% in 1986 (Table 1.4). In contrast, the male participation rate declined over the same period, from 87.5% in 1931 to 76.7% by 1986.

TABLE 1.4: Labour Force Participation Rates of Adults (over 15 years), by Sex and Marital Status, Canada, 1931-1986

	Men	Women			
	All	All	Married	Single	Other
	%	%	%	%	%
1931	87.5	19.7	3.5	43.8	21.3
1941	85.8	20.7	4.5	47.2	17.3
1951	83.8	24.1	11.2	58.3	19.3
1961	77.7	29.5	22.0	54.1	22.9
1971	77.3	39.4	37.0	53.5	26.5
1981	78.4	51.7	50.5	64.6	35.1
1986	76.7	55.1	56.1	66.1	35.3

Source: Adapted from Margrit Eichler, *Families in Canada Today* (Toronto: Gage, 1988), pp. 54 and 192.

This growth in women's labour force participation was particularly dramatic for married women. In 1931 only 3.5% of married women were labour force participants. Married women, especially those with young children, were just not expected (and, in some cases, permitted) to have paid employment. During the 1960s this began to change, and in the 1970s married women entered the labour market in such large numbers that by the 1980s the majority were labour force participants. Even more striking is that 56% of women with children under the age of three were in the labour force in 1986, and 66% of these were employed full-time.[17]

The many reasons for increased labour force participation by women include:

- the increased demand for female employees created by strong growth in service sector jobs, many of which are extensions of the kind of work women do in the home (e.g., nurses, waitresses, social services workers);
- the growth in the number of part-time jobs, giving women flexibility to work for pay as well as to work in the home;
- declining fertility, which means that women have fewer children and thus carry out child-care responsibilities for shorter periods of time;

- rising unemployment, which means that the incomes of husbands are no longer as secure as they were in the past;
- the financial demands associated with purchasing housing and other goods in a consumer society;
- increases in women's educational attainment and potential earning power; and
- the increasing, although inadequate, availability of child care.

More women have entered the labour force because their labour is needed by burgeoning service industries and because families increasingly need more than one earner to maintain adequate standards of living. As we explore in Chapter Five, a variety of economic changes have reduced the ability of some men to maintain a family on one paycheque. The cost of housing, particularly in Canada's urban centres, makes it almost essential for a family to have at least two earners. Women's earnings play an important role in maintaining overall family income. In 1961, 65% of all families in Canada were traditional one-earner families where the husband was the breadwinner and the wife was the homemaker. By 1986 only 12% of families were one-earner couples, while slightly over half of all families had both spouses in the labour force (Table 1.5). The two-earner family is now the norm; the one-earner family is the exception.

TABLE 1.5: Family Types in Canada, Selected Years, 1961-1986

	1961	1971	1981	1986
	%	%	%	%
Husband-and-wife families				
One-earner couples (husband only)	65	32	16	12
Two-earner couples (both spouses)	14	36	49	52
Other families	16	23	24	23
Single-parent families	6	9	11	13
Total	100	100	100	100

Source: Figures for 1961, 1971, 1981 from Monica Townson, *Women's Labour Force Participation, Fertility Rates and Implications for Economic Development Policy* (Ottawa: Institute for Research on Public Policy, 1987). The 1986 figures were calculated on the same basis from Statistics Canada, *1986 Census, Families,* Part 2, Table 1 (Ottawa: 1987), cat. no. 93-107, and from Statistics Canada, *Income Distributions by Size In Canada* (Ottawa: 1986), cat. no. 13-207, 1986, p. 80. All figures refer to income recipient families.

> “ . . . sometimes they like to make it sound like women are just working for their career . . . to 'get ahead' . . . that's nonsense . . . you have to work to support your family . . . there is no way that we could support our kids and pay for our house without both of us working . . . it's hard enough as it is . . .
>
> *Married factory worker, British Columbia* ”

It must be emphasized that women seek paid employment in the 1990s for many reasons, just as men do. However, some of these reasons differ from those of men because women have a different history. Traditionally, women have worked without pay at home, in both the production of commodities (e.g., weaving cloth from home-spun wool) and in family care. Now that paid work is often available, many women welcome the opportunity to work for pay. Every woman makes the actual decision to seek a job after considering a variety of factors related to her own circumstances, including:

- the costs and benefits of the available work;
- her need or desire for what the income could provide;
- the psychological benefits of paid work;
- whether she has a steady relationship and the income of her partner;
- her desire to avoid the negative aspects of dependency;
- the degree to which her partner participates in family care, etc.;
- the number of children and their ages and the availability and affordability of child care; and
- her self-concept and her desire or need to maintain social, intellectual, and workplace skills.

SINGLE MOTHERS

Growth in the number of unattached individuals, and especially single parents, is one of the main reasons for the feminization of poverty since the early 1970s. Between 1961 and 1986, single-parent families (82% of which are single mothers with children) increased from 6% of all families to 13% (Table 1.5). In 1971 a slight majority of poor adults lived in couple families with single (unmarried) children (Table 1.6). By 1986 only 30% of poor adults lived in couple families. By contrast, other family types — unattached individuals, single parents, and couple families with no single children — all grew as a proportion of the total population in poverty. In 1986, individuals living in single-parent family units constituted 16.1% of poor individuals, up from 11.2% in 1971.

TABLE 1.6: Changes in the Distribution of Poverty, Adult Individuals by Type of Family Unit in Which They Reside, Canada, Selected Years, 1971-1986

Type of Family Unit	1971	1977	1981	1986
	%	%	%	%
Unattached individual	27.8	37.8	37.1	35.8
Couple with single children	53.3	43.2	30.2	30.0
Single parent with single children	11.2	12.9	13.9	16.1
Couple families with no single children	7.7	6.1	18.8	18.1
Total	100.0	100.0	100.0	100.0

Source: Tabulations by Analytical Services, Health and Welfare Canada and Statistics Canada on Statistics Canada, Survey of Consumer Finances, Public Use Micro-data Tape: Incomes of Individuals, 1986.

The increasing number of single-parent families reflects dramatic changes in the family and in the dependency relationships of women. There are several paths to single parenthood; it can be the result of the death of a spouse, divorce, separation, or the birth of a child to an unmarried non-cohabiting woman. Of these, the first — widowhood — has not increased, while the others have risen dramatically.

In 1966, there were roughly 50 divorces per 100,000 population in Canada. By 1985 this had increased to almost 250 per 100,000. Over the same time, the number of marriages declined although not as much as the increase in divorces. The number of marriages per 100,000 population in Canada fell from a high of 920 in 1972 to 730 in 1985. In addition, more women are choosing to have and keep children outside of marriage or a couple relationship. The number of births to single mothers quadrupled from 14,000 in 1951 to 59,600 in 1985.[18] These are the underlying factors contributing to the growth of female-headed households — one of the most striking social changes occurring in Canada and all industrialized nations over the past twenty years. Because female-headed households in Canada are overwhelmingly poor, the importance of this for an understanding of women's poverty cannot be overstated.

THE POVERTY OF SINGLE MOTHERS

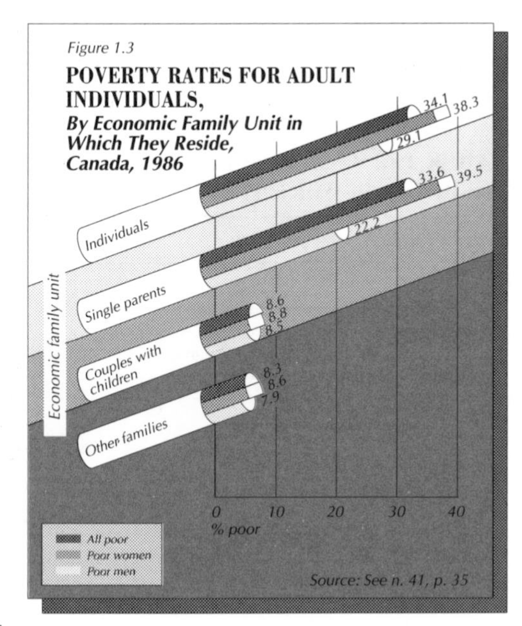

The likelihood of poverty for individuals (women and men) living in single-parent households in 1986 was 33.6% — much higher than the 8.6% rate of poverty for individuals living in couple families (Figure 1.3). The poverty rate for female heads of single-parent families (not shown in Figure 1.3) was even higher, at 44.1%. Poverty among single parents is the major factor underlying the high level of child poverty in Canada. Seventeen per cent of Canada's children — just over one million — are poor, and 35.5% of these live in single-parent families headed by women.[19]

> " *. . . when I split up it was a difficult decision . . . I was raised with two parents . . . when I finally left it was because I thought the situation was bad for the kids . . . now [after the separation] I have no choice but to work . . .*
>
> *Single mother with two children, grocery clerk, Saskatchewan* "

It is important to emphasize that, in 1986, the majority (58.5%) of single parents worked in the labour market; their earnings from this work significantly lowered their incidence of poverty. The rate of poverty for single mothers who worked full-time for the full year was 12.8%. Those who worked part-time or full-time for less than the full year had a poverty rate of 54.2%, while for those who did not work in the labour market the rate was 62.3%. (Data are averages from Figure 1.4.)

The age and number of children also influence the incidence of poverty for single parents, but employment status remains a more important determinant of poverty. Single mothers with more than one child, or with at least one child under seven years of age, were especially likely to be living in poverty (Figure 1.4). However, the incidence of poverty for single mothers working full-time with at least one child under 7 was 25.7%, considerably lower than the 75% poverty rate for similar mothers working part-time, and the 91.2% poverty rate for non-employed single mothers with young children under 7 years of age. Single mothers were at the lowest risk of poverty (11%) if they had one child not under 7 years of age and were employed full-time.

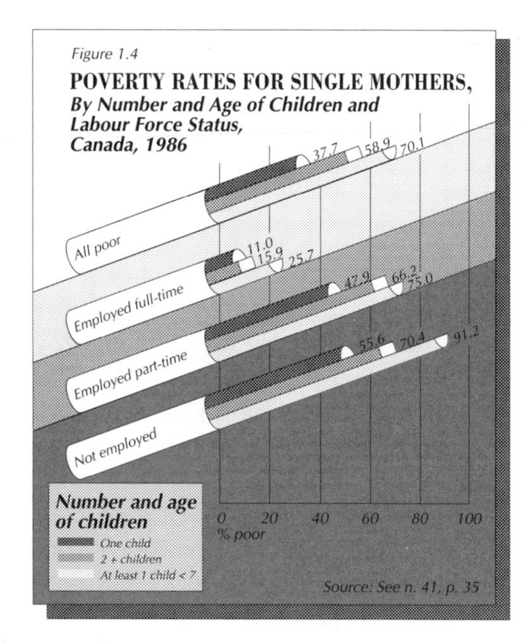

Figure 1.4
POVERTY RATES FOR SINGLE MOTHERS,
By Number and Age of Children and Labour Force Status, Canada, 1986
Source: See n. 41, p. 35

Childrearing places heavy demands on couple families; parenting alone is a monumental task. With few exceptions, the burden of childrearing has always been the responsibility of women. The single mother often shoulders the complete responsibility. She has the bulk of the financial burden for children and she is severely restricted in her ability to earn an adequate living. For example, even if child care is available, a woman with responsibility for children will be restricted in the number of hours she can work, is less able to work shift work, and will require a job with flexibility so that sick children and other circumstances demanding her attention can take priority over her paid work. These are only some of the factors limiting women's ability to work for adequate wages.

While employment does not guarantee that a single mother will escape poverty, it does improve her chances considerably. If the labour market itself offered better employment opportunities for women, the poverty of single mothers could be reduced significantly. But improvements in the labour market through better wages and steady employment are only part of the solution.

. . . I didn't want to work after my eldest was born . . . I wanted to stay home when my kids were small . . . but after we broke up . . . I had no choice . . . I had to work . . .

Single mother, part-time grocery clerk, Saskatchewan ”

The poverty of single parents is a complex phenomenon, in part, because the single-parent population is diverse. In the mid-1980s, one-quarter of single mothers were widowed, and 15% were unmarried or not cohabiting. The majority (57%), however, were separated or divorced, and this looms as a major factor contributing to the poverty of women.[20] The effects of divorce or separation are very different for men and women. Studies in the United States and Canada show that the economic consequences of divorce or separation usually entail a significant reduction in women's standard of living and a significant improvement in that of men.[21] Hence the well-known expression, "a woman is just one man away from poverty".

“ *. . . after the separation it seemed as if I had lost everything . . . he was supposed to help with the mortgage payments but we lost the house . . . I had to move into an apartment with the children . . . he didn't make regular support payments . . . at first I went to welfare . . . part-time work in a dress shop couldn't support us now . . .*

Divorced mother with four children, currently employed part-time with nursing home, trying to leave social assistance, Ontario ”

Overall, the incomes of single mothers averaged about $25,000 in 1986, compared to about $44,000 for husband-wife families with children.[22] The vast majority of dissolved marriages or cohabiting unions with dependent children results in women acquiring custodial responsibility for their children. In theory, women should receive maintenance payments or at least child support from their estranged husbands. In practice, only about 65% of custodial parents are awarded something for their children, and these payments are generally extremely low. Even if awards are adequate, many spouses default on their obligations. Despite recent efforts to improve the enforcement of court-awarded maintenance and child support by garnisheeing wages and even income tax refunds and transfer payments, problems with child support remain. Research in the United States indicates that child support enforcement policies may be effective in reducing welfare program costs, but they do not have a major impact in reducing poverty or the welfare dependency of single mothers.[23] One reason is that some non-custodial parents simply do not have the economic resources themselves to provide adequate financial support for their children.

The most important source of income for single parents, as for husband-wife families, is earnings from employment. On average, 64% of the total income of single parents is derived from wages and salaries. Nevertheless, a very high proportion of single parents are on welfare. It is estimated that about one-third of all female single parents in Ontario receive assistance.[24] About one-third of Canada's social assistance recipients are single parents and they are all, by definition, poor.[25]

RHONDA
(Nova Scotia)

Rhonda is a single mother with two children aged 5 and 18 years. She has a grade 11 education and vocational training in photography. After her second child was born, Rhonda was diagnosed as having muscular sclerosis, a disease that affects the central nervous system. She was unable to work and was forced to apply for social assistance to support her family. Rhonda's health has improved over the past two years and she has been trying to find permanent work and be independent of welfare. She has worked on a number of short-term government-financed projects and has combined unemployment insurance, social assistance, and wages from temporary work. This time her contract is only for six months. As hard as she tries, Rhonda cannot seem to break the cycle of short-term work. With two children to support she cannot take shift work or low-paying jobs in restaurants or stores. Last year her income from transfer payments and work totalled approximately $15,000.

We highlight diversity among single parents because the stereotype of single mothers as welfare recipients reinforces both negative and incorrect generalizations. Research is pointing increasingly to the transitional nature of much of the poverty of single parents, particularly those who become single through separation or divorce.[26] The majority of single mothers will leave welfare, whether through remarriage, finding work, or both. On the other hand, the poverty of an older homemaker following divorce or the death of a spouse is likely to be long-term if she has been out of the labour force for many years and has no independent means of support. Those at high risk of long-term welfare dependency are teenage, unmarried, and uneducated mothers who face multiple barriers to becoming employed. Their poverty is more than just transitional; they need solutions that deal with multiple problems, such as the need for child care, training, and job search skills.

WOMEN IN COUPLE FAMILIES

Not surprisingly, women's labour force earnings also have a significant effect on the incidence of poverty among couple families, even though the overall incidence of poverty among couple families is low by comparison with poverty among other types of families. Families with only one earner face considerably higher poverty rates than two-earner families. In 1986, 9% of two-earner couple families (or 527,000 couples) were poor in Canada. Without the earnings of wives in these families, the rate of poverty of couples would have been 16%, with 438,000 more couples added to the ranks of those considered poor (Figure 1.5). One study found that employed wives lowered the overall incidence of poverty in Canada by 28.1% in 1977.[27]

Figure 1.5

POVERTY RATES FOR COUPLE FAMILIES,
With and Without Wives' Earnings, Canada, 1986

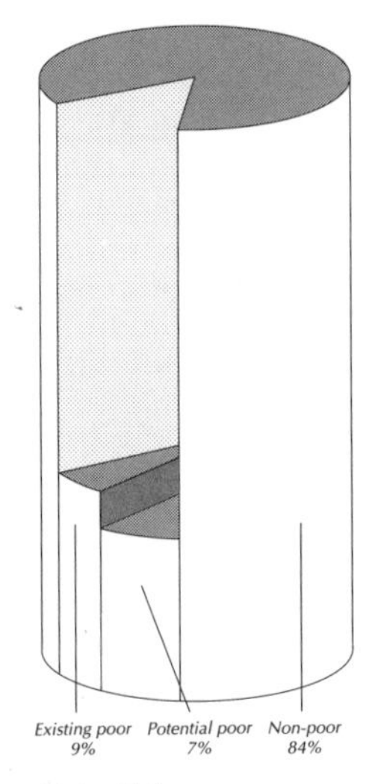

Potential poor = couples who would be poor if wives' earnings were removed

Source: See n. 41, p. 35

Again, the critical issue for understanding women's poverty is that women continue to have primary responsibility for domestic work and childrearing in addition to their role as paid workers. Studies have shown that the presence of children, especially young children, reduces both the likelihood that a woman will be employed, and, for an employed woman, the number of her expected hours of work.[28] However, as with single mothers, and despite the constraints facing women who do have children, paid full-time full-year work in the labour market is the best predictor of lower rates of poverty for women.

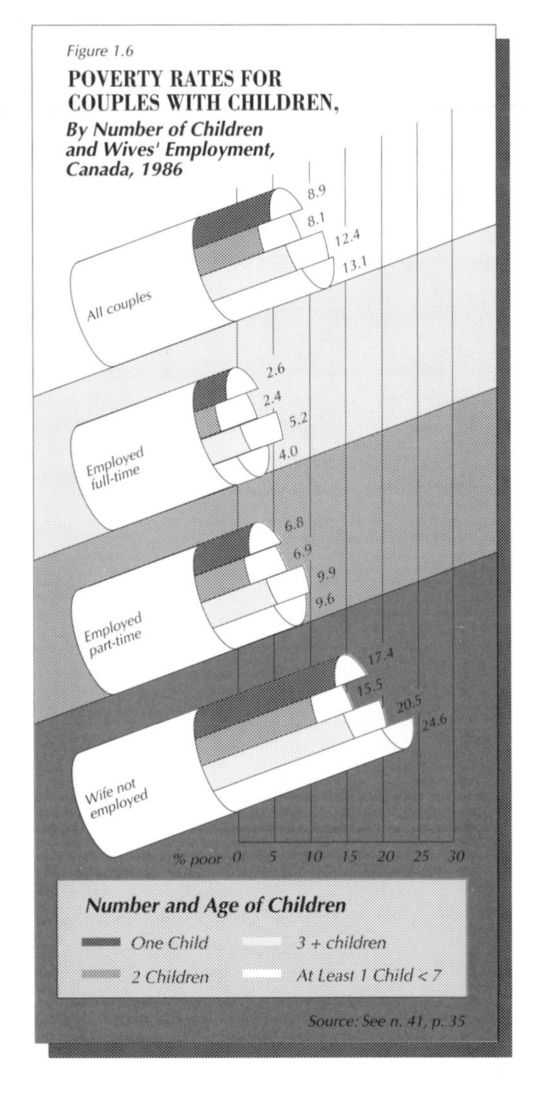

In the case of couples with children where the wife was employed (and where it was assumed that men were employed), poverty rates in 1986 were significantly lower than for couples where the wife did not work in the paid labour force (Figure 1.6). If a wife worked part-time the couple was more than twice as likely to be poor than if she worked full-time; a couple in which a wife who did not work in the labour market was about five times more likely to be poor than a couple in which a wife was employed full-time. However, it is especially important to note that, although the likelihood of poverty increased as the number of children increased (especially if children under seven years of age were present), if the wife had paid employment the family was much less likely to be poor, regardless of the size of the family and the age of the children. This was true both for wives, and, as we have seen, for single mothers.

JOY AND DENNIS
(Saskatchewan)

Joy and Dennis are in their mid-20s, married with two children both under 6 years old. Dennis works shift work at an airport; Joy works part-time evenings as a clerk in a shop. Neither has completed high school. Despite the fact that they both are employed, their combined income places them slightly below the poverty line. Joy would like to work extra hours but she cannot afford to pay child-care fees on her current salary. She relies on friends and relatives to help babysit when Dennis is working evenings. Dennis works overtime to make extra money. Until recently the couple took in boarders to help pay the mortgage. Dennis has made a number of applications for higher-paying positions. Joy would like to attend courses to increase her skills but she is unable to afford tuition or the time it would take from her job or her children. Joy is considering taking children into her home during the day to raise extra money.

FAMILY RESPONSIBILITY CONSTRAINTS

> “ *. . . at the height of the season we're working thirteen, sometimes fifteen hours a day . . . it's difficult when you have children . . . my husband helps out, but he's working long hours too . . . sometimes you just don't get to see the kids . . . I have to put a limit on the overtime I do now . . . I can't manage long hours with the baby . . .*
>
> *Married factory worker,*
> *British Columbia* ”

HOURS OF WORK IN THE LABOUR MARKET AND AT HOME

The dramatic changes in women's labour force participation have also been associated with significant changes in their hours of work, both in the labour market and in the household. On the whole, women work fewer hours **in the labour market** than do men. They work more part-time hours; they work in occupations and industries that conventionally involve shorter hours; they work less overtime. Even when women work full-time in the labour force, they tend to have a shorter (paid) work week than men.[29]

But if women work fewer hours in the labour market, women tend to have a much longer **total** work week, especially when young children are present. Husbands typically spend very little time (less than an hour per day) on housework, including child care.[30] Study after study shows that when wives hold jobs outside the home, their combined workload (known as the double day) is significantly greater than that of their husbands.[31] Moreover, when their wives hold paid jobs, husbands increase their time spent on housework and child care only marginally.[32] This slight increase in the amount of time devoted to housework is almost exactly offset by a reduction in labour market work, so that men's total work week remains almost unchanged.

The household work of wives is reduced by roughly one-half when they also engage in paid employment. As well, their hours of paid employment are not as high as men's. However, the combination of work in the home **and** work in the labour force produces a longer total work week for women. Clearly, wives who work full-time in the labour market have a longer work week than their husbands (48.7 versus 44.1 hours) when both household work and labour market work are considered (Table 1.7).[33] This difference greatly understates the work week if weekends are included, because wives tend to continue their household tasks on the weekend.

Given this unequal division of household tasks when both partners are employed, it is not surprising that absenteeism is higher for females than males in labour market jobs — just as absenteeism is higher for males than females on household jobs! It is also not surprising that women enter certain occupations or restrict their hours of work or the location of their jobs to be compatible with their household work. This is the critical point: the labour market behaviour of females cannot be understood in isolation from their broader role in the family and society at large.

Some women are under considerable pressure to give up their (often lower-paying) jobs or reduce their career aspirations to accommodate their husband's (usually higher-paying) career. Many do so, thereby perpetuating wage and employment inequality in the labour market. Others do not, and often face family tensions as well as social pressures and guilt as a result. Guilt is often related to the societal perception that women working in the labour force have "created a generation of latch-key children". This pressure invariably falls on the wife, not on the husband.

TABLE 1.7: Typical Five-day Work Week (Household plus Labour Market) for Husband and Wife With Child Under 15, by Wife's Labour Market Status, Toronto, 1980

Wife's Labour Market Status	Husband	Wife
	(hours)	(hours)
Non-employed wives		
Housework and child care	5.5	36.3
Labour market work	40.8	0.0
Total work	46.3	36.3
Employed wives (full-time)		
Housework and child care	6.6	16.0
Labour market work	37.5	32.7
Total work	44.1	48.7

Source: Calculated from Canadian Advisory Council on the Status of Women, *Integration & Participation: Women's Work in the Home and in the Labour Force* (Ottawa: 1987), p. 4, which in turn is based on unpublished data from William Michelson, *From Sun to Sun: Daily Obligations and Community Structure in the Lives of Employed Women and their Families* (Towata, New Jersey: Rowan and Allenheld, 1985).

The toll of the double work day on women is considerable and is one of the main reasons underlying inequalities between men and women in the labour market. The problem becomes cumulative as husbands specialize in labour market tasks (thereby acquiring the experience and seniority that enhances their earnings) while wives juggle both household and labour market tasks (thereby adversely affecting their labour market earnings). Employers may bypass women for promotion or place them in dead-end jobs where turnover does not matter, in anticipation of child-related career interruptions.[34] Women may thereby be penalized by a stereotype even if they do not have children or do not significantly interrupt their labour force participation to have children.

Dissatisfaction with work time is clearly illustrated in the results of the Survey of Work Reduction conducted by Statistics Canada as a supplement to the June 1985 Labour Force Survey.[35] About one-third of the work force was content with their work time arrangements. Approximately 31% wanted a reduction in their work time (for a corresponding reduction in pay), and approximately 32% wanted an increase (with a corresponding increase in pay). Females tended to prefer the reduction in work time, although the differences were not great for **all** females versus all males (32% and 30% respectively). The greatest preference for work time reductions, however, was among females in the traditional childrearing years (ages 25 to 34) and females with children under five years of age (about 40% of both categories preferred a reduction in their work time). In fact, wanting the extra time to take care of children and household work was ranked as most important by 42% of women, compared to 20% of the men. These findings provide further evidence that differential household responsibilities, especially the care of children, have a dramatic effect on labour market behaviour and hence the incomes of women.

> *. . . they want me to work nights but it's hard . . . I have the kids and they need my time . . . and I can't afford a sitter . . ."*
>
> *Single mother,*
> *employed on job training program as family support worker,*
> *Nova Scotia* ”

There is nothing inherently unjust in the dual role of household and labour market work. What is unjust is that only women have been socially assigned to the role of domestic labourers, and that household labour and child care, both socially necessary tasks, have been undervalued. Many female-dominated jobs (nursing, teaching, and service occupations) are extensions of the kinds of work women do at home. Because women are unpaid when they do similar work in the household, it is easy to see how such work may be undervalued when done in the labour market. And because of their homemaker and childrearing responsibilities, women have been segregated into low-wage, part-time, and insecure jobs.

These issues raise concerns about how to provide support to women who have to integrate work in the home with work for pay, as well as ways to improve the division of household labour. As issues of concern to women, they are more pressing in Canada than in almost any other industrialized country because:

- the increase in female labour force participation has been greater in Canada than in most other developed countries;
- the female participation rate in Canada is still below that of many other industrialized countries; and
- Canada has poorly developed support policies for families with both parents in the labour market.[36] In fact, Canada is quite far behind other industrialized countries in removing barriers that inhibit labour force participation by women.

CHILD CARE AND CHILD-CARE EXPENSES

" *. . . the first thing you have to do is find a good babysitter or daycare . . . most of the time daycare is too expensive . . . there aren't enough subsidized spaces . . . or you don't qualify . . . you put an ad in the paper and just take your chances . . . the first time I had a sitter for my baby I worried about whether or not she was getting fed . . . and you hear lots of stories . . ."*

Single mother with three children, teacher's aide, Saskatchewan "

Given women's child-care responsibilities, the lack of adequate child care becomes an important constraint on their labour market behaviour. Inadequate child care has been noted by numerous studies, government commissions, and task forces. In 1986, the Task Force on Child Care reported that the number of available spaces in licensed child-care centres was substantially below the need.[37] A 1988 report of the National Council of Welfare noted that although 1.9 million children under the age of 13 need some form of care because their parents work or study outside the home, there were only 243,545 licensed child-care spaces in Canada.[38] Most children are in unlicensed or informal child-care arrangements that are often less than adequate.[39]

The inhibiting effect of child-care expenses is an especially important barrier for women who would normally receive low wages in the labour market. A person who works in a paid job and has to pay for child-care expenses, as well as transportation, clothing, and other work-related expenses, is often financially worse off employed than on social assistance. A study by the Social Planning Council of Metropolitan Toronto, published in 1986, concluded that most single mothers in that city would have to find jobs paying $8 an hour, or twice the minimum wage, to be better off than they are on welfare.[40] In our interviews we were struck by the fact that many women held jobs despite the fact that the financial rewards were greater if they did not work. Evidently there is a powerful incentive to work, regardless of the financial disincentives.

LINDA
(Nova Scotia)

Linda is a single parent, divorced with three children. She lives with the two youngest children in a resource-based community in Nova Scotia. She has always worked outside the home but was laid off from her position with a federal Crown corporation two years ago and has been unable to find a permanent position since that time. She did have some savings but was forced to use that money when she was laid off. Her severance pay was applied to expenses for the first six months when she was considered ineligible for unemployment insurance benefits. She was unemployed briefly again last spring but has managed to secure a number of temporary positions as a clerk in the federal public service. Linda completed high school and has attended a number of college courses to upgrade her skills, including computers, French language, and business entrepreneurship. Still, she has been unable to find permanent work. Her current contract has been extended twice but she anticipates being unemployed at the end of the current three-month contract. She finds it impossible to plan ahead but is adamant about not collecting social assistance. Still, she resents the fact that she is ineligible for many of the benefits available to people on social assistance or with lower incomes. She cannot afford formal child care for her youngest child and has no drug or dental coverage.

SUMMARY

In Canada, there are more poor women than poor men, and women are much more likely to be poor than are men.

Between 1971 and 1986 the number of women in poverty increased by 110.3% while the number of men in poverty increased by only 23.8%. All of the relative increase in women's poverty occurred in the 1970s. In 1971 women made up 45.6% of those in poverty; by 1981 they had become 60.3% of the poor. Since the early 1980s this proportion has stabilized at just below 60%.

The majority of women are no longer totally economically dependent on men. Most women are in the paid labour force, and there has been a dramatic increase in divorces, separations, and births to single mothers, all of which have led to a significant increase in the number of single-parent families.

In 1971, the majority of poor adults lived in couple families. In 1986, the majority of poor adults lived as unattached individuals or in single-parent families, the majority of which were headed by women. In 1986, individuals living in single-parent family units constituted 16.1% of poor individuals, up from 11.2% in 1971 and growing.

Women still carry most of the responsibility for domestic work and child care. These responsibilities and the cost of purchasing alternative services, such as child care, act as major constraints on women's ability to have careers, to work sufficient hours for pay, and to have adequate incomes. These constraints are particularly acute for single mothers, and this accounts in large measure for their exceedingly high risk of poverty.

The fact remains that paid work, even with all the barriers facing women in the labour market, appears to be the best ticket out of poverty for women, whether they are single women (with or without children) or members of a couple.

NOTES (Chapter One)

1. These figures refer to the notion of the **incidence of poverty**; that is, the proportion of all people in a particular group who are poor. This is also referred to as the **poverty rate** and is an indicator of the probability of being poor.
2. These figures refer to the **distribution of poverty**, that is, how the poor are distributed across the categories men and women. Distributions can be across any specified category such as age groups, education levels, family status, etc.
3. Diana Pearce, "The Feminization of Poverty: Women, Work, and Welfare", *Urban and Social Change Review*, vol. 2, no. 1 & 2 (1978), pp. 28-36. The claim that this is the first reference to the feminization of poverty is made in Wendy Sarvasy and Judith Van Allen, "Fighting the Feminization of Poverty: Socialist-Feminist Analysis and Strategy", *Review of Radical Political Economics*, vol. 16, no. 4 (1984), pp. 89-110.
4. In global terms, women comprise half of the world's adult population but perform nearly two-thirds of all the work hours, receive only one-tenth of the world's income, and own less than one one-hundredth of the world's property. These United Nations figures are cited in Erica Bell-Lowther, "World Feminization of Poverty: A Conference Report", *The Social Worker*, vol. 53, no. 2 (Summer 1985), p. 70.
5. To be described as participating in the labour force, a person must either be employed or unemployed and have actively looked for work in the past four weeks. Retirees and married women without paid work are not categorized as participating in the labour force.
6. Total income includes all money income that a family makes in one year from wages and salaries, self-employment, investment (including any rental income), government transfers, and pensions or annuities. The level of income referred to as a poverty income is total income before tax.
7. There are basically two ways of defining poverty (and therefore determining a poverty line):
   - having less than an objectively defined absolute minimum — the absolute needs approach;
   - having less than others in society — the relative needs approach.

   Statistics Canada's LICOs are based on the absolute needs approach, but they incorporate a relative standard as well. They are set by determining the income levels where, on average, 58.5% of income is spent on the basic necessities of food, clothing, and shelter. This figure was derived from adding 20% to the national average proportion of income spent on food, clothing, and shelter for all Canadian families. This comes from Statistics Canada's 1978 Family Expenditure Survey which found that the average Canadian family spent 38.5% of its income on these necessities. The addition of 20% is arbitrary, but at least has been used consistently over time. The 58.5% ratio is referred to as the 1978 base.

8. Statistics Canada does not call them poverty lines, nor do they promote their use as such, especially for program or administrative purposes.
9. Of the many poverty lines, the commonly used poverty lines in Canada (other than the Statistics Canada LICOs) are those of the Canadian Council on Social Development and the Senate Committee on Poverty, both of which are higher than the Statistics Canada LICOs. See: Roger Love, "A Note on the Measurement of Poverty in Canada", *Canadian Statistical Review* (June 1984).
10. An **economic family** is a statistical concept meaning any group of people who share a common dwelling and are related by blood, marriage, or adoption. An economic family can also be an unattached individual. An economic family differs from a **household**, which may contain other non-related individuals, such as a boarder or friend, whose income would not be included in the total income of the economic family. A **census family** differs from an economic family in that it consists of parents and single (unmarried) children only, or unattached individuals, but it does not include other relatives such as grandparents, aunts, uncles, or married children who may be living in the same household and sharing income.
11. Margrit Eichler, *Families in Canada Today*, 2nd edition (Toronto: Gage, 1988), p. 127.
12. Another problem relates to the concept of "head" of an economic family, a concept used in the Survey of Consumer Finances, our primary data base. This definition is sexist in that it always refers to the man in a couple family, regardless of the woman's income. A woman can be a head of an economic family if she is unattached or a single parent. Nevertheless, the concept of "head" of an economic family could not be avoided in this report given that it is built into the way that poverty is defined. We sometimes refer to a person in relation to the head of a family, and in a couple relationship the woman is the wife even if the couple is not married, and the man is always the head, even if his wife earns more income.
13. Jan Pahl, "The Allocation of Money and the Structuring of Inequality Within Marriage", *Sociological Review*, vol. 31, no. 2 (1983), pp. 237-262.

14. Lars Osberg, *The Future of Work in Canada: Trends, Issues and Forces for Change* (Ottawa: Canadian Council on Social Development, 1988), p. 4; David Ross, Peter Usher, and George McRobie, *From the Roots Up: Economic Development as if the Community Mattered* (Croton-on-Hudson, N.Y./Ottawa: Bootstrap Press/Vanier Institute of the Family, 1986), pp. 67-68, 87-90.
15. Meg Luxton, *More Than a Labour of Love: Three Generations of Women's Work in the Home* (Toronto: Women's Educational Press, 1980), pp. 18-21, 117-159; Marilyn Waring, *If Women Counted: A New Feminist Economics* (San Francisco: Harper & Row, 1988), pp. 136-138; Margrit Eichler, "The Connection Between Paid and Unpaid Labour", in *Women's Paid and Unpaid Work: Historical and Contemporary Perspectives,* ed. Paula Bourne (Toronto: New Hogtown Press, 1985), pp. 61-78; and Veronica Strong-Boag, "Discovering the Home: The Last 150 Years of Domestic Work in Canada", in *Women's Paid and Unpaid Work,* ed. Bourne, *ibid.*, pp. 35-60. See also: issue of *INSTRAW News,* no. 12 (Summer 1989), which focused on "Women's Work: the Informal Sector".
16. *Supra,* note 5.
17. Monica Townson, *Women's Labour Force Participation, Fertility Rates, and the Implications for Economic Development and Government Policy* (Ottawa: Institute for Research on Public Policy, 1987), p. 44.
18. Maureen Moore, "Women Parenting Alone", *Canadian Social Trends* (Winter 1987), p. 32.
19. National Council of Welfare, *Poverty Profile 1988* (Ottawa: 1988), p. 28.
20. Moore, "Women Parenting Alone", *supra,* note 18, p. 32.
21. Eichler, *Families in Canada Today, supra,* note 11, pp. 249-250.
22. Moore, "Women Parenting Alone", *supra,* note 18.
23. Philip K. Robins, "Child Support, Welfare Dependency, and Poverty", *The American Economic Review,* vol. 76, no. 4 (September 1986), p. 768.
24. Ontario, Ministry of Community and Social Services, Social Assistance Review Committee, *Transitions* (Toronto: 1988), p. 30.
25. See Chapter Seven for an analysis of women and the welfare system.
26. Sheila B. Kamerman and Alfred J. Kahn, *Mothers Alone* (Dover, Mass.: Auburn House, 1988), Chapter Four; and Douglas J. Bersharov and Alison J. Quin, "Not all female-headed families are created equal", *The Public Interest,* no. 89 (1987).
27. Robert Swidinsky, "Working Wives, Income Distribution and Poverty", *Canadian Public Policy,* vol. 9, no. 1 (March 1983), p. 76.

28. Alice Nakamura and Masao Nakamura, "A Survey of Research on the Work Behaviour of Canadian Women", in *Work and Pay: The Canadian Labour Market,* ed. W. Craig Riddell (Toronto: University of Toronto Press, 1985), p. 178.
29. In the Canadian context, these patterns are discussed in Roberta Edgecombe Robb and Morley Gunderson, *Women and Overtime* (Toronto: Ontario Task Force on Hours of Work and Overtime, 1987); and Canada, Commission of Inquiry into Part-time Work (Joan Wallace, Commissioner), *Part-time Work in Canada: Report of the Commission of Inquiry into Part-time Work* (Ottawa: Labour Canada, 1983).
30. Calculated from data given in M. Meissner, E. Humphreys, S. Meis, and W. Scheu, "No Exit for Wives: Serial Division of Labour and the Cumulation of Household Demands", *Canadian Review of Sociology and Anthropology,* vol. 12, no. 4 (1975), pp. 434, 435. The calculations were based on five times the daily work day (given on p. 434) plus two times the day-off work times (given on p. 435).
31. Summarized in Francine Blau and Marianne Ferber, *The Economics of Women, Men and Work* (Englewood Cliffs, N.J.: Prentice Hall, 1986), pp. 125-132. Canadian evidence from the Time Use Pilot Survey of 1981 also indicates that women who work in the labour force spend about twice as much time on child care and house-related work as men who work in the labour force. This is illustrated in Canada, Statistics Canada, *Women in Canada: A Statistical Report* (Ottawa: 1985), p. 19.
32. Joseph H. Pleck, *Working Wives, Working Husbands* (Beverly Hills, Calif.: Sage, 1985), p. 31.
33. Our assessment is that these are conservative estimates of the differences in the amount of time husbands and wives spend on housework, especially as they relate to child care. This is because time devoted to child care is reported as such only when direct care of a child is involved. For example, this averaged only 1.1 hours per day for women who did not work in the labour market and who had a child under 10 years of age. Our judgement is that such women also **indirectly** spend more time in child-care tasks but that these were counted in other time-budget categories, such as reading, driving or walking, visiting, talking or writing, and even relaxing. This would be especially the case for women who also work in the labour market since they spend considerable time in organizing and making arrangements for their children, activities that may not always be reported as child-care time.
34. This phenomenon has been named the "mommy track".
35. Prem Benimadhu, *Hours of Work: Trends and Attitudes in Canada* (Ottawa: Conference Board of Canada, 1987).

36. See: Canada, Task Force on Child Care (Katie Cooke, Chairperson), *Report of the Task Force on Child Care* (Cooke Report) (Ottawa: Status of Women Canada, 1986), Chapter Twelve. See also: Sheila B. Kamerman and Alfred J. Kahn, *Child Care, Family Benefits, and Working Parents: A Study in Comparative Policy* (New York: Columbia University Press, 1981).
37. Canada, Task Force on Child Care, *Report of the Task Force on Child Care, ibid.*, Chapter Three.
38. National Council of Welfare, *Child Care: A Better Alternative* (Ottawa: 1988), p. 3.
39. Canada, Task Force on Child Care, *Report of the Task Force on Child Care, supra*, note 36, pp. 45-47.
40. See: Toronto, Social Planning Council of Metropolitan Toronto, *Living on the Margin* (Toronto: October 1986), p. 115.
41. Tabulations by Analytical Services, Health and Welfare Canada on Statistics Canada, Survey of Consumer Finances, Public Use Micro-data Tape: Incomes of Individuals, 1986.

PART ONE: THEORY, DESCRIPTION, AND ANALYSIS

Chapter 2: Perspectives on Poverty, Women, and the Labour Market

In recent years, increasing attention has been devoted to the analysis of women's poverty and women's inequality in and out of the labour market.[1] These analyses have attempted to shed light on the reasons women are so vulnerable to poverty and why they experience inequality. As we have seen, a central issue is the role of women as mothers and wives. Despite general recognition of the limitations these roles impose on women's ability to earn adequate incomes, there is wide variation in the interpretation of why this is so and what should be done about it.

Acknowledging the risk of oversimplification, we identify two main perspectives on poverty and the labour market: first, market perspectives which include supply side and demand side perspectives; second, political economy perspectives. Supply side or human capital perspectives focus on the characteristics of individuals or families as primary determinants of their poverty. Demand side perspectives focus on the characteristics of society, the economic environment, and the nature of the labour market in which women work. Political economy perspectives, such as feminism, focus on class structures, gender[2] differences, and patriarchy.

MARKET PERSPECTIVES

SUPPLY SIDE PERSPECTIVES

The oldest explanations for the existence of poverty focus on the deficiencies of the poor themselves who are thought to be deprived through their own choice or misfortune. From this perspective, poverty is seen as a way of life resulting from various characteristics of poor people: a lack of motivation to work or pursue more education, family structures such as single parenthood or large families, inadequate skill in interpersonal relations, individual circumstances such as youth or disability, and a lack of job or life skills. The poor are thought to be different from the non-poor and for cultural or social reasons their poverty is perpetuated over time.

Modern sociological and anthropological variations of this approach have attempted to explain low income primarily by reference to cultural or biological variables. One of the most important contemporary representations of the culture of poverty perspective is the literature surrounding the experience of being Black and living in U.S. urban ghettoes.[3] The idea that women's unique ability to give birth determines their roles as mothers, wives, and homemakers is rooted in the ancient theory of biological determinism.[4]

The economic variant of the supply side approach to explaining poverty is human capital theory. The human capital perspective argues that people have low wages because of their personal or human capital characteristics.[5] Human capital theory attempts to link low income or poverty to the "stock of human capital" that each person brings to the labour market. Human capital refers to factors such as education, training, mobility, or labour market information — all of which require a costly investment but yield a return in the form of higher earnings. More extreme versions of this perspective hold that people who are poor or whose incomes are low lack motivation, have a taste for leisure as opposed to income-generating activity, or are present-oriented rather than future-oriented and hence not willing to undertake investments for a future return.[6]

This perspective, often associated with neoclassical economics, alleges that such decisions are often matters of choice by individuals. For example, the argument goes, some women may choose part-time work because it is compatible with their full-time household responsibilities. According to this view, women may also choose to invest less in education and training, on the assumption that these investments in human capital will not pay off in the long run because they will be out of the labour market as homemakers, caregivers, or mothers for lengthy periods in their lives. Some individuals may choose certain lower-paying jobs because they are simply temporary positions or perhaps a stepping stone to higher-paying positions.

The main emphasis of human capital remedies for reducing poverty tends to be on policies that would enhance the human capital (education, training, mobility, and information) possessed by the poor. The critical assumption is that once this is done, jobs would be there, as would opportunities for upward occupational mobility.

> *. . . it is not much different among my friends . . . many have university educations but do not have much money . . . I have a friend who cleans offices . . . she makes $8.00 an hour . . . it's not a great job but it's a high wage . . . another friend works for a youth group and they try to pay higher wages . . . but where else can we work that pays higher? . . .*
>
> *Single, 24-year-old waitress, Quebec*

Recent empirical work on poverty has substantially weakened the "culture of poverty" perspective.[7] Studies of poverty over long periods have found that the population in long-term poverty is a relatively small group. A major study of poverty in the United States found that, between 1969 and 1978, only 2.6% of the population was poor in eight of the ten years, while 24.4% of the population was poor for at least one year in this decade.[8] No similar studies exist in Canada because we lack comparable data, but it is generally believed that a similar dynamic pattern of poverty exists here. Studies of welfare recipients in Ontario have found a comparable pattern of movement on and off assistance. Only 15% of the single parents who began to receive social assistance in Ontario in 1975 remained on assistance in 1984.[9]

Other studies have suggested that the poor are not substantially different from the non-poor. Many of the poor have full-time employment and levels of educational attainment similar to the non-poor. The poor are a diverse group made up of the elderly, children, single mothers, husband-wife families, disabled people, and young men and women who find themselves poor from time to time as a result of a variety of circumstances — separation, divorce, unemployment, a disabling accident, or sickness.

Nor are biological theories credible in their explanation of why women are poorer than men. Biological differences do exist, but these differences do not explain why women are segregated into low-wage jobs in the modern industrial labour market. And technological advances have largely removed the perceived need for sex distinctions based on physical strength.[10]

The human capital perspective of neoclassical economics has a difficult time explaining the existence of discrimination in employment against women as anything other than a marginal aberration. The significant wage differentials between men and women in the same jobs and the occupational segregation of women into low-paying jobs are not well explained by a theory that emphasizes individual choice and individual ability.

LISE AND CAROLE
(Quebec)

Lise is single, 24 years old, and a waitress in a small delicatessen. Carole is single, the same age, and works as a clerk with a cosmetics company on a temporary basis. The two women are friends and share an apartment in a large city. They are university-educated: Lise is two credits short of a Bachelor of Arts degree and Carole has completed her degree. They have had a series of short-term and low-paying jobs as waitresses and office clerks. Lise has worked at the same position for the past four months and makes $4.65 an hour. Carole has had a temporary position for two months but continues to file her cards for an earlier unemployment insurance claim (she does not collect benefits). She is earning $7 an hour, which she considers high relative to the other positions she has been able to get. Both women find themselves in a cycle of low-paying work that is difficult to break. Employers have told them that they need experience, but they cannot find work in a field that requires a university education. Both are making payments on their student loans and cannot afford to work part-time or for lower-paying jobs. Neither has financial support from her parents. While they would both prefer to work at jobs in their respective fields, they see few alternatives to their current situation.

DEMAND SIDE PERSPECTIVES

In contrast to supply side perspectives, the demand side perspective emphasizes the characteristics of the society, and especially labour markets, as principal determinants of incomes. People are poor not so much because they do not have the qualifications that are rewarded in the market, but because society places limits on what individuals can do. The "blame" for poverty shifts from the inadequacies of the individual to the inadequacies of the environments in which people operate.

Idealism is a major sociological tradition used to explain why women are treated differently than men. This theory suggests that women do not have any real limitations on their abilities but are socialized from an early age to choose traditional feminine roles and to limit their own abilities. Men, too, are socialized to treat women as less than capable. It is these ideas about masculine and feminine roles that determine the structure of jobs and the division of labour between men and women in the home and in the workplace.[11] According to this perspective, it is misinformation or incorrect ideas about women that lead to discrimination, inequality and, ultimately, to poverty. Emphasis is placed on the need for education to change stereotyped ideas about women. Measures to change the behaviour of employers, such as anti-discrimination legislation, are also important, together with policies on issues such as child care to remove the structural barriers to female participation in paid employment.

> “ *. . . in this region there are only so many jobs for women . . . stores, restaurants, office clerk . . . there aren't many factories . . . it's all at low or minimum wage . . . women try hard to get jobs in the hospital or with government . . . the wages are higher and there's some security . . .*
>
> *Nursing home worker,*
> *Ontario* ”

The economic variant of the demand side perspective on poverty is often referred to as the dual labour market perspective.[12] According to this view, labour markets are segmented into a variety of non-competing groups. The core or primary labour market consists of higher paying jobs, usually with good working conditions, fringe benefits, and opportunities for promotion and advancement. These are often unionized jobs occupied by males. In contrast, the secondary or peripheral labour market has the opposite characteristics. In addition, the dead-end, low-wage nature of secondary jobs often leads to high absenteeism and turnover, as well as low commitment on the part of workers. Over time the structure and characteristics of jobs have become identified with the individuals most likely to hold those jobs, thus creating a self-perpetuating cycle. The majority of women are concentrated in the secondary labour market.

The dual labour market perspective, while not denying the importance of human capital attributes, redirects the policy emphasis away from enhancing the qualifications of individual workers and toward ensuring that the labour market is able to provide jobs at reasonable wages. This can be done by breaking down the barriers, such as discrimination, that lead to segmented labour markets. Such an approach is consistent with the supply side emphasis on making markets more competitive. However, the segmented labour market perspective is also the basis for advocating policies like affirmative action and equal pay for work of equal value, and for improving jobs through improving wages, even if such policies are not consistent with free market competition.

The dual/segmented labour market perspective does not advocate breaking down all barriers to entry into the primary labour market; many of the barriers afford a desirable degree of protection, albeit only for those in the primary labour market. The higher wages, due process, and seniority protection that comes from unionization, for example, are considered desirable — to be **extended** to the non-union sector, not eradicated. In fact, a major policy thrust of the segmented labour market perspective is to use legislation to **extend** the benefits of the primary labour market into the secondary labour market. This is deemed necessary because workers in the secondary labour market tend to have neither the individual nor the collective bargaining power to achieve these gains. Such legislation can include minimum wage laws, employment standards laws (regulating hours of work, vacations, overtime, maternity and other types of leave, pensions, and termination), health and safety legislation, and wage extension legislation whereby wage rates (often from the union sector) are extended throughout the industry by government decree.

The main contribution of dual labour market theory is the recognition that segmentation of the labour market into non-competing groups means that wages are not clearly related to individual productivity. As such, discrimination is no longer just an aberration; it is a pervasive feature of the labour market. Empirical work on wage discrimination in Canada has revealed an unexplained residual, reflecting wage differences between men and women that cannot be accounted for on the basis of human capital attributes. It is reasonable to assume that much of this difference is the result of discrimination against women. Affirmative action and better wages for low-paid workers are central to the dual labour market approach to solving the problem of poverty.

Demand side theorists emphasize the ideas, the social environment, and especially the jobs that produce poverty rather than the people who are poor. In so doing they have encouraged the development of policies that have contributed to mitigating market-determined inequalities. But as many analysts have concluded, despite the adoption of a wide variety of anti-poverty programs and policies to improve the status of women in the labour market, poverty has not been alleviated, nor has women's disadvantaged position in society been altered significantly. What is not readily explained by demand side theories is **why** structures of inequality exist. Why, for example, are **women** at the bottom of the job hierarchy and concentrated in part-time jobs? On these questions other perspectives have much more to offer.

RUTH
(Nova Scotia)

Ruth is a single mother with two children aged 12 and 10. She lives in a rural single-industry community. She completed grade 11 and has a two-year data processing diploma from a vocational school. She left an abusive husband when her children were young and was forced to rely on social assistance to support her family. She returned to vocational school to upgrade her skills but has not found a job that requires her training. While on social assistance she worked part-time as a waitress at a local diner. At the time of the interview she was working on a Canadian Jobs Strategy project earning approximately $350 a week. Still she cannot afford the $75 weekly cost of child care for her two children and is forced to leave them alone during the day while she works during the summer months. When she took the job, her rent in public housing increased substantially and she was forced to begin repayment on a debt of $7,500 incurred when she returned to school for the data processing course. Now her take-home pay is less than what she would have received on social assistance. Her job ends in two months. She does not want to return to social assistance, but is not sure how she will manage on unemployment insurance benefits.

POLITICAL ECONOMY PERSPECTIVES

Political economy perspectives differ from supply and demand side perspectives in emphasizing the importance of politics in determining the structure of social and economic relations. Poverty, gender inequality, and low wages are not the result of rational choices within the context of neutral market forces as in the supply side perspective. Nor are they solely the result of imperfections in the market that can be corrected by effective legislation. In the political economy perspective, poverty and inequality are the outcomes of economic processes that are driven primarily by relations of power. The economy, the labour market, and ultimately society are shaped by this primarily political process. Key variables, which are emphasized to different extents by the various streams of political economy, include interest groups, class power, relations of production, the political process, ideology, and patriarchy.

The Canadian political economy tradition has focused on understanding the unique history of the development of the Canadian economy as a capitalist market economy. Many forces have shaped the Canadian political economy and therefore its social relations: its early colonial status, its role as an exporter of staple goods, regional interests, class interests, and the particular nature of the Canadian state, media, and official cultural institutions. At its most general level, this perspective attributes the existence of poverty to class status. People are poor because they are members of a subordinate class (in relation to employers or capital). Consequently they lack the power to appropriate a fair share of the social product. According to this view, the extent of working poverty in Canada will be determined largely by broader political issues and the extent to which various interests, especially labour and capital, have influence over labour market policy and labour market outcomes.

In reflecting on the Canadian reality, political economists point out that labour and non-business groups are weak in Canada compared to other industrialized countries.[13] Compared to business, labour tends to have little direct influence over policies that affect the labour market, especially the structure of employment. Indeed, labour's weakening power base is evident in deregulation, privatization, and deunionization.[14] From a political economy perspective, political choices such as these are linked to the interests of elites, or the capitalist class. They are more important than human capital decisions or even segmented labour markets in explaining why people are poor. Evidence to support this view comes from comparative political research, which suggests that it is primarily political factors, such as the level of unionization and the extent to which labour and business interests are organized and institutionally represented in government, that determine differing welfare and income distribution outcomes in the various capitalist nations.[15]

Political economy can help explain the causal mechanism whereby occupational and sectoral segregation prevail and keep wages low for particular groups. For example, employers may create artificial barriers or systems of stratification to reinforce divisions between groups and to forestall union organization. In the area of discrimination, sociologist Patricia Marchak argues that the occupational and industrial segregation of women into low-paid, part-time service sector jobs reflects a rational development from the point of view of employers as a class because it establishes a lower-paid segment against which men will not readily compete.[16] This has been particularly important to the phenomenal growth of service sector jobs over the past several decades.

Feminist perspectives emphasize the importance of the oppression of women that runs across class divisions and all aspects of human activity. The common strain linking political economy perspectives with feminism is the recognition that social relations, such as inequality between men and women, are conditioned by economic structures and processes. For both perspectives, power is a "fundamental category", and the key issue is to understand the interests served by women's inequality and poverty.[17] Intellectually, feminism and political economy are natural, but uneasy, partners. They have major, and as yet not totally resolved, problems related to the synthesis of gender with other major categories of inequality such as class. Attempts to reduce women's inequality to class inequality are rejected by feminism.[18] Women clearly have an inferior status to men in society at all levels, and this inferior status is unique and distinct from other forms of inequality.

Various streams of feminist thought emphasize differing causes of sex/gender oppression. Radical feminist theories emphasize the male domination of women, or patriarchy, as the main source of female inequality. Socialist feminist theories emphasize women's role in relation to production. Women as childbearers have a unique relation to production since they "reproduce" the labour force, which is essential but unpaid work. The way that society treats women's work in the home separates out and subordinates women within classes and pervades all levels of human activity.[19] Liberal feminism identifies several sources of inequality, including male power and class but also socialization.

The differences between these strands of feminist thought are less important than what binds them. From all feminist perspectives, women's unequal treatment and poverty are the result of a mutually reinforcing cycle that traps women in certain roles in the home and in the labour market.[20] The vicious circle of women's disadvantage begins with women's overriding responsibility for domestic work and child care, i.e., an unequal division of domestic labour between the sexes. This also contributes to the concentration of women in part-time work and occupational segregation in "women's work". Unequal division of domestic labour and paid work of any kind produces the well-known double workday for women. At the same time, the unequal division of domestic labour contributes to women having interrupted careers, which affects their ability to pursue education and training. All of this results ultimately in lower pay for women.

Whether individual women actually have children or are wives does not affect how they are treated in the labour market. The biological reality of women's ability to give birth has been socially reconstructed into "appropriate" roles for women and men. Women enter the labour market always as past, present, or future mothers. Women are allocated to jobs not so much on the basis of their ability to do the job, but rather on the basis of such factors as custom, tradition, social attitudes, historical stereotypes, and outmoded personnel practices. Their socially assigned role as housekeepers and mothers is reinforced by the family (in the fact that they do most of the domestic labour and child care), public policy (in the lack of adequate child care, maternity leave, and access to abortion), and the labour market (in that low-paid jobs for women make it rational for their higher-paid husbands to work in the labour market while they take care of the children and the home). This cycle is also recognized by human capital theorists. But as Irene Bruegel points out, "the human capital approach tends to look at each part of the cycle in isolation, rather than looking at the cumulative process".[21]

> *. . . I feel like I missed one whole season working [the] graveyard [shift] at the diner . . . I'd get home just on time to send the kids to school . . . then I'd sleep until noon and make their lunch . . . I'd never get back to sleep . . . I just felt like yelling all of the time . . . I just had to quit . . .*
>
> *Single mother, trying to leave social assistance, Nova Scotia*

Feminism relies on the historical analysis of political economy to add an important dimension to its view of inequality in the work force and in the home. In pre-industrial times all members of the family worked, and the labour of all, including children, was valued because the family was a "system" of production. This is very different from the notion that women are relatively recent entrants to the work force. Feminist political economy has helped demonstrate the dual nature of women's work, in the home and the workplace, and established the critical importance of domestic labour to the system of production. With the emergence of the factory wage system, men became "productive" because they were associated with the production of commodities that could be sold for profit in the public sphere, while women were "unproductive" although they gave birth and worked in the private sphere — the home. They were described as "unproductive" because they were economically dependent. The need to support wives and children led to demands for a "family wage", and female financial dependency became a central issue for trade union bargaining and for welfare state provision.[22] Feminists emphasize that the economic dependency of women, which is such an important part of the vicious circle, is a relatively recent historical occurrence and should not be taken as a given.[23]

Feminism rejects the unregulated labour market as a viable mechanism for improving the economic position of women. Support for policies like equal pay for work of equal value repudiates the idea that market forces should determine the worth of jobs. Policy options to assist poor women must go beyond conventional supply side policies (education, training, mobility) and policies to reduce labour market segmentation (anti-discrimination and wage improvement policies). Policies must focus instead on altering the structure of demand for women in the economy and changing the unequal division of labour in the home. From a feminist perspective, an important role of public policy is to provide a range of supports for families that will alleviate women's responsibility for child care. The provision of child care is an essential precondition to equality of the sexes. Public policy should also be extended to assistance in creating a more equitable sharing of domestic and child-care responsibilities (e.g., parental leave). Women may not have full access to family resources; besides, such access is increasingly precarious given changing family structures. Reliance on the family as a source of income may also simply perpetuate the stereotype of dependency.

SUMMARY

Supply side theories emphasize that women's role in the labour market is severely constrained by their household responsibilities, especially those associated with the care of children. However, these theories tend to see women's domestic responsibilities as choices they make or as part of the natural order.

Demand side theories are better at explaining the occupational differences between men and women in terms of the division of markets into non-competing segments and the existence of discrimination, but the question of the unequal division of domestic responsibilities and its genesis is left unanswered.

Political economy perspectives on women's poverty and inequality emphasize the idea that they are products of an unequal distribution of political and economic power. Major shifts in the social and institutional power relationships between labour and capital and between women and men are essential to any fundamental redistribution of jobs and income in Canada.

Feminism emphasizes the importance of changing the division of labour between women and men in the home and in the workplace. The struggle for women's equality is fundamentally a political task that requires building coalitions with other groups that also experience oppression. Public policy can be an important mechanism for achieving equity goals through intervention in the market and support for changing the concrete basis for the unequal division of labour in society.

NOTES (Chapter Two)

1. See, for example: Pat Armstrong, *Labour Pains: Women's Work in Crisis* (Toronto: Women's Educational Press, 1984); Pat Armstrong and Hugh Armstrong, *The Double Ghetto: Canadian Women and Their Segregated Work* (Toronto: McClelland and Stewart, 1984); Canada, Commission on Equality in Employment (Rosalie Silberman Abella, Commissioner), *Equality in Employment: Report of the Commission on Equality in Employment* (Ottawa: 1984); Canadian Advisory Council on the Status of Women, *Integration & Participation: Women's Work in the Home and in the Labour Force* (Ottawa: 1987); National Council of Welfare, *Women and Poverty* (Ottawa: 1979).
2. Feminist literature generally makes a distinction between "sex" which is biologically determined, and "gender" which is socially constructed.
3. Daniel Patrick Moynihan, *The Negro Family: The Case for National Action* (Washington, D.C.: U.S. Department of Labor, Office of Family Planning and Research, 1965).
4. This perspective is discussed critically in Armstrong and Armstrong, *The Double Ghetto, supra*, note 1, p. 107.
5. "Classic" writings in the human capital tradition include Gary Becker, *Human Capital* (New York: Columbia University Press, 1964); Jacob Mincer, *Schooling, Experience and Earnings* (New York: Columbia University Press, 1974); and various articles in Theodore Schultz, ed., "Investment In Human Beings", *Journal of Political Economy*, vol. 70, no. 5, part 2 (1962).
6. As stated in Harry G. Johnson, "Some Micro-Economic Reflections on Inequality and Wealth Inequalities", *Annals of the American Academy of Political and Social Science* (special issue on "Income Inequality"), vol. 409 (September 1973), p. 57.

   > "People can legitimately differ in their preferences: some may prefer an early, austere, hard-working and productive life for the sake of a comfortable old age as an independent worker or affluent retired person; others may prefer to live it up in their youth while hoping that the future will take care of itself. They can also legitimately differ in their preference for either family formation and child upbringing or more personal leisure and material consumption . . . They may choose between a fixed commitment to regular, but limited, hours of work and the freedom to work in concentrated spurts, punctuated by periods of voluntary idleness; or between either high material consumption and scanty leisure or low material consumption and ample leisure."

7. For a review of this literature see, for example: Martha S. Hill, "The Changing Nature of Poverty", *Annals of the American Academy of Political and Social Sciences*, vol. 479 (May 1985); Frances Fox Piven and Richard Cloward, "The Contemporary Relief Debate", in *The Mean Season: The Attack on the Welfare State* (New York: Pantheon, 1987).
8. Isabel V. Sawhill, "Poverty in the U.S.: Why Is It So Persistent?", *Journal of Economic Literature*, vol. 27, no. 3 (September 1988), p. 1080.
9. Patricia M. Evans, *A Decade of Change: The FBA Caseload, 1975-1986. A background paper prepared for the Social Assistance Review Committee* (Toronto: Ontario Social Assistance Review Committee, June 1987), p. 15.
10. Armstrong and Armstrong, *The Double Ghetto, supra,* note 1, p. 125.
11. *Ibid.*, p. 127.
12. A classic work on the dual, segmented labour market perspective is Peter B. Doeringer and Michael J. Piore, *Internal Labour Markets and Manpower Analysis* (Lexington: D.C. Heath, 1971). Econometric evidence on labour market segmentation in Canada is given in William Merrilees, "Labour Market Segmentation in Canada: An Econometric Approach", *Canadian Journal of Economics*, vol. 15, no. 3 (1982), pp. 458-473; and Lars Osberg, R. Muzany, Richard Apostle, and Don Clairmont, "Job Mobility, Wage Determination and Market Segmentation in the Presence of Sample Selection Bias", *Canadian Journal of Economics*, vol. 19, no. 2 (1986), pp. 319-346.
13. Keith G. Banting, "The State and Economic Interests: An Introduction", in *The State and Economic Interests*, ed. Keith Banting (Toronto: University of Toronto Press, 1986), pp. 16-29; and Daniel Drache and Harry J. Glassbeek, "The New Fordism in Canada: Capital's Offensive, Labour's Opportunity", *Osgoode Hall Law Journal*, vol. 25 (Winter 1987).
14. Leo Panitch and Donald Swartz, *The Assault on Trade Union Freedoms: From Consent to Coercion Revisited* (Toronto: Garamond Press, 1988).
15. See, for example: Andrew Martin, "The Politics of Employment and Welfare: National Policies and International Interdependence", in *The State and Economic Interests*, ed. Banting, *supra*, note 13.
16. Patricia Marchak, "Rational Capitalism and Women as Labour", in *Feminism and Political Economy: Women's Work and Women's Struggles*, ed. Heather Jon Maroney and Meg Luxton (Toronto: Methuen, 1987).
17. Heather Jon Maroney and Meg Luxton, "From Feminism and Political Economy to Feminist Political Economy", in *Feminism and Political Economy*, ed. Maroney and Luxton, *ibid.*, p. 6.

18. For an early classic of feminist literature that attempts to establish the relationship between class and gender, see: Margaret Benston, "The Political Economy of Women's Liberation", in *Roles Women Play: Readings Towards Women's Liberation*, ed. Michele Hoffnung Garsoff (Belmont: Brook/Cole, 1971), pp. 194-205.
19. Pat Armstrong and Hugh Armstrong, "Beyond Sexless Class and Classless Sex: Towards Feminist Marxism", *Studies in Political Economy*, vol. 10 (1983), p. 39.
20. Irene Bruegel, "Women's Employment, Legislation and the Labour Market", in *Women's Welfare, Women's Rights*, ed. Jane Lewis (London & Canberra: Croom Helm, 1983), p. 158.
21. *Ibid.*, p. 157.
22. Eli Zaretsky, "Rethinking the Welfare State: Dependence, Economic Individualism and the Family", in *Family, Economy and State*, ed. James Dickinson and Bob Russell (Toronto: Garamond Press, 1986), pp. 90-92.
23. Brigitte Kitchen, *Employment Strategies For Women and the Sexual Division of Labour* (Toronto: School of Social Work, Atkinson College, York University, 1988).

PART ONE: THEORY, DESCRIPTION, AND ANALYSIS

Chapter 3: The Working Poor: A Descriptive Picture

THE CONCEPT OF THE WORKING POOR

The labour market-related poverty of women is the main focus of this book. A term often used to describe the group that experiences this type of poverty is the "working poor". This terminology is problematic because it implies that people who do work outside the labour market do not work. In particular, people (mostly women) who work in the home or on farms and who care for children have been victimized by the idea that they are not workers. In this study we use the concept and the term "working poor" (which is widely known and used), but we wish to emphasize that in no way does this imply that people's work outside the paid labour force is not socially valuable work.

As a group, the working poor are frequently compared to the "other" poor — people with no attachment to the labour force. There is, however, no universally accepted definition of the working poor. It is used generally to describe people who work in the labour market but still do not earn sufficient income to avoid economic hardship. Often the term refers to people who work in the labour market full-time or at least have a major attachment to the labour market, yet remain poor.

> "*. . . at first it was a bit insulting to think that I would be considered poor . . . sure I don't have much money . . . but I have a job . . . and I'm supporting myself . . . and I really don't want to be working as a waitress for the rest of my life . . .*
>
> *Single, 24 years old, waitress, university degree, Quebec*"

Two issues need to be resolved in an effort to define the working poor in any objective sense: who is to be included, and how is labour market attachment to be defined? Some researchers exclude certain groups such as elderly people and youth because they are not expected to work or because they have relatively weak attachment to the labour force. However, excluding such groups can understate the extent of working poverty, because they are disproportionately likely to be working poor, and their weak attachment to the labour force may be involuntary.

The second concern is the definition of labour market attachment. Most researchers have attempted to identify some level of labour market attachment as an acceptable minimum demonstrating a willingness to work. At one extreme, the definition of working poor would include all families where at least one family member worked at some point during a year, even if the work was part-time or of short duration. The more restrictive definition would consider the working poor to include only those families where the family head worked full-time for the full year.

We believe the labour market attachment of many women involves part-time, part-year employment as well as dropping out of the labour market to raise children. Such women should not be excluded from the concept of working poverty because much of their poverty is related to the limitations of the labour market. Moreover, even if they are not employed continuously, they do have an attachment to the labour market over the long term.

Distinguishing the working poor from the other poor is important because policies to alleviate poverty are most effective if they clearly identify the source of poverty. The working poor are normally expected to engage in paid employment. The poverty of the working poor is believed to be related to low wages, unemployment, or too few hours worked — problems that are related to labour market policy. The other poor, who are usually not expected to engage in paid employment, often includes disabled people, the elderly, or single mothers. Their poverty is thought to be related to inadequate income security programs, onerous family responsibilities, or personal characteristics that are associated with poverty — problems that are not generally related to the labour market and are normally dealt with through a variety of social policies.

In many cases the distinction between working poverty and other poverty is useful but in some cases it is difficult to know where to draw that distinction. One example of this is the poverty of elderly women which is related to deficiencies in both the pension system and the labour market. Women doing domestic work and child care, at home full-time for a number of years, are not allowed to contribute to the Canada/Quebec Pension Plan and they are employed in low-wage and part-time work, which results in a small pension or no pension.

The traditional concept of full-time, full-year poor workers has strong appeal because it demonstrates unambiguously that some people can work full-time for the whole year but still be poor. This furnishes strong evidence that their poverty is attributable not to any personal shortcoming, but to their lack of income from employment. But considering only full-time, full-year labour market attachment in the definition of labour market-related poverty ignores the labour market hardship of those people, many of them women, who do not have such attachment. The poverty of elderly women or disabled people, for example, is often linked to inadequate pensions or income security protection; but since many income security benefits are tied to employment, their poverty is in many ways related to the labour market.

In addition, society's expectations about work vary over time and across communities, social groups, provinces/territories, and especially countries. Our idea of who is expected to work for wages has changed over the years, especially with respect to women. Now that the majority of women, and especially married women, are active members of the labour force, the view that women should not be in the labour market is diminishing. This change is especially evident in the shifting, if not ambivalent, attitude toward single mothers.

To avoid excluding important groups from our description of labour market-related hardship, we have adopted a broad definition of the working poor. In this study, the working poor are defined as **adult individuals (15 years or older) who worked at any time during the year of the survey and lived in an economic family whose income fell below the poverty line**.[1] To provide evidence of narrower concepts of working poverty, we also divided the working poor into the full-time working poor and the part-time working poor. In our analysis, full-time refers to those individuals who worked more than 30 hours a week for 49 weeks or more. Part-time refers to all others, that is, those who worked full-time for less than 49 weeks (i.e., part-year) and those who worked less than 30 hours a week, for any portion of the year.

The study's broad definition of the working poor encompasses people with very low attachment to the labour market. It can include young people who are students and the elderly poor who work to supplement pension income with labour market earnings. On the other hand, it excludes people who did not work or were unemployed for the twelve-month period covered by the survey, despite the fact that they may have wanted to be employed or were employed in the year before or after the survey. Although the broader concept of the working poor is used in this study, breakdowns by personal, family, geographic, and labour market characteristics help determine the size of various groups and the importance we should attach to their labour market poverty.

RITA AND DALE
(British Columbia)

Rita and Dale are in their mid-30s, married with a 1-year-old child. Rita is eight months pregnant with their second child. Both work at a fish packing plant. Their work is seasonal, extending for about eight months of the year. Their hourly wage rate is about $13.50 an hour, and there is considerable overtime available at the height of the season. The work is unionized and both have several years of seniority with the company. When they both work the full season, their combined income (with unemployment insurance in the off-season) places them above the poverty line. Last year the couple was forced to rely on Dale's salary alone. Rita's first pregnancy was not planned, and the birth occurred at a time when she was not eligible for paid maternity leave under unemployment insurance because she did not have enough qualifying weeks of employment. They were determined not to have to apply for welfare but they exhausted all their savings trying to get through the winter months. This year Rita will qualify for maternity leave, but the family will again have to rely on reduced earnings.

The distinction between the working poor and the other poor remains arbitrary, and the boundary should be regarded as flexible. Labour market involvement should be seen as a spectrum, with full-time, full-year workers at one extreme and people with no labour market involvement at the other. In between there is a range of levels of involvement. The extent to which people can and do use the labour market to avoid poverty will depend on a number of factors: the state of the economy and whether job opportunities exist, the availability of supports such as child care and training, and personal desire and ability. People in the category sometimes referred to as the "welfare poor" (a narrower term for the other poor) may not work at all, but under different labour market conditions and with different social supports, they might well become active labour market workers. If a single mother on welfare did not work for one year she would be excluded from the working poor definition used in this study. But it would be wrong not to consider her poverty as related at least in part to the severe lack of opportunities in the labour market.

THE DATA

The data for this description of the working poor in Canada were derived from the Survey of Consumer Finances (SCF), a major survey conducted annually by Statistics Canada using interviews with people in 36,000 dwellings in Canada. It yields information on incomes of individuals, families, and households as well as on geographic location, demographic characteristics, and labour force activity. Most of our data are from special tabulations of individual adults from the *Public Use Micro-data Tape: Incomes of Individuals, 1986*. Historical data are taken from tapes of previous years; supplementary data are from the micro-data tape *Incomes of Economic Families, 1986.*[2]

The Survey of Consumer Finances has some important limitations. Because it is a relatively small but representative sample of the population of Canada, it cannot yield estimates for small population areas such as the Yukon or Northwest Territories or for specific urban areas. Because it does not sample people on Indian reserves and does not determine whether a person is disabled, or a member of a racial minority community, we cannot separate out these groups in our descriptive profile of poverty, even though studies indicate that they tend to have low incomes and difficulties in the labour market.[3] However, we do deal with these groups and their labour market difficulties in subsequent chapters.

As discussed in Chapter One, the general incidence of poverty refers to the percentage of all adults in a particular category who are poor. The incidence of **working poverty** (a subset of poverty) is the proportion of people **in the work force** who are poor.[4] The work force is defined here as all adults in Canada who worked part-time or full-time at any time in the year of the survey.

POVERTY AND LABOUR MARKET POVERTY

In 1986, approximately 1.3 million people in Canada did not escape poverty although they were employed (Table 3.1). The working poor represented 9.3% of all people who worked in the labour market and 46.8% of all poor people. Women made up about 46.4% of the working poor, slightly more than their 43.8% representation in the work force. A minority of poor women (37%) were working poor even using our broad definition, while a majority of poor men (60.8%) were working poor.

TABLE 3.1: The Working Poor: A Basic Description, Canada, 1986

Category	Both Sexes		Female		Male	
	N (000s)	%	N (000s)	%	N (000s)	%
Work force	13,952		6,111		7,842	
Distribution by sex		100.0		43.8		56.2
Working poor	1,292		599		693	
Distribution by sex		100.0		46.4		53.6
Incidence		9.3		9.8		8.8
As % of all poor		46.8		37.0		60.8

Note: Numbers may not add up due to rounding.
Source: Tabulations by Analytical Services, Health and Welfare Canada on Statistics Canada, Survey of Consumer Finances, Public Use Micro-data Tape: Incomes of Individuals, 1986.

The incidence of working poverty was slightly higher for women (9.8%) than it was for men (8.8%). The difference in rates of **working** poverty between males and females was not as large as the difference in **overall** poverty rates for men and women, and not as large as we might expect given women's disadvantaged position in the labour market. This somewhat surprising finding may be explained in several ways. First, disproportionately more women than men are members of the group we call the "other" poor. Second, and more important, the concept of poverty is based on total family income, and the estimates of working poverty here are the number of individuals who live in economic family units that are poor. While women on average have lower wages than men, they are also part of economic family units with other contributors to family income; thus, the total family income may be sufficient to exceed the poverty level.

It is important to keep in mind that although women may live in families with incomes above the poverty line, they also may experience labour market hardship as **individuals**; this will not show up in estimates of working poverty. Poverty indicators are useful but they can tell us only so much. They have to be supplemented with other indicators of labour market hardship, such as unemployment rates and wage levels, to form a more complete picture of labour market-related difficulties. In addition, as we discussed in Chapter One, any understanding of women's poverty has to take into account the likelihood that total family income is not shared equally within all families.

FULL-TIME AND PART-TIME WORKING POVERTY

Full-time work does not guarantee that a person will escape poverty. In fact, 29.6% of the working poor, or 383,000 people (127,000 women and 256,000 men), worked full-time for the entire year in 1986 (Table 3.2). Working poor men were almost twice as likely as working poor women to be employed full-time (36.9% versus 21.2%).

Working poor women were more likely to be employed part-time or full-time for less than a full year; while 78.8% of working poor women were employed part-time, 63.1% of working poor men were employed part-time. Consequently, men constituted about two-thirds (66.8%) of the full-time working poor, while women constituted slightly more than half (51.9%) of the part-time working poor.

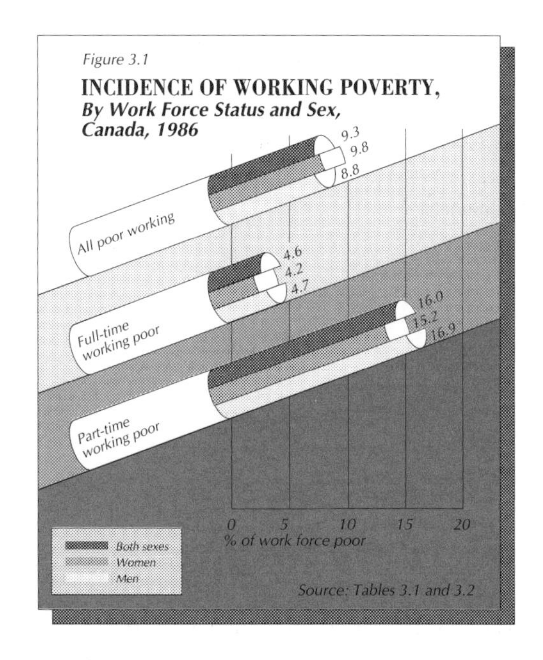

The incidence of poverty for full-time, full-year workers was 4.6%, considerably lower than it was for those working part-time at 16% (Table 3.2 and Figure 3.1). As with the overall rate of working poverty, there was little difference between women and men in their

TABLE 3.2: Full-time/Part-time Labour Force Status of the Working Poor, Adult Individuals, Canada, 1986

Number and Distribution	Both Sexes		Female		Male	
	(000s)	%	(000s)	%	(000s)	%
Full-time working poor	383		127		256	
Distribution by sex		100.0		33.2		66.8
Part-time working poor	909		472		437	
Distribution by sex		100.0		51.9		48.1
Distribution by work force status						
Full-time working poor		29.6		21.2		36.9
Part-time working poor		70.4		78.8		63.1
Total working poor		100.0		100.0		100.0
Incidence						
Full-time working poverty rate (% of full-time work force who are poor)		4.6		4.2		4.9
Part-time working poverty rate (% of part-time work force who are poor)		16.0		15.2		16.9

Source: Tabulations by Analytical Services, Health and Welfare Canada on Statistics Canada, Survey of Consumer Finances, Public Use Micro-data Tape: Incomes of Individuals, 1986.

poverty rates when they both work full-time. This highlights the importance of part-time work as a determinant of working poverty, especially for women.[5]

CHANGES IN WORKING POVERTY

The actual number of people experiencing labour market-related poverty has increased dramatically since the early 1970s, at a faster rate than non labour market-related poverty. The proportion of people in

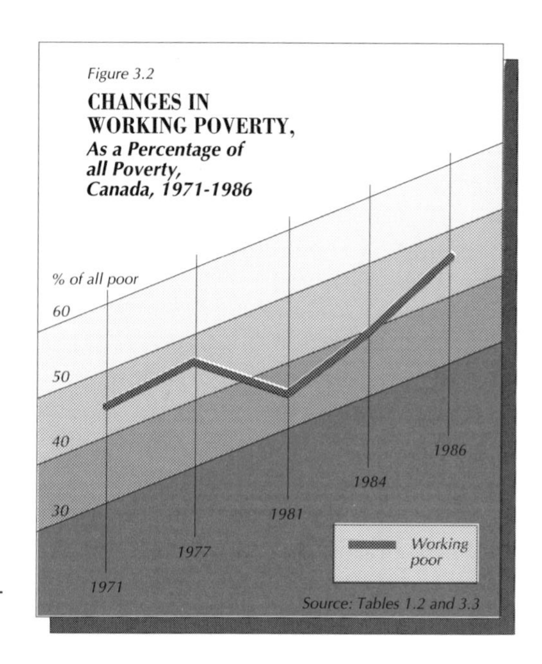

the labour market who experience poverty (the incidence of labour market poverty) also rose, but much less dramatically. In 1971, a total of 770,000 people were working and poor (Table 3.3). By 1986 this had risen to 1,292,000, an increase of 67.8%. Although not shown in the table, non labour market-related poverty (the other poor) grew by 59.3% over the same period. It is of more immediate concern that, since 1981, working poverty has increased relative to all poverty (Figure 3.2). In part this may be due to a decline in the elderly poor population, most of whom would be classified as other poor, as a result of increases in federal pension benefits.[6] As well, the women who are now 65 to 70 years of age had a greater likelihood of working in the paid labour force than those aged 70 to 75 and 75 to 80 (Table 1.4, Chapter One).

TABLE 3.3: Time Pattern of Working Poverty, Canada, Selected Years, 1971-1986*

	1971		1977		1981		1984		1986		Increase
	(000s)	%	(000s)	%	(000s)	%	(000s)	%	(000s)	%	1971-86
Both sexes											
Working poor	770		1,010		961		1,234		1,292		67.8%
Incidence		8.6		8.8		7.7		9.6		9.3	
% of all poor		45.6		46.3		36.8		40.0		46.8	
% part-time		59.7		64.4		68.9		71.2		70.4	
Women											
Working poor	230		410		431		584		599		160.4%
Incidence		7.7		9.0		8.2		10.6		9.8	
% of working poor		29.9		40.6		44.8		47.3		46.4	
% part-time		78.3		75.6		77.5		77.6		78.8	
Men											
Working poor	540		600		530		650		693		28.3%
Incidence		9.1		8.6		7.3		8.8		8.8	
% of working poor		70.1		59.4		55.2		52.7		53.6	
% part-time		51.9		56.7		62.0		65.5		63.1	

Note: * 1971 data uses 1969 LICO base; 1977 to 1986 data uses 1978 LICO base.
Source: Tabulations by Analytical Services, Health and Welfare Canada and Statistics Canada on Statistics Canada, Survey of Consumer Finances, Public Use Micro-data Tape: Incomes of Individuals.

Women experienced the bulk of the increase in labour market-related poverty. The number of working poor women rose from 230,000 in 1971 to 599,000 in 1986, an increase of 160.4% — substantially higher than the 28.3% increase for working poor men (Table 3.3). In addition, women's poverty overall increased 110.3%, compared to the 23.8% increase for men (Table 1.2, Chapter One). It should be noted that while women's poverty increased between 1971 and 1986 (110.3%), women's working poverty increased much more substantially (160.4%).

This has significantly changed the distribution of working poverty by sex. In 1971, women were 29.9% of the working poor; by 1986 they had become 46.4% of the working poor, a trend that might be described as "the feminization of working poverty" (Figure 3.3). As was the case for overall poverty, the most significant increases in the proportion of working poor women occurred in the 1970s. But unlike overall poverty, the feminization of working poverty continued in the 1980s, with a slight decrease in the proportion of women who were working poor occurring between 1984 and 1986.

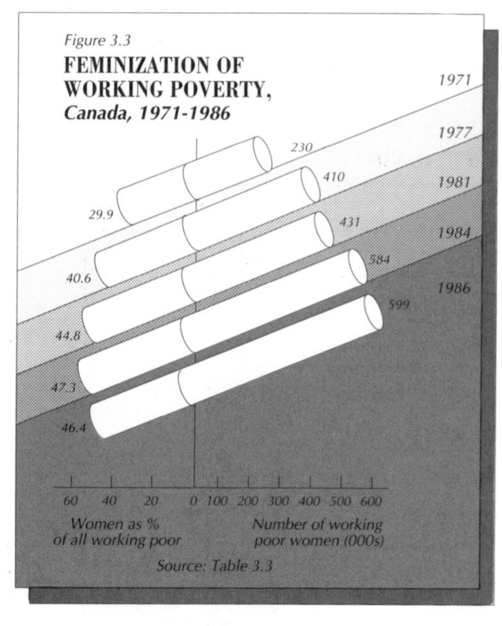

Figure 3.3
FEMINIZATION OF WORKING POVERTY,
Canada, 1971-1986

This change in the sex distribution of working poverty between 1971 and 1986 is also reflected in an increase in the percentage of working poverty that is part-time, since women are more likely to be part-time working poor than full-time working poor. In 1971, 59.7% of the working poor were part-time working poor; by 1986 this figure had increased to 70.4% (Table 3.3).

There were more than twice as many working poor women in 1986 than in 1971, but over that period the proportion doing part-time work remained nearly constant, at slightly above 75%. The increase in numbers of working poor men was relatively small but the proportion of them in part-time work increased in the same period from 51.9% to 63.1% (Table 3.3).

> “ *. . . Part-time work is the evil of our time . . . there are twelve people working in my department for a 22½-hour week . . . there are no benefits . . . maybe they could hire fewer people for more wages . . .*
>
> *Retail clerk, department store chain, Ontario* ”

The incidence of working poverty also increased from 8.6% in 1971, reaching a high of 9.6% in 1984 at the end of the recession (for central Canada) before declining slightly to 9.3% in 1986 (Table 3.3 and Figure 3.4). Again the pattern of working poverty diverges somewhat from the pattern of other poverty. While the incidence of poverty overall declined from 16.1% in 1984 to 13.9% in 1986 (Table 1.2, Chapter One), the decline in the incidence of working poverty was much more modest, from 9.6% to 9.3%. Men fared worse than women in this regard; men's 8.8% rate of working poverty remained unchanged between 1984 and 1986, while the women's rate declined very slightly from 10.6% to 9.8%.

From 1984 to 1986, the Canadian economy as a whole (although not all regions) experienced a recovery from the severe recession of the early 1980s. The recovery does appear to have reduced poverty overall, but although unemployment rates dropped significantly between 1984 and 1986, the rate of working poverty did not. This raises questions about what is happening with wages and hours of work, issues we will take up in Chapter Six.

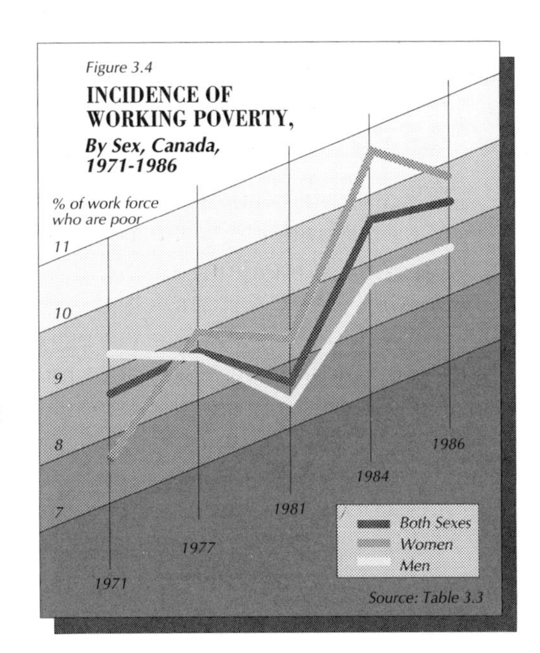

Figure 3.4
INCIDENCE OF WORKING POVERTY,
By Sex, Canada, 1971-1986

Source: Table 3.3

THE PERSONAL CHARACTERISTICS OF THE WORKING POOR

What effect do personal characteristics have on the likelihood that a person in Canada will be a member of the working poor? As we have seen, the likelihood that women will be working poor is only slightly higher than the likelihood that men will be working poor, even though women have a much higher likelihood of being poor. Other personal characteristics are significant, however, and these do vary by sex.

> "*. . . it's hard to find work when you can't read or write very well . . . I left school after grade 8 . . . I hated the principal . . . and I never seemed to do very well . . . at first my mother found me a job where she worked at the factory . . . but they let me go . . . they said I was too slow . . . it took awhile to find another job . . .*
>
> *Single, 18 years old, full-time babysitter, Nova Scotia*"

The effect of personal characteristics on the likelihood of being working poor can be seen by comparing the incidence figures for specific groups with the average incidence for all individuals (Table 3.4). For example, while both men and women had a much higher incidence of being working poor if they were young (15-24 years of age), less educated (below grade 9), or recent immigrants, the effect of low education and youth is more pronounced for women than for men.

The distribution figures indicate that more than 35.2% of the working poor were under 25 years old; 14% of the working poor had less than a grade 9 education; and 10.8% were immigrants that came to Canada after 1970. A slightly higher proportion of working poor women than working poor men were young. On the other hand, a slightly higher proportion of working poor men had less than a grade 9 education. There were only slight differences in the distribution of male and female working poor by immigrant status. Although the likelihood of being poor was higher for recent immigrants, the vast majority (more than 80%) of working poor males and females were Canadian born. This highlights how incidence and distribution figures can differ dramatically depending upon the size of the group.

TABLE 3.4: Incidence and Distribution of the Working Poor, by Personal Characteristics, Canada, 1986

	Incidence of Working Poverty			Distribution of Working Poor		
	Both Sexes	Female	Male	Both Sexes	Female	Male
All individuals	9.3	9.8	8.8	100.0	100.0	100.0
Age of individual						
15-24	14.0	15.3	12.9	35.2	38.8	32.0
25-34	9.6	9.3	9.8	29.2	27.8	30.5
35-54	6.5	6.7	6.3	26.4	25.6	27.1
55-64	7.7	8.5	7.3	7.8	6.7	8.7
Over 65	7.2	9.5	6.3	1.4	1.2	1.7
Education						
Below grade 9	12.6	16.5	10.7	14.0	12.5	15.4
9-13	10.1	10.7	9.7	55.1	55.7	54.6
Some post-secondary	9.9	10.7	9.2	11.9	13.0	11.0
Post-secondary certificate	7.8	7.6	8.1	12.3	13.1	11.6
University	4.5	4.3	4.6	6.6	5.7	7.4
Immigrant status						
Canadian born	9.3	9.9	8.8	83.3	84.3	82.4
Immigrated pre-1971	5.5	5.3	5.6	5.9	5.1	6.6
Immigrated post-1970	14.7	14.8	14.6	10.8	10.6	11.0

Source: Tabulations by Analytical Services, Health and Welfare Canada on Statistics Canada, Survey of Consumer Finances, Public Use Micro-data Tape: Incomes of Individuals, 1986.

FAMILY AND HOUSEHOLD

The likelihood of being working poor was significantly greater if a person was unattached or living in a single-parent household. Unattached individuals and individuals in single-parent families had rates of working poverty of 23.5% and 22.5% respectively, compared to 6.2% for people living in couple families (Table 3.5). Heads of families, by definition always male in couple families,[7] had a higher incidence of labour market poverty (12.3%) than did wives (5%) or children over 15 years of age living with their parents (6.6%). This was simply because

TABLE 3.5: Incidence and Distribution of the Working Poor, by Household and Family Characteristics, Canada, 1986

	Incidence of Working Poverty			Distribution of Working Poor		
	Both Sexes	Female	Male	Both Sexes	Female	Male
All individuals	9.3	9.8	8.8	100.0	100.0	100.0
Economic family characteristics						
Unattached individual	23.5	25.0	22.1	33.6	34.6	32.8
Single parent with children	22.5	27.5	14.7	15.5	25.1	7.3
Couple with children	6.2	5.3	6.8	36.2	27.5	43.7
All other family/couple types	5.2	4.8	5.6	14.6	12.8	16.2
Relationship to head of economic family						
Head	12.3	25.9	9.4	70.9	55.4	84.2
Wife	5.0	5.0	n/a	14.1	30.5	n/a
Child*	6.6	6.9	6.4	13.4	12.5	14.2
Other	9.9	10.1	9.5	1.6	1.6	1.6
Census family characteristics						
Head of 2-parent family	6.8	n/a	6.8	26.8	n/a	50.0
Individual or single-parent head	21.9	24.3	19.4	45.8	56.7	36.4
Wife in 2-parent family	5.0	5.0	n/a	14.2	30.7	n/a
Not head or wife	6.8	7.4	6.4	13.2	2.7	13.7
Household living arrangements						
Unattached alone	16.9	17.0	16.7	15.3	16.0	14.7
Unattached in household with other economic families or individuals	35.0	42.3	30.3	18.3	18.6	18.1
All other families	7.1	7.4	6.8	66.4	65.4	67.2

Notes: * 15 years of age and over, living with parents.
n/a denotes not applicable.

Source: Tabulations by Analytical Services, Health and Welfare Canada on Statistics Canada, Survey of Consumer Finances, Public Use Micro-data Tape: Incomes of Individuals, 1986.

many heads of families are unattached individuals or heads of single-parent families, groups with much higher rates of working poverty. It is interesting to note under household living arrangements that unattached individuals had a dramatically higher incidence of working poverty (35.0%) if they lived in a household with other people rather than in their own household (16.9%). This may be because many poor single people live in institutions such as group homes or have to share a residence to survive.

> "*... the only way people can afford to work part-time ... or for low wages ... is to live with someone else ... the young women at work are moving in with their boyfriends ... or other friends ... they don't want to marry but it's cheaper to share rent ...*
>
> *Department store clerk,*
> *Ontario*"

Male-female differences were reflected in a number of categories. Unattached females had a slightly higher incidence of working poverty (25%) than unattached males (22.1%), and a much higher incidence (42.3%) than males (30.3%) if they were unattached and lived in a household with other people. Females in single-parent households had a rate of working poverty of 27.5%, compared to 14.7% for males in the same situation. Most, although not all, of these adults were the heads of these households. Female heads of families had a very high probability of being working poor (25.9%) compared to male heads (9.4%). Again, this difference reflects the fact that, by definition, men are always heads of couple families. As we discussed in Chapter One, the poverty of single motherhood is one of the most significant categories of women's poverty.

With respect to the distribution of working poverty by family and household characteristics, about one-third of the working poor were unattached individuals; a further third lived in couple families with unmarried children. Approximately 15% lived in single-parent households. The male-female differences in this distribution show a higher concentration of the female (25.1%) than male (7.3%) working poor in single-parent households. They also show a higher proportion of working poor men in couple families with unmarried children (43.7%)

compared to similarly situated women (27.5%). The majority of the working poor (70.9%) were heads of families, 14.1% were wives, and 13.4% were unmarried children 15 years of age and over living with their parents.

JANICE AND GREG
(Saskatchewan)

Janice and Greg live in an urban centre in Saskatchewan; they are married and have three children aged 8, 10, and 12. Until recently, Greg was self-employed and Janice did not work outside the home. A year ago he was forced to stop work as the result of a debilitating illness. Initially he qualified for worker's compensation but his claim was terminated when it was determined that his illness was not work-related. To earn money the couple tried hauling wood for a short period in the winter months, but Greg's disability became too serious to continue. When Greg was employed the family income ranged from $36,000 to $45,000. They owned their own home and made monthly mortgage payments of about $1,500. After he was forced to stop working, Greg was not eligible for unemployment insurance and the couple exhausted their savings before applying for social assistance. Now the assistance payments barely cover their mortgage, and they are facing the possibility of losing their home. Greg has applied for disability coverage under the Canada Pension Plan but there is a waiting period of several months. He has also applied for a student loan to return to community college for retraining. The combined income from a disability pension and a student loan will be slightly less than their current income on social assistance, but the couple is looking forward to leaving assistance.

REGION AND RESIDENCE

People in Canada were more likely to be working poor if they lived outside Ontario where the incidence of working poverty was 6.6% (Table 3.6). Rates of working poverty in the Atlantic provinces, Quebec, the Prairie provinces, and British Columbia were all in excess of 9% of the work force in 1986. The likelihood of being working poor was highest for people in the labour force in Newfoundland (14.8%), Saskatchewan (13.8%), and Manitoba (12.1%). The incidence of working poverty in all other provinces was close to the overall average.

TABLE 3.6: Incidence and Distribution of the Working Poor, by Region and Residence, Canada, 1986

	Incidence of Working Poverty			Distribution of Working Poor		
	Both Sexes	Female	Male	Both Sexes	Female	Male
All individuals	9.3	9.8	8.8	100.0	100.0	100.0
Region						
Atlantic	10.4	11.4	9.7	9.1	9.1	9.1
Quebec	10.7	10.3	11.1	28.8	25.3	31.8
Ontario	6.6	7.5	5.9	26.9	29.3	24.8
Prairies	11.5	12.0	11.1	21.7	21.6	21.9
British Columbia	10.8	12.3	10.1	13.1	14.1	12.2
Province						
Newfoundland	14.8	13.8	15.5	3.0	2.6	3.4
P.E.I.	9.0	10.0	8.1	0.5	0.4	0.5
Nova Scotia	9.0	10.5	7.9	3.1	3.3	2.9
New Brunswick	9.2	11.0	7.9	2.6	2.9	2.3
Quebec	10.7	10.3	11.1	28.8	25.3	31.8
Ontario	6.6	7.5	5.9	26.9	29.3	24.8
Manitoba	12.1	12.6	11.9	5.4	5.3	5.4
Saskatchewan	13.8	14.7	13.1	5.6	5.5	5.6
Alberta	10.3	10.9	10.0	10.8	10.8	10.8
British Columbia	10.8	12.3	9.8	13.1	14.1	12.2
Population of Area of Residence						
City 100,000+	9.3	9.7	9.1	58.5	58.7	58.3
Town < 100,000	8.8	10.1	7.7	23.2	25.2	21.5
Rural	9.7	9.8	9.6	18.3	16.1	20.2

Note: Numbers may not add up due to rounding and the exclusion of a small category of special individuals not classified by province for reasons of confidentiality.

Source: Tabulations by Analytical Services, Health and Welfare Canada on Statistics Canada, Survey of Consumer Finances, Public Use Micro-data Tape: Incomes of Individuals, 1986.

Significant differences between provinces were evident in male and female rates of working poverty. For example, in Newfoundland and Quebec, men were more likely to be working poor than women, while in all other provinces the reverse was true. There were many more working poor women than working poor men in British Columbia, Nova Scotia, and New Brunswick. The population of the place of residence had little impact on the incidence of working poverty overall, although women living in towns of less than 100,000 population had a higher incidence (10.1%) than did men (7.7%).

> *... sure, there aren't many good jobs here for women ... but how would I be better off in a larger community where I would pay more rent and be away from my family and friends ... I would have to make a lot more money to make it worth it ...*
>
> *Single mother, secretary for social service agency, Nova Scotia*

The distribution of the working poor by region showed more than half the working poor living in Quebec and Ontario. Similarly, well over half the working poor lived in cities or towns with populations greater than 100,000.

LABOUR FORCE ACTIVITY

Because the majority of people make most of their income from earnings in the labour market, the inability to earn is a major factor related to poverty. As discussed in the section on family and household characteristics, the likelihood of poverty rises as the size of an economic family declines, because there are fewer potential earners. As we might expect, the incidence of working poverty was 2.7% for people living in families with three or more earners, 5.3% for individuals living in two-earner families, and 21% for those in one-earner families (Table 3.7). Women had a higher incidence of working poverty than did men in one-earner families (25.4% compared to 18.1%). Distribution figures reveal that the majority of working poor women (59.5%) lived in families with only one earner.[8]

TABLE 3.7: Incidence and Distribution of the Working Poor, by Labour Market Activity, Canada, 1986

	Incidence of Working Poverty			Distribution of Working Poor		
	Both Sexes	Female	Male	Both Sexes	Female	Male
All individuals	9.3	9.8	8.8	100.0	100.0	100.0
Number of earners in family						
1	21.0	25.4	18.1	60.4	59.5	61.2
2	5.3	5.5	5.2	26.0	27.2	24.9
3+	2.7	2.9	2.6	7.9	8.0	7.8
Other	69.8	74.4	65.6	5.7	5.3	6.1
Weeks Employed						
0 weeks	--	--	--	--	--	--
1-24 weeks	21.0	19.8	22.2	36.9	38.1	36.0
25-48 weeks	14.3	15.1	13.6	23.7	25.9	21.9
49+ weeks	5.3	5.5	5.2	39.3	36.1	42.2
Weeks unemployed						
0 weeks	7.3	8.1	6.6	63.9	67.4	60.8
1-24 weeks	14.5	14.8	14.3	18.6	18.2	18.9
25-48 weeks	21.8	19.8	23.3	16.4	13.7	18.8
49+ weeks	40.0	28.6	47.6	1.1	0.7	1.4

Source: Tabulations by Analytical Services, Health and Welfare Canada on Statistics Canada, Survey of Consumer Finances, Public Use Micro-data Tape: Incomes of Individuals, 1986.

The length of time a person worked in paid employment also had an important influence on the likelihood of being poor. The longer a person was employed in a year, the more likely that she or he was not poor. The incidence of poverty for someone who worked 1 to 24 weeks was 21%, compared to 14.3% for someone with 24 to 48 weeks of employment and 5.3% for someone with a full year of employment. Conversely, the more a person was unemployed,[9] the greater the likelihood that she or he would be working poor. The overall incidence of working poverty for those with no unemployment was 7.3%; with 1 to 24 weeks unemployment it was 14.5%; and with 25 to 48 weeks it was 21.8%. For those who remained unemployed for the entire year, the incidence was 40%.[10]

> *. . . It is difficult working for low money and not having a permanent job . . . I always have to be thinking of the next job . . . maybe I have money today . . . or this week . . . but I may be unemployed next week . . . or maybe my hours will be cut . . . it is impossible to plan . . .*
>
> *Single, employed by temporary office placement agency, Quebec*

Figures on the distribution of working poverty illustrate that about two-thirds of the working poor experienced no unemployment during the survey year, while the other third experienced some unemployment during the same time period. Working poor women had a slightly greater tendency to have experienced no unemployment during the survey year than did working poor men.

OCCUPATION AND INDUSTRY

> *. . . sure it's seasonal work but where else can women make over $12.00 an hour . . . most of us have grade 12 or less . . . we don't have office skills . . . even if we did we would make less than we can at the plant . . . there aren't many jobs for women that pay enough money . . .*
>
> *Married, fish packing plant worker, British Columbia*

The probability of being working poor varied significantly by industry and occupation. Overall, the incidence of working poverty was high for people who worked in personal services (19.9%) and agriculture (18.3%) (Table 3.8). Slightly higher than average rates of working poverty were also evident in the construction (11.8%) and the business and miscellaneous services sectors (10.9%).

Despite very significant differences between men and women in several industrial sectors, the pattern worked both ways. In some sectors, such as "other primary" (primarily forestry and mining) and non-durable manufacturing, women had much higher rates of working poverty than did men. In other sectors, such as construction and wholesale

TABLE 3.8: Incidence and Distribution of the Working Poor, by Industry and Occupation, Canada, 1986

	Incidence of Working Poverty			Distribution of Working Poor		
	Both Sexes	Female	Male	Both Sexes	Female	Male
All Individuals	9.3	9.8	8.8	100.0	100.0	100.0
Industry						
Agriculture	18.3	19.1	18.2	8.2	5.5	10.6
Other primary	8.4	11.4	8.0	2.3	0.8	3.6
Non-durable manufacturing	8.3	11.2	6.3	7.7	9.2	6.5
Durable manufacturing	5.8	5.9	5.6	5.0	2.2	7.4
Construction	11.8	7.6	12.1	7.2	1.1	12.6
Transportation/communications/ other utilities	6.5	6.0	6.5	5.1	2.5	7.3
Wholesale trade	6.9	3.2	8.2	3.2	0.9	5.1
Retail trade	9.2	9.7	8.6	13.0	15.0	11.3
Finance/insurance	5.7	5.6	6.3	3.3	4.1	2.5
Community services	6.7	6.2	7.8	12.2	16.7	8.3
Personal services	19.9	20.1	19.4	20.8	29.6	13.1
Business and miscellaneous services	10.9	11.5	10.5	8.4	8.4	8.4
Public administration	4.1	5.1	3.3	3.2	3.4	2.9
Occupation						
Managerial/administration	3.9	4.2	3.8	4.7	3.8	5.4
Professional/technical	5.7	7.7	4.8	3.1	2.8	3.4
Health related	4.0	3.9	4.7	2.0	3.3	0.9
Teaching/recreation/arts	7.1	7.0	7.3	4.9	6.0	3.9
Clerical	6.9	6.9	7.0	12.4	21.3	4.8
Sales	8.8	9.1	8.5	8.8	9.1	8.5
Services	16.8	18.3	14.8	26.7	35.3	19.3
Farming/fishing	17.1	19.6	16.4	10.4	5.2	14.8
Processing/machining	7.6	13.9	6.3	4.3	2.7	5.7
Fabrication/assembly/repair	9.0	12.5	7.9	7.4	5.1	9.4
Construction	11.2	23.0	11.0	7.0	0.7	12.5
Transportation/equipment operating/ materials handling	9.4	14.8	8.5	7.8	3.9	11.1
Not applicable	7.4	7.4	0.0	0.1	0.3	0.0

Source: Tabulations by Analytical Services, Health and Welfare Canada on Statistics Canada, Survey of Consumer Finances, Public Use Micro-data Tape: Incomes of Individuals, 1986.

trade, men had much higher rates of working poverty than did women. However, these sectors have very small numbers of women employees.

In terms of occupations, the probability of being working poor was considerably higher for people working in services (16.8%) and farming and fishing (17.1%). Rates of working poverty were very low for people working in managerial/administrative occupations (3%), health and related occupations (4.1%), and professional and teacher occupations (5.7%). Substantial differences between men and women existed in several occupations. For example, in processing and machining occupations, women had a 13.7% chance of being working poor, compared to a 6.3% chance for men. Similarly in fabrication, assembly, and repair occupations, 12.7% of women were likely to be poor, compared to 7.9% of men.

> “ *. . . I am just panicked right now . . . what am I going to do to get me through this winter? . . . I have to do something . . . I have to find work . . . but then I look around and there are only jobs like department stores hiring part-time . . . or waitressing . . . I cannot afford to work for those wages or to work shifts . . .*
>
> *Single mother, community worker on temporary contract, Nova Scotia* ”

Working poor women were very highly concentrated in the personal service industries (29.6%) and service occupations (35.3%), those industries and occupations with the highest incidence of female working poverty. These industries and occupations also employ large numbers of immigrants and members of racial minority communities. This suggests that some groups of women are significantly more affected than others by occupational and industrial segregation, and that the poverty of women is integrally related to the nature of their employment. This issue will be explored more extensively in Chapters Four and Five.

INCOMES

It is easy to understand why women are more likely to be poor when we look at differences in the incomes men and women receive. The average total income from all sources of all adult individuals (poor and non-poor alike) was $18,816 in 1986. But the average total income for men was $23,960, while the average for women was $13,251, or 55.3% of men's average income (Table 3.9).

TABLE 3.9: Average Incomes of Individuals, by Sex and Work Force Status, Canada, 1986

	Both Sexes	Men	Women	Women as % of Men
	$	$	$	
All individuals	18,816	23,960	13,251	55.3
Full-time working poor	9,424	10,160	7,915	77.9
Part-time working poor	6,356	7,418	5,886	79.3
Other poor	6,966	6,856	7,019	102.3

Source: Tabulations by Analytical Services, Health and Welfare Canada on Statistics Canada, Survey of Consumer Finances, Public Use Micro-data Tape: Incomes of Individuals, 1986.

By comparison, the full-time working poor in Canada had average incomes of $9,424 ($10,160 for men and $7,915 for women), so that the average income of full-time working poor women was 77.9% of their male counterparts' income. Part-time working poor men made $7,418, compared to $5,886 (79.3%) for part-time working poor women. The average incomes of "Other poor" — people who did no work in the labour market — was $6,966; interestingly, women in this category had slightly higher average incomes than men ($7,019 versus $6,856), presumably because women receive child-related social benefits/tax deductions and credits.

> "*If one month something happens and you get behind . . . you're messed up for four months trying to catch up . . . sometimes I think that it's just not fair . . . I work for every darn thing . . . and we never seem to have enough . . . If we just had some extra money . . . things would be much easier . . . I may look for a part-time job in the fall . . .*
>
> *Single mother with two children, government employee, Nova Scotia*"

In general, working poor women tended to be poorer than were working poor men. If we look at how these men and women were distributed within family income groupings, we see that women were slightly more concentrated in the lowest income categories (less than $10,000), while men were slightly more concentrated in the higher income categories ($20,000 plus) (Figure 3.5). By definition, working poor people — be they men or women — were economically deprived. However, to the extent that there was an income hierarchy within the working poor population, men had a tendency to be at the top and women had a tendency to be at the bottom.

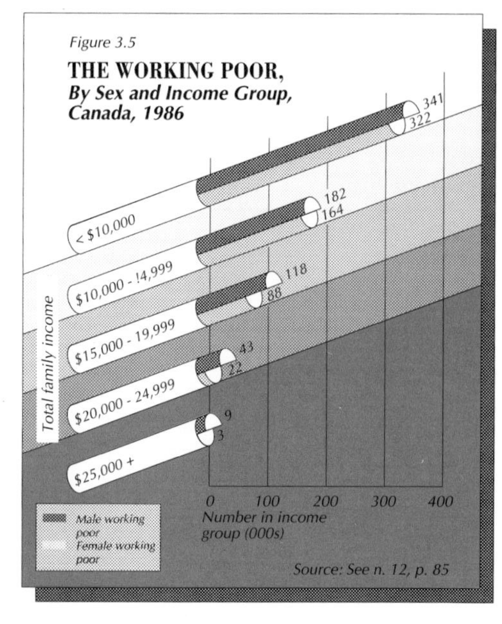

THE WORKING POVERTY GAP

> “ *. . . when it comes to working I'm not asking for a lot of money . . . I just want to make it to the poverty line . . . I need about $8.00 to $10.00 an hour to bring me to the poverty line with my family . . . I think we could live quite well on that money . . . just for once in my life . . . [I'd like] to live on the poverty line . . .*
>
> *Single mother with two children, Nova Scotia* ”

In any analysis of poverty it is useful to know not only how many people fall below the poverty line, but also by **how much** their incomes fall below. The difference between the actual incomes of the poor and the poverty cut-off is called the poverty gap. It is also useful to know whether some kinds of families have a bigger gap between their income and the poverty line than others. Finally, it is useful to know the extent of the total shortfall across the whole of society; this is called the total poverty gap. This total poverty gap indicates how much it would take in total dollar terms to eliminate poverty in Canada. In this chapter, we estimate the poverty gap associated with labour market-related poverty as we have defined it. After looking at the gap in terms of earnings alone and in terms of total income (which includes government transfers), we break this down by family type.[11]

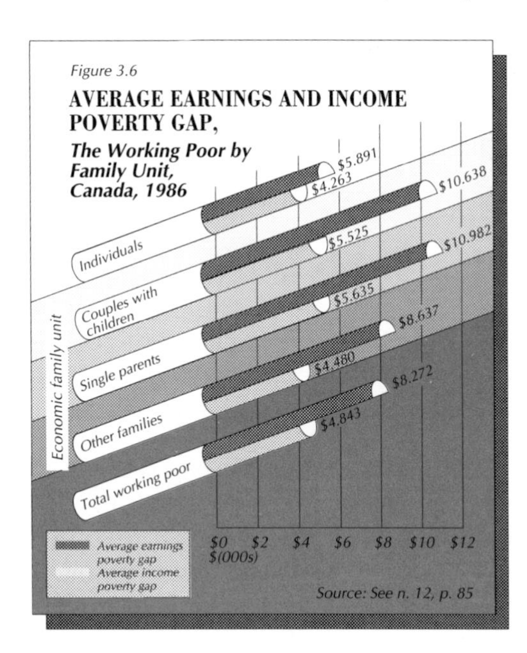

Figure 3.6
AVERAGE EARNINGS AND INCOME POVERTY GAP,
The Working Poor by Family Unit, Canada, 1986
Source: See n. 12, p. 85

The **average** income poverty gap for the working poor was $4,843 in 1986. This means that working poor families in Canada had incomes that were on average almost $5,000 below the poverty line (Figure 3.6). This average varied by family type but single-parent families experienced the largest income poverty gap at $5,635. The shortfall was about twice as large when based on earnings alone (as opposed to total income). This indicates that the working poor receive a significant portion of their income from sources other than earnings from employment. One question that arises from this analysis is whether policies to alleviate working poverty should attempt to improve earnings from employment or from other income, especially government transfers. These issues are explored in the subsequent chapters.

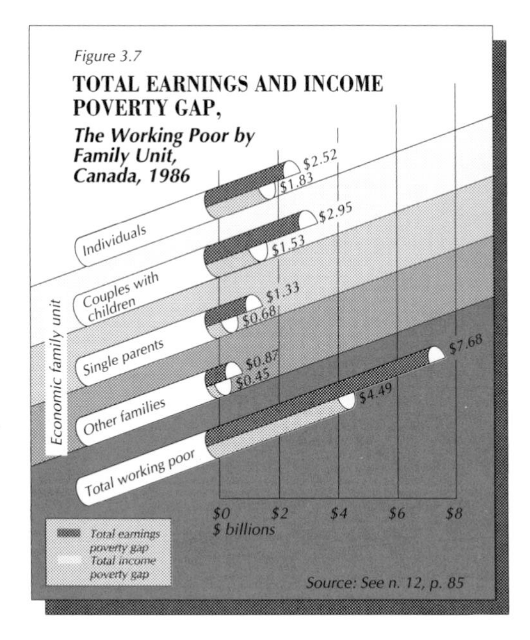

Figure 3.7
TOTAL EARNINGS AND INCOME POVERTY GAP,
The Working Poor by Family Unit, Canada, 1986
Source: See n. 12, p. 85

The total earnings poverty gap is the difference between the total earnings of the working poor and the poverty line. In 1986, it would have cost $7.7 billion to bridge this gap, i.e., bring the working poor up to the poverty line (Figure 3.7). However, government transfer payments totalled $3.19 billion, reducing the total earnings poverty gap of the working poor from $7.7 billion to $4.5 billion. This $4.5 billion, which is referred to as the total income poverty gap, breaks down into $1.83 billion for individuals, $1.53 billion for couples with children, $0.68 billion for single parents, and $0.45 billion for other families.

SUMMARY

Slightly less than one-tenth of the work force in Canada was poor in 1986, with the incidence of women's working poverty being slightly higher than men's. Forty-six per cent of the working poor were women.

Approximately 30% of the working poor (383,000 people) were employed full-time for the entire year and were still poor. Slightly more than one-fifth of working poor women were employed full-time for the entire year. People who were employed for less than the full year or were employed part-time were much more likely to be working poor than full-time, full-year workers.

The number of working poor women in Canada increased by 160.4% between 1971 and 1986, much higher than the 28.3% increase in the number of working poor men. While the overall number of working poor people rose significantly over the period, women's share of this growing number increased from 29.9% to 46.4%.

The incidence of working poverty for women was higher in 1986 than in the early 1970s, but the incidence of working poverty for men declined slightly.

The likelihood of being a member of the working poor was significantly greater for people with the following characteristics: under the age of 25, less than grade 9 education, a recent immigrant, an unattached individual or living in a single-parent household, living outside Ontario, living in a family with only one earner, and experiencing some unemployment.

Individuals working in service industries and occupations, which are dominated by women, are much more likely to be working poor than are men or women in other occupations and industries.

Working poor women are much worse off economically than are working poor men.

Eliminating the total labour market-related poverty gap in Canada would have cost an additional $4.5 billion in 1986; for single parents who do paid work, the cost would be $0.68 billion.

NOTES (Chapter Three)

1. For a detailed analysis of the concept of labour market-related poverty and a range of possible measures, see: Robert Taggart, *Hardship: The Welfare Consequences of Labour Market Problems: A Policy Discussion Paper* (Kalamazoo, Michigan: W.E. Upjohn Institute For Employment Research, 1982).
2. Statistical analysis based on the family usually disadvantages women because data on poor women tend to become invisible. The interests of women as individuals are better served when the unit of analysis is the individual rather than the family. Researchers normally use the *Incomes of Economic Families* micro-data tape. However, we have used the individuals tape, the Survey of Consumer Finances, because we wanted a count of individuals who were poor, not economic families. Although the concept of poverty is based on economic family income, we have used figures on the numbers of working poor male and female individuals, the majority of whom are, of course, living in families.
3. Pamela White, *Native Women: A Statistical Overview* (Ottawa: Department of the Secretary of State of Canada, 1985); Ian McDowell and Ed Praught, *Report of the Canadian Health and Disability Survey, 1983-1984* (Ottawa: Statistics Canada, 1986).
4. In this we differ from other studies and more conventional measures of working poverty, which use the entire population, not just the work force, as the measure against which poverty is made. We believe that the percentage of the work force that is poor is a more meaningful measure of labour market-related poverty.
5. Paradoxically, the rates of full- and part-time working poverty are slightly lower for women even though the overall rate of working poverty is slightly higher for women. This is explained by the different weighting of men and women in each work force. Women workers are more or less equally divided between the part-time and full-time/full-year work forces, while about two-thirds of men are full-time full-year workers.
6. National Council of Welfare, *Poverty Profile 1988* (Ottawa: 1988), p. 41.
7. See Chapter One for a discussion of the definition of heads of families and its sexist nature.
8. A small percentage (5.7%) live in families with no earners. This is what is meant by the "other" category in Table 3.7. The fact that there are some working poor with no earnings suggests that some people do work in the labour force but don't get paid. This could include family farm workers, small business owners with no income, or workers who were employed for a short period in the year of the survey but received their pay in the subsequent year.

9. The concept of unemployment refers to more than simply not working. Here it refers to a specific form of not working, in that to be unemployed a person must not only not be working, but must also be **searching for work**. See endnote 5, Chapter One.
10. Caution should be used with this last figure since the sample upon which it is based is very small.
11. Because we are looking here at the incomes of economic families, not the incomes of individuals, we have shifted to the use of Statistics Canada's Survey of Consumer Finances, Public Use Micro-data Tape: Incomes of Economic Families, 1986.
12. Tabulations by Analytical Services, Health and Welfare Canada on Statistics Canada, Survey of Consumer Finances, Public Use Micro-data Tape: Incomes of Individuals, 1986.

PART ONE: THEORY, DESCRIPTION, AND ANALYSIS

Chapter 4: Poverty and the Labour Market

IMPORTANCE OF LABOUR MARKET EARNINGS

Understanding what happens in the labour market is obviously essential to understanding poverty. Labour market earnings are important not just because they provide a decent standard of living, but because employment and earnings from the labour market contribute to an individual's prestige and self-worth. The working poor suffer not only the economic consequences of low earnings, but also the indignity associated with the status of low income.

" *. . . my work is part of who I am . . . sure it's hard sometimes . . . I worry about my kids . . . I worry about whether I can pay the bills . . . whether my job is going to continue . . . but it's important to be able to say I'm working . . . and to tell my kids that I'm supporting them . . .*

Single mother, clerk in the federal public service, Nova Scotia "

Because employment is an important source of social interaction, restricted access to employment limits a person's social life. Social interaction may also be conditioned by the types of jobs people hold. Segregating people into low-wage, low-status jobs — as is often the case for women — denies them access to the status that is (rightly or wrongly) frequently associated with the higher-paying jobs. Low-wage dead-end jobs can lead to higher absenteeism and turnover and poor work performance. This in turn keeps people in those positions or contributes to a pattern of constantly shifting from one low-wage job to another.

However, some types of labour market work enable workers to acquire skills and information that can enhance future earnings power. It is a source of on-the-job training (both formal and informal) as well as information about other job prospects. In addition, it conveys signals to employers about a worker's commitment, willingness, and ability to hold a job.

Finally, labour market earnings are important because society deems it appropriate that people earn their income rather than receive it in the form of transfer payments. This attitude is held by both taxpayers and recipients of transfers. One of the recurring comments we heard from poor women is that they would welcome the opportunity to get off the welfare rolls, if only they had the chance.

Clearly, labour market earnings are important for both their economic and their non-economic social consequences. Hence the importance of understanding why the labour market does not provide sufficient earnings to enable a significant portion of the population to escape poverty, let alone earn a decent standard of living.

GAIL
(Saskatchewan)

Gail is in her mid-30s, a single mother with two children aged 8 and 10. She has been separated from her husband for several years, and he now lives with another woman with three children. He spends time with their children but cannot afford support payments. Gail initially went on social assistance after the separation but worked two days a week part-time for a photocopier company. Two years ago she decided that she wanted more independence and entered a training program to help women move from welfare to work. To find a job she moved to a smaller rural community and now works as a clerk in a small shop. Her employer pays her slightly higher than minimum wage, but she now makes less than she would have on social assistance. She is fortunate in that she has some drug and dental coverage at work. Still, she finds it difficult to afford extra expenses such as school supplies, and she cannot afford extra child-care expenses when the children are sick. She rents a two-bedroom trailer but is on the waiting list for public housing. Even though she now has less money, Gail is adamant about not returning to social assistance.

SYSTEMIC BARRIERS IN THE LABOUR MARKET

SEX DISCRIMINATION IN WAGES AND EMPLOYMENT

Discrimination is a central factor that affects women's wages and employment opportunities. According to the latest 1986 census figures, female employment income was 55.6% of male employment income for all workers and 65.6% for full-year, full-time workers.[1] The extent to which this residual wage gap reflects discrimination is a controversial question that has been subject to considerable empirical analysis.[2] Much of the controversy stems from whether differences in such factors as hours of work, labour market experience, occupation, and industry reflect choice or discrimination. As we saw in Chapters One and Two, even when choice is involved, women's choices are severely constrained by household responsibilities.

Notwithstanding the controversy, there is substantial agreement that at least some of the earnings gap reflects discrimination **inside** the labour market. In any case, differences in wage-determining factors (such as hours of work, labour market experience, industry, and occupation) also reflect discriminatory factors, many of which originate **outside** the labour market. They could originate in the unequal division of labour with respect to household work and child care, or from gender stereotyping in schools or the family itself.

" *. . . it's disgusting the jobs that are put off on women . . . being a waitress or a sales clerk . . . and then they give them the most menial pay and call them unskilled . . . even bank tellers aren't well paid . . . and if you happen to be supporting a family you can't work for those wages . . .*

Single mother, working at a temporary job and trying to leave social assistance, Nova Scotia "

Based on the extensive literature on the determinants of the male-female earnings gap, the Ontario *Green Paper on Pay Equity*[3] suggested that the 1982 male-female earnings gap of 0.38 (i.e., 1 minus the ratio of female to male full-time earnings of 0.62) could be attributed to the following factors:

- differences in hours worked (0.16);
- factors such as experience, education, and unionization (0.05 to 0.10);
- occupational segregation (0.10 to 0.15);
- wage discrimination within the same narrowly defined occupation and establishment (0.05).

This analysis highlights the potential importance of some policies and the limitation of others in enhancing women's wages and employment opportunities. Especially evident are the limitations of conventional equal pay for **equal work** policies, because such policies would deal with only a small (0.05) portion of the gap attributable to wage discrimination within the same establishment and narrowly defined occupation. Equal employment opportunity policies (including affirmative action) have a potentially broader scope because they can deal with the larger portion of the gap (i.e., 0.10 to 0.15) attributable to the segregation of women in lower-paying occupations. Similarly, equal pay for **work of equal value** policies (often termed comparable worth in the United States and pay equity in Canada) have the potential for greater impact than conventional equal pay for equal work policies because they allow comparisons across otherwise dissimilar occupations. Their scope is severely limited, however, by the fact that they are currently restricted to comparisons within the same establishment. This is especially confining because many low-wage, female-dominated jobs are in all-female establishments (like child-care centres) where there are no male occupational groups with which to make comparisons. The empirical evidence on the male-female earnings gap also highlights the limitations of policies that deal with discrimination in the labour market. Much of the gap arises from constraints existing outside the labour market, as well as from the inability or unwillingness of employers to accommodate the changing nature of family life. Hence the importance of policies such as child care, alternative work arrangements, income supplementation, tax policy, and family law (discussed in Chapter Seven).

OCCUPATIONAL SEGREGATION BY SEX

> "*. . . it's interesting . . . you hear a lot about people needing to get experience and that it makes a difference in getting a job . . . but I have lots of experience at low-paying jobs . . . I've worked most of my life . . . but that doesn't seem to help me get out of this . . .*
>
> *Retail clerk,*
> *Saskatchewan*"

The segregation of women into lower-paying occupations is also an important reason for their low pay relative to men's. In 1981, 59.2% of women were employed in clerical (35.2%), sales (9%), and service (15%) jobs. Even though these figures are disproportionately high, they actually represent a slight **increase** from 1951, when a total of 58.4% of women held clerical (30.1%), sales (8.8%), and service (19.5%) jobs (Table 4.1).

Overall, women represented 43.3% of workers in all occupations; however, they were disproportionately represented in lower-paying clerical (78.9%), sales (45.4%), and service (54.9%) jobs (Table 4.2).[4] These jobs had average wages of $13,885, $16,284, and $11,270 respectively, compared to an average of $18,910 for all occupations.[5] As low as they are, these figures underrepresent the actual picture of women's occupational segregation. The broad occupational groupings in Table 4.1 also mask considerable occupational segregation **within** each group; women tend to dominate in the lower-paying positions. For example, in the managerial and administrative categories, females tend to occupy the administrative, not the executive positions; in teaching they occupy the lower-paying elementary school positions, not the higher-paying principal jobs; and in medicine and health they tend to be nurses, not doctors. This segregation of women into jobs that resemble unpaid domestic labour (cleaning, nurturing, teaching, health care) contributes to the undervaluation of women's work.

TABLE 4.1: Percentage Distribution of Female Labour Force, by Occupation, Canada, Selected Years, 1951-1981

Occupation	1951	1961	1971	1981
Managerial, administrative	3.3	3.3	2.0	5.2
Natural sciences, engineering	0.4	0.4	0.6	1.1
Social science	0.5	0.7	1.0	2.0
Religion	1.0	0.6	0.1	0.2
Teaching	6.7	7.3	7.1	6.0
Medicine and health	6.5	8.6	8.2	8.4
Artistic	0.9	1.1	0.7	1.4
Clerical	30.1	30.6	31.8	35.2
Sales	8.8	8.4	8.4	9.0
Service	19.5	19.5	15.1	15.0
Farming	2.8	4.3	3.6	2.2
Other primary	0.0	0.0	0.1	0.2
Processing	4.9	2.7	2.0	2.1
Machining and fabricating	10.2	7.2	5.5	5.1
Construction	0.3	0.2	0.2	0.3
Transport	0.1	0.1	0.3	0.6
Other	2.7	2.7	2.6	2.3
Unspecified	1.1	2.4	10.8	3.6
All Occupations	100.0	100.0	100.0	100.0

Note: Numbers may not add up due to rounding.
Source: Alice Nakamura and Masao Nakamura, "A Survey of Research on the Work Behaviour of Canadian Women", in *Work and Pay: The Canadian Labour Market,* ed. W. Craig Riddell (Toronto: University of Toronto Press, 1985), p. 180.

TABLE 4.2: Average Employment Income*, by Major Occupation and Sex, Canada, 1985

Occupation	Average Employment Income			Female Income as % of Male Income	% Female in each Occupation
	Female	Male	Both**		
Managerial, administrative	21,328	37,939	32,664	56.2	31.8
Natural sciences, engineering	19,878	30,756	28,828	64.6	17.7
Social sciences	15,792	34,938	23,757	45.2	58.4
Religion	12,526	16,975	16,045	73.8	20.9
Teaching	20,137	33,009	24,973	61.0	62.4
Medicine and health	18,051	46,679	24,050	38.6	79.0
Art, literary, recreation	12,060	18,945	15,984	63.7	43.0
Clerical	12,746	18,147	13,885	70.2	78.9
Sales	9,594	21,840	16,284	43.9	45.4
Service	7,362	16,028	11,270	45.9	54.9
Farming	6,235	11,986	10,764	52.0	21.2
Fishing, trapping, related	6,145	14,867	14,045	41.3	9.4
Forestry and logging	6,193	18,783	17,945	33.0	6.7
Mining and quarrying oil and gas	17,056	25,944	25,789	65.7	2.3
Processing	9,907	21,498	18,623	46.1	24.8
Machining	13,473	22,717	22,034	59.3	7.4
Product fabricating, assembly, and repair	11,117	21,633	19,084	51.4	24.2
Construction	12,655	19,685	19,502	64.3	2.6
Transport	11,100	22,076	21,186	50.3	8.1
Materials handling	10,761	17,825	16,116	60.4	24.2
Other	11,966	25,261	22,284	47.4	22.4
Unspecified	9,575	14,098	13,263	67.9	18.5
Total, all occupations	13,027	23,411	18,910	55.6	43.4

Notes: * For persons who reported employment income and weeks worked.
** Average income of female and male employees, weighted by number of employees.
Source: Morley Gunderson, *Employment Income,* 1986 Focus in Canada Series (Ottawa: Statistics Canada, 1989), cat. no. 98-129.

Although precise comparisons of these data with data for previous years are difficult, there is some recent evidence of a small decline in occupational segregation. Increased representation of women has been most prominent in higher-paying managerial, administrative, and scientific jobs (Table 4.3). However, because these jobs represent only a small fraction of all jobs, they do not represent a realistic route to occupational advancement for most women — and certainly not for working poor women. This is illustrated most clearly in Table 4.1 which gives the distribution of the female labour force by occupation. In 1951, only 4.2% of the female labour force was employed in higher-paying managerial, administrative, and scientific jobs. Even though this proportion more than doubled between 1951 and the 1980s, it remained at only a little more than 8% of the female labour force.

The increasing educational levels of women with professional, job-oriented degrees like law, medicine, and business reflected women's increased access to higher-paying occupations.[6] Between 1966 and 1981, women doubled their representation in graduate degree programs, from 18% to 37%. By 1981, they constituted 50% of those with a bachelor or first professional degree, and their representation among those receiving doctoral degrees tripled between 1966 and 1981. In terms of percentages, progress was made in professional fields like law, medicine and business, and even in male-dominated bastions like engineering and science. However, progress in terms of actual numbers of women was less dramatic.

Such educational advances may prove beneficial for individual women, but their effect on aggregate outcomes is limited by the fact that women university graduates still earn only about as much as male high school graduates.[7] As well, most poor people do not acquire advanced education and those that do (often single parents attending community colleges part-time) often have substantial debts from student loans by the time they graduate. Student loan programs were designed generally for young, recent secondary school graduates, who are often single and seldom have dependants or other debts. The reality is that most women will be left behind in the occupational advances being made by a small number of already privileged women. Because low levels of education are an important determinant of working poverty for both men and women, a great deal of emphasis must be put on securing education and training, and this in turn must be linked to changes in the nature of employment.

TABLE 4.3: Women as Percentage of Total Labour Force, by Occupation, Canada, Selected Years, 1951-1981

Occupation	1951	1961	1971	1981
Managerial, administrative	8.7	10.4	15.7	25.0
Natural sciences, engineering	6.9	4.8	7.3	13.9
Social sciences	27.8	29.4	37.4	50.8
Religion	39.7	28.9	15.7	26.5
Teaching	67.2	64.4	60.4	59.4
Medicine and health	68.5	72.1	74.3	77.6
Artistic	30.7	31.2	27.2	39.5
Clerical	56.1	61.0	68.4	77.9
Sales	33.3	32.0	30.0	42.1
Service	45.1	46.7	46.2	52.7
Farming	3.9	11.7	20.9	22.7
Other primary	0.1	0.3	1.3	4.5
Processing	14.8	13.7	17.8	22.1
Machining and fabricating	18.0	17.9	18.7	20.0
Construction	1.0	0.8	0.9	2.0
Transport	0.5	0.6	2.4	6.5
Other	16.3	13.6	15.7	20.4
Unspecified	20.6	26.0	43.4	42.7
All Occupations	22.0	27.3	34.3	40.0

Source: Alice Nakamura and Masao Nakamura, "A Survey of Research on the Work Behaviour of Canadian Women", in *Work and Pay: The Canadian Labour Market,* ed. W. Craig Riddell (Toronto: University of Toronto Press, 1985), p. 186.

BARBARA
(Nova Scotia)

Barbara is in her late 30s, a single mother of two teenagers. She is divorced from her husband and receives no support. She worked at several jobs while the children were young and has supported the family since her separation. She worked shift work as a security guard for seven years but left when she felt the children needed more of her time at home. After two years on social assistance she returned to school and completed a diploma as a medical secretary. She immediately found work on a training program with the provincial government and worked as a secretary with a social service agency for more than a year at minimum wage. Later she was classified as "temporary" and worked at a slightly higher wage for three years before receiving her "permanent" classification this year. Barbara hated being on assistance but felt at the time she had no choice. She took in boarders for extra money. She went into debt when she first left social assistance to work for minimum wage. This year will be the first that she will be making about $19,000 — $7,000 more than she made last year. Still, she is just managing to make ends meet. She is considering applying for an additional part-time job to help pay off the expenses she incurred when her job was less secure.

DISCRIMINATION AGAINST ABORIGINAL PEOPLE, RACIAL MINORITIES, AND PEOPLE WITH DISABILITIES

> "... If you don't get a job working for the Band ... it's hard to find work ... you aren't likely to get a job at one of the stores in any of the towns near here ... they don't hire native people ...
>
> *Aboriginal woman, part-time Band office worker, Ontario*"

We have looked at wage discrimination and occupational segregation and how they contribute to women's low pay and fringe benefits and hence to their working poverty. Aboriginal people, racial minorities (often termed "visible minorities"), and disabled people have also been identified — notably by the Abella Commission — as particularly disadvantaged in the labour market. This stems in part from wage discrimination and occupational segregation. These groups, along with women, have been targeted for employment equity initiatives (affirmative action) in the federal jurisdiction.

It is important to emphasize that the category "women" is not a homogeneous group. Women differ substantially with respect to education, labour market experience as well as occupational and industrial distribution, giving rise to substantial differences among women in terms of earnings, unemployment, and poverty rates. Women can be doubly disadvantaged when they are members of designated groups — disabled persons or members of the Aboriginal and racial minority communities — as well as of other groups that experience discrimination. Approximately one-third of women in Canada are immigrants or members of racial minority communities.

There is an element of arbitrariness in designating targets for anti-discrimination initiatives. Other non-targeted groups (e.g., recent immigrants, francophones in English-speaking Canada) may experience similar problems. As well, some members of designated groups are better off than most people outside the designated groups. These differences in treatment by public policy can create inequities and conflicts between designated and non-designated groups, as well as competition between designated groups. Furthermore, for Aboriginal people, racial minorities, and especially disabled persons, there is a degree of subjectivity involved in categorizing individuals in a particular group, which depends upon who is doing the categorizing.

An alternative to group designations based on personal characteristics would be to designate according to the labour market characteristics that give rise to the problem in the first place. Important characteristics could include low-wage status or being subject to wage or occupational segregation. Of course, there would be considerable overlap between the people identified using personal characteristics and those based on labour market characteristics; on that basis, using personal characteristics may be simpler.

Table 4.4 illustrates the occupational segregation of the four designated groups. The occupation groups are the thirteen "employment equity occupations" — groupings that have been formulated to capture occupational hierarchy. While women constituted 44% of the experienced work force in 1986, they occupied only 17.4% of upper level managerial positions and 8.1% of the foremen/women positions. Conversely, they were overrepresented in clerical and service jobs. Aboriginal people and disabled people were also underrepresented in higher-level occupations and overrepresented in service and manual jobs. Racial minorities were underrepresented at the managerial levels and in foremen/women positions.

TABLE 4.4: Occupational Distribution* of Designated Groups, Canada, 1986

	Females	Aboriginal People	Visible Minorities	Disabled People
All occupations	44.0	2.1	6.3	5.4
Upper level managers	17.4	1.4	4.1	1.8
Middle and other level managers	33.1	1.4	4.7	3.3
Professionals	53.3	1.4	7.1	3.1
Semi-professionals, technicians	50.5	2.3	6.2	5.0
Supervisors	47.9	1.6	7.5	6.3
Foremen/women	8.1	1.7	3.6	6.3
Clerical workers	79.9	1.7	6.2	4.2
Sales	48.0	1.4	5.1	4.8
Service	61.3	2.8	8.3	6.4
Skilled crafts and trades	8.3	1.9	3.8	6.4
Semi-skilled manual	14.0	2.6	4.8	8.8
Other manual	29.2	3.0	7.9	7.3
Occupation not stated	45.9	3.9	8.4	4.6

Note: * Per cent in the occupation who are members of the designated groups.

Source: Data for females, Aboriginal people, and visible minorities are from: Canada, Employment and Immigration Canada, *Employment Equity Availability Data Report on Designated Groups from the 1986 Census of Canada, For Employers under the Employment Equity Act and the Federal Contractors Program* (Ottawa: 1989). Data for disabled people are from the same publication, based on the Health Activity Limitation Surveys of 1986. Work force population figures are for persons aged 15 and over who worked in 1985 or 1986. Persons with disabilities refer to labour force participants aged 15 to 64 who worked any time between 1981 and 1986.

Income figures on persons with disabilities are even more sketchy. Results from the Canadian Health and Disability Survey of 1983-84 show that disabled persons were at the lower end of the income spectrum. For example, in 1983-84, 63.2% of disabled people had incomes (including disability payments) of less than $10,000 per year, compared to 43.8% of all people in Canada.[8] The greater the severity of the disability, the lower the income. Work-related problems of disabled people are particularly acute because they often face additional work-related expenses and problems of workplace access and accommodation to their needs.

Compared to the national unemployment rate of 10.3% in 1986, unemployment rates were particularly high for Aboriginal people (22.7%) and persons with disabilities that limit them in their labour force work (20%).[9] For women and racial minorities, unemployment rates were slightly higher than average, at 11.2% and 10.8% respectively. These unemployment rates do not take into account the hidden unemployment that results when people cease participating in the labour force altogether because they assume that no jobs are available. (These people are known as discouraged workers.) For example, relative to the average labour force participation rate of 66.5%, the participation rate for persons with disabilities was only 37.7%; the participation rate for disabled females was even lower at 28.4%.

OCCUPATIONAL BENEFITS

PENSIONS

The poverty of women begins with low employment earnings and is perpetuated in retirement because pensions are usually based on earnings. This is an especially important issue for women because they make up the majority of all poor people and, because they generally live longer, they make up the majority of the elderly. As a result of these two factors, about two-thirds of the elderly poor are women. This issue is a neglected area of concern in studies of poverty related to the labour market.

Canada's pension system comprises a complex array of public and private programs. Every person over age 65 is eligible for the flat-rate, Old Age Security payment, although a portion is taxed back from pensioners with higher incomes. Those with inadequate incomes can receive the income-tested Guaranteed Income Supplement and Spouse's Allowances; the latter is also available to people over age 60 under certain circumstances. People who work in the labour market pay into and are ultimately eligible to receive public pension benefits from the Canada/Quebec Pension Plans. These benefits are related to earnings and the worker's cumulative history of contributions. As well, workers may be members of employer-sponsored occupational pension plans. Because they are based on labour market activity, employer-sponsored occupational pension plans are of particular relevance to working poor women.

Women in the labour force are much less likely than are men to be covered by an occupational pension plan. In 1984, 30% of the female labour force was covered, compared to 42% of the male labour force.[10] The difference reflects the fact that females are more likely to be non-paid workers in family businesses or part-time employees (who are usually ineligible), and because they tend to be employed in small establishments or industries and occupations where pension coverage is rare.[11] The low level of pension coverage in predominantly female establishments, industries, or occupations is rooted in the stereotype that women do not need independent retirement income because they do not support a family and are themselves dependent.[12]

In addition to their lower rate of pension coverage, women are less likely to be covered by flat-benefit plans where the benefits are independent of earnings. Flat-benefit plans dominate the unionized sector, which is disproportionately male. By contrast, women are disproportionately enrolled in earnings-based plans, with benefits usually based on earnings in the final few years of work. This tends to disadvantage women because of their lower earnings.

Women are also likely to receive lower pension benefits **within** a given earnings-based pension plan because such plans are based on a combination of final earnings and service credits (e.g., 2% of final earnings for each year of service). Women tend to accumulate fewer service credits because of career interruptions and job turnover. Their lack of service credits also make them less likely to be eligible for subsidized early and special retirement features. Most important, the lower wages of women (because of wage discrimination or segregation into low-wage occupations) lead to lower pension benefits in earnings-based plans.

> "... when I was first laid off I thought of retiring . . . I'm 55 years old and I've worked for the same company for 21 years . . . I got all the papers together . . . but the thought of it was too scary . . . I'm too young to retire . . . and a pension of $61 a month is just not enough . . .
>
> *Unemployed department store clerk, Ontario*"

OTHER OCCUPATIONAL BENEFITS

As with pension benefits, women are likely to receive fewer occupation-related benefits (disability payments, health benefits, paid vacations above the statutory minimum number of weeks, court-awarded personal injury settlements, etc.) than are received by men. This occurs because women are more likely to work in occupations, industries, or establishments that do not offer fringe benefits; even if they do, women are likely to receive smaller benefits because many are wage-related or have eligibility requirements based on length of service. If women are less likely to accumulate service requirements or receive lower wages than is true for men, they will also receive lower levels of benefits.

Many fringe benefits take the form of perks to minimize taxes. As such, they are available disproportionately to people with higher incomes and higher marginal tax rates. Because men tend to dominate these higher-income positions, they tend to benefit more than women do from these non-taxable perks.

The large and growing importance of occupational benefits highlights the fact that labour market earnings are central to women's long-term income security. Earnings are important not only in their own right, for the buying power and prestige they bring, but also for the fringe benefits that accompany them. These issues are particularly acute for working poor women who are self-employed or work part-time, many of whom are not eligible for a wide range of occupational benefits. This is also the case for the marginalized work force in subcontracted jobs or in jobs with limited-term contracts.

> “ *. . . my husband was off for 1½ months on crutches after he slipped on the ice . . . we lost six weeks' pay . . . luckily our income tax [rebate] came in . . . but we could hardly afford groceries . . . right now I have a prescription in my purse that I can't fill . . . my husband takes only one week of vacation every year . . . we need the extra money . . . if you need tires for the car or something for the house . . . the money comes in handy . . .*
>
> *Married retail clerk,*
> *Saskatchewan* ”

SUMMARY

Labour market earnings are important not only because of the buying power they bring, but also because they are a source of status, prestige, and self-worth. These and other features of good quality jobs are often denied the working poor.

The disadvantagement or working poverty of women is primarily the result of wage discrimination and segregation in low-wage occupations.

Women can be doubly disadvantaged when they are also members of groups such as Aboriginal people, racial minorities, or disabled persons —all of whom are also disadvantaged in the labour market. For these groups, the labour market often does not provide decent jobs (or any jobs) at decent wages.

The effects of working poverty on women are compounded by the fact that poor quality jobs deliver fewer occupational benefits because benefits tend to be tied to earnings.

NOTES (Chapter Four)

1. Morley Gunderson, *Employment Income, 1986*, Focus in Canada Series (Ottawa: Statistics Canada, 1989), cat. no. 98-129 .
2. Canadian studies on this topic are summarized in Morley Gunderson, "Discrimination, Equal Pay, and Equal Opportunities in the Labour Market", in *Work and Pay: The Canadian Labour Market*, ed. W. Craig Riddell (Toronto: University of Toronto Press, 1985), pp. 219-265.
3. Ontario, Attorney General and Minister Responsible for Women's Issues, *Green Paper on Pay Equity* (Toronto: 1985).
4. With regard to the categories of Social Sciences, Farming, Teaching, and Medicine and Health which have a high proportion of females (Tables 4.2 and 4.3), it should be remembered that those categories employ a fairly low percentage of all workers (Table 4.1).
5. The negative relationship between the proportion of the occupation that is female and the average wage of that occupation has been documented in econometric studies, reviewed in Donald Treiman and Heidi Hartmann, *Women, Work and Wages* (Washington, D.C.: National Academy Press, 1981), pp. 28-32.
6. Figures for this paragraph are from Alice Nakamura and Masao Nakamura, "A Survey of Research on the Work Behaviour of Canadian Women," in *Work and Pay*, ed. Riddell, *supra*, note 2, pp. 200-201.
7. Gunderson, *Employment Income, supra*, note 1.
8. Ian McDowell and Ed Praught, *Report of the Canadian Health and Disability Survey, 1983-1984* (Ottawa: Statistics Canada, 1986), p. 86. Since the disability survey did not collect data on the income of non-disabled persons, the 1984 Survey of Consumer Finances is used for all the Canadian figures.
9. Canada, Employment and Immigration Canada, *Employment Equity Availability Data Report on Designated Groups from the 1986 Census of Canada, for Employers under the Employment Equity Act and the Federal Contractors Program* (Ottawa: 1988), tables 8 and 14.
10. Canada, Statistics Canada, *Pension Plans in Canada, 1984* (Ottawa: 1986), cat. no. 74-401, p. 12.
11. *Ibid.*, p. 12, for Canadian data on this point. U.S. information on this is discussed in Cynthia Cohen, "The Impact on Women of Proposed Changes in the Private Pension System", *Industrial and Labor Relations Review*, vol. 36, no. 2 (1983), pp. 258-270; and Wesley Mellow, "Determinants of Health Insurance and Pension Coverage", *Monthly Labor Review*, vol. 105, no. 2 (1982), pp. 30-32.

12. Freda Paltiel, "Women and Pensions in Canada", *International Social Security Review*, vol. 35, no. 3 (1980), pp. 333-334; and Susannah Rowley, "Women, Pensions and Equality", in *CharterWatch: Reflections on Equality*, ed. Christine Boyle et al. (Toronto: Carswell, 1986), pp. 297-298.
13. Evidence on these various effects for Canadian women is given in: James Pesando, Morley Gunderson, and John McLaren, "Pension Benefits and Male-Female Wage Differences: A Canadian Perspective", Toronto, University of Toronto, 1988, mimeo.

PART ONE: THEORY, DESCRIPTION, AND ANALYSIS

Chapter 5: Changes in the Labour Market

UNEMPLOYMENT AND RECESSION

In the early 1980s, the Canadian economy experienced a pronounced and deep recession that produced levels of unemployment exceeded only during the Great Depression of the 1930s. In 1983, Canada's unemployment rate peaked at 11.9%. Although the rate of unemployment for women had been consistently higher than the rate for men, female unemployment peaked at 11.6% in 1983, slightly less than the male unemployment rate of 12%.[1]

Despite a rebounding economy after the 1981-82 recession, unemployment has remained high in all regions of Canada (with the exception of southern Ontario). Regions like the Atlantic provinces have been especially affected. For example, the 1986 unemployment rate in Newfoundland was 20%, almost three times Ontario's rate at 7%. Historically it had been about twice the Ontario rate. Clearly, the recovery has been uneven, with dramatic labour shortages in southern Ontario, but continued high unemployment in the Atlantic region.

> "*. . . my husband lost his job as a steam fitter last year . . . the economy just slowed down . . . it was impossible to support the family on my job with only 27 hours a week . . . during the summer months I found another job as a clerk in the local delicatessen . . . minimum wage . . . that kind of pay was okay when I was in my early twenties . . . but to work for $4.50 an hour when I'm 45 years old . . . my husband was receiving unemployment insurance . . . but there wasn't enough money . . . now he has a job paying $6.90 an hour . . . that's a third of what he was making before . . .*
>
> *Teaching assistant for children with learning disabilities, British Columbia*"

Since 1966, when the female and male unemployment rates were both a little over 3%, the unemployment rate for women has generally been rising both absolutely and relative to the rising male rate. The female rate dropped below the male rate in the peak unemployment years of 1982-83 because of the strong growth of male unemployment as a result of plant closures and layoffs in manufacturing.

MADELEINE
(Northern Ontario)

Madeleine lives in a single-industry town in northern Ontario. She is in her mid-50s, divorced, and living alone in a two-bedroom apartment. She has five children, aged 19 to 24, who no longer live at home. She has a grade 8 education and worked as a supervisor with a large department store chain for 21 years before the store was closed last summer. Until she was laid off, Madeleine was relatively satisfied with her income. She made approximately $7.50 an hour but her expenses were reduced after the children left home. She receives an additional $150 a month as part of her divorce settlement. Since the store closed, however, Madeleine has not been able to find full-time work. She has applied to a number of retail stores but they are only hiring part-time staff. If she decided to retire now, her company pension would pay only $61 a month. She has decided to return to community college for upgrading and training in office skills. She admits that it is not an easy decision. She has not attended school since she was a child. She has limited savings and plans to apply for a student loan. The alternative is to try to survive on a short work week at minimum wage.

Most people who become unemployed experience only a short period (2 to 2.5 months) of unemployment. Nevertheless, a considerable amount of total unemployment is accounted for by those few who experience long spells of unemployment.[2] The average duration of unemployment is shorter for women than it is for men; but because women have a higher overall unemployment rate, the shorter average duration implies that women also have a greater frequency or incidence of unemployment, which more than offsets their shorter duration.[3] Longer-term unemployment for women is likely to be disguised, however, by the fact that when jobs are not available, women are likely to leave the labour force completely (the discouraged worker effect).

The burden of unemployment always tends to hit disadvantaged people hardest. In a severe recession like the 1982 downturn, the groups most likely to suffer the largest increase in unemployment are those with the most tenuous hold on jobs: single mothers, Aboriginal people, disabled people, and young people, among others. One study that focused on the differential burden of the 1982 recession in Canada concluded:

> It is the long-term or chronically unemployed who are most likely to be pushed into poverty when jobs become scarce. Such unemployment is most prevalent among workers in primary industries such as fishing, logging and construction, transport or material handling, among workers in the Atlantic provinces and Quebec, among those possessing skills which earn low wage rates, among poorly educated youths, native peoples, and older workers who have lost their jobs.[4]

The relationship between unemployment and poverty is clear. As we saw in Chapter Three, as the length of a person's unemployment increases, they are much more likely to be working poor. This is true both for men and women, although the relationship is stronger for men. On a provincial basis, the same relationship holds. Provinces with high unemployment rates generally have high rates of working poverty, and vice versa. The notable exceptions are Manitoba and Saskatchewan which have high rates of working poverty but low rates of measured unemployment. This reflects the availability of low-wage agricultural work and the lack of unemployment insurance benefits for many farmers.

The effect of the recession of the early 1980s on working poverty is noteworthy. As the economy moved into recession, the extent of working poverty increased for both men and women. The incidence of working poverty declined after its peak of 1984, but it remained disturbingly high, despite the expansion of the mid-1980s. Prolonged periods of recession appear to have a lingering effect on working poverty; sustained high levels of working poverty are related to changes in the structure of employment.

Several studies have examined the relationship between poverty and the business cycle. An early but comprehensive study, based on U.S. data, indicated how an expanding economy dramatically helps the poor, in spite of the fact that it is also associated with inflation.[5] That study analysed the effect of expansion on three factors that affect the position of the poor: their income from labour market earnings and transfer programs; the real value of their assets; and prices for the goods they consume. Each of these components was found to change in a manner beneficial to poor people when the economy is expanding.

First, the labour market earnings of the poor increase relative to the average in periods of expansion. This is because the poor are more likely to get a job, they are more likely to have other members of the family participating in the labour market, their hours increase, and their wages rise faster than average. The study found that transfer payments also generally kept up with inflation, although this is obviously a potential problem given current concern about containing the growth of government spending.

Second, the real value of the assets of the poor does not decrease much as a result of the associated inflation because the poor have few assets, those assets they do have tend to increase in value with inflation, and the poor tend to be net debtors rather than creditors.

Third, the prices of goods consumed by the poor do not increase by as much as average prices in a period of inflation.

The study concludes that although the poor are adversely affected by inflation, they benefit more from the improved employment opportunities than they lose as a result of inflation.

Empirical work in the United States provides more recent evidence on how business cycle fluctuations have a disproportionate effect on the poor.[6] Over the period 1948-83, high unemployment was associated with a significant decrease in the income share going to the bottom 40% of income earners, while the share going to the top 20% increased. Those earners in the upper middle portion of the income distribution experienced negligible effects. Similar results, showing how the poor are affected negatively and disproportionately by recession and the accompanying unemployment, were found in a range of empirical studies from the United States.[7]

In fact, based upon a comprehensive review of various U.S. studies, one authority attributes the persistent and relatively constant rate of poverty in the United States between 1967 and 1985 mainly to rising unemployment during that period.[8] Higher unemployment (and, to a lesser extent, demographic change) exactly offset the reduction in poverty that otherwise would have occurred because of increased transfer payments and human capital investments such as education and training. The poverty rate, which was roughly 14% in 1967 and 1985, would have fallen to somewhere between 10% to 11.6% were it not for the rising unemployment over that period.

In Canada, similar empirical work has come to the same conclusion, i.e., that the proportion of people living in poverty increases dramatically as the state of the economy deteriorates.[9] The proportion of people in poverty declined steadily during the economic expansion of the 1970s, then rose dramatically during the recession of the early 1980s.

The single most important determinant of changes in poverty rates between 1970 and 1985 was change in economic growth rates and the fact that poverty tends to increase in cyclical downturns and periods of high unemployment.[10] While increased transfer payments offset part of the loss of earnings from employment, they were insufficient to offset the entire loss of earnings. As a result, poverty and inequality tended to increase whenever employment growth slackened or declined. The only group for which transfer payments had a significant impact during cyclical downturns was the elderly.

EROSION OF LABOUR MARKET EARNINGS

One of the most important indicators of the degree to which the labour market provides a decent standard of living is the real wage rate — that is, the money wage rate adjusted for inflation. Based on this indicator, the Canadian labour market has not provided an improved standard of living for the average person in Canada.[11]

Over the period 1975 to 1987, **nominal** labour income (wages plus supplementary benefits) did rise by a substantial 140%. However, this was about equal to the inflation rate, so that **real** labour income rose by only 1.5% over that 12-year period. In fact, there was an actual drop of 6.2% occurring between 1977 and 1987. This decline in real wages after 1977 was offset by an increase in supplementary benefits, including employers' contributions to health insurance, pension plans, workers' compensation, and unemployment insurance benefits.

Provincial figures on labour income have been available only since 1979. The largest drops in real income (adjusted for provincial consumer price indexes) occurred in Newfoundland, British Columbia, and Quebec, with the largest gains in Manitoba and Nova Scotia. Other provinces showed little change. Separate figures are not available for men and women or for the working poor. However, given that the adverse consequences of labour market adjustment have already been shown to fall disproportionately on the working poor, it is reasonable to assume that they, and perhaps especially women, also experienced real income losses.

Of particular relevance to low-wage workers is the infrequent upward adjustment of the minimum wage to compensate for the substantial inflation that occurred in the 1970s and 1980s. Specifically, since 1975 the **real** minimum wage (adjusted for inflation) has fallen by more than 30% in Alberta, British Columbia, and Quebec and by more than 20% in the other seven provinces.[12] In 1975, minimum wages (expressed in annual income terms) averaged a little more than 10% above the poverty line for single persons without dependants and for two-income, four-person families. For single parents with one child, the minimum wage income averaged 86% of the poverty line. By 1985, minimum wage incomes had fallen to about 84% of the poverty line for single persons without dependants and for two-income, four-person families. For single parents with one child, minimum wages averaged 65% of the poverty line, and were as low as 56% of the poverty line in British Columbia.

The erosion of real wages has hit low-wage workers as well as the average worker in Canada. In fact, the erosion has been worst for those at the minimum wage. In no province would working full-time for the full year at the legal minimum wage enable even single persons without dependants or two-income families with two children to escape poverty. Single parents with one child could not even come close to escaping poverty in such circumstances.

“ *. . . I simply cannot work for wages that will not support my three children and me . . . They keep telling you that to get started you have to start at the bottom . . . if the bottom is minimum wage I can't get started . . . Maybe married or single people can work for those wages . . . I can't . . . How can you support a family with this type of money?*

Single mother with three children,
trying to leave social assistance,
Saskatchewan ”

Clearly, the experience of recent years highlights the failure of the Canadian labour market to maintain a decent standard of living for all people in Canada. One study of family income changes in Ontario between 1970 and 1985 found that while total income from all sources rose by 22.7%, the earnings from the employment component of that income rose by only 17.5%.[13] Even more important, the earnings component of low-income families did not increase at all, and although the real total income of poor people did rise, this was primarily because of increases in transfer income over the period. The main reasons for these increases were growth in the number of single mothers as a proportion of all low-income families, and the lack of growth in young people's earnings. It is increasingly difficult for single-earner families to have the same standard of living they did even a decade ago. Wage erosion has resulted from numerous factors:

- the depressed economic conditions of the early 1980s;
- unemployment;
- international competition;
- industrial restructuring and the wage polarization associated with low-wage service jobs and part-time jobs;
- public sector retrenchment; and
- the rapid influx of workers at the low end of the wage spectrum — women from the household, immigrants, and (until recently) youth.

All these changes have contributed to the erosion of labour market earnings for the average worker but especially for low-wage workers, many of whom are women. This highlights the importance of focusing on the labour market as a source of income and as a determinant of working poverty.

CHANGES IN THE NATURE OF EMPLOYMENT

INTERNATIONAL COMPETITION AND FREE TRADE

The effects of increased international competition, in particular free trade between Canada and the United States, are controversial, especially with respect to their impact on women. Whatever the pros and cons of the Canada-U.S. free trade agreement, it will undoubtedly have considerable adjustment consequences. Many of these will be in female-dominated industries like textiles, footwear, clothing, food processing, and electrical products. Other female-dominated jobs in the business service sector (e.g., data processing, financial services, telecommunications, transportation, and culture) may also be jeopardized,[14] while some growth may occur in the low-wage personal service sector. Of greater importance is that employers in Canada, faced with increased competition under free trade, may become even more opposed to the expense of programs like pay equity and employment equity, which specifically benefit women.

The potential for positive consequences from free trade has also been identified: net new job creation;[15] rationalization of industry to be able to compete with increasing world competition;[16] the opportunity for changing to better jobs;[17] the chance to use employment equity initiatives in the newly created jobs; and lower consumer prices, especially on food and clothing, which may be particularly important for the poor.[18]

"*. . . both of us have fairly good seniority . . . even for a seasonal job . . . but we always have to think that something could happen to the fishing industry . . . to the company . . . I worked for another company a number of years ago that closed . . . and we always think the same thing could happen again . . . we depend on the weather, the season, the fish . . . now there are changes to GATT and [the] free trade [agreement] to worry about . . . fish plant workers in the United States only make $5.00 an hour . . .*

Married, husband and wife are both employed
in fish packing plant,
British Columbia"

Whether the positive consequences of free trade have the potential to offset the negative effects remains unanswered. What is certain, however, is that Canada's international competitiveness will depend increasingly on our ability to improve productivity and quality by harnessing the potential of advanced technology, effective management, and skilled workers.[19]

TECHNOLOGICAL CHANGE

Since the 1960s, the Canadian labour market has been subject to rapid changes in technology. The changes have now gone beyond conventional mechanization to encompass robotics, computerization and, in the office, personal computers, facsimile machines, and electronic mail. As the information society replaces the industrial society, technological change is demanding changes in work organization and work relations.

The effect of technological change in the office has been particularly important for women, given their dominance in clerical and office occupations and the low-wage nature of many of these jobs. Unfortunately, the impact of technological change has been difficult to isolate and study because it has been concurrent with other important changes.

The impact of technological change on employment growth **overall** has probably been neutral; many new jobs have been created as others have become redundant. Technological innovation has likely slowed the growth of clerical work and changed its nature from typing and filing to word processing and information storage and retrieval. Even if the overall impact is neutral, however, it masks the fact that a process of job creation and job destruction creates considerable **adjustment** consequences on **both** the upside and the downside. Adjustment may be particularly difficult for women.

On the downside, involuntarily unemployed women may have special difficulties finding new jobs if they entail either mobility or relocation from the community. With regard to relocation, women's options may be more limited because their husbands generally earn more than they do and because, in this society, women are expected to put their husbands' jobs/careers ahead of their own. As well, discrimination in recruiting and hiring obviously makes job changes more difficult. Women earning low wages, especially if there is no family support, can find it particularly difficult to finance the transition between jobs.

On the upside, adjustment problems may also prevail. Technological change can create opportunities for interesting and well-paying jobs in designing, implementing, and operating the new technology, especially in offices. It also offers the potential for substantial productivity improvement and therefore the ability to compete on the basis of high productivity rather than low wages. However, this requires that the new high-tech jobs be open to women and that women have the basic education (often in math, science, and technology) to take advantage of these opportunities. It also requires flexibility (e.g., from household ties) for any retraining and relocation that may be necessary. These conditions are not always present for women, especially single mothers, although they are more free to relocate than married women.

> *. . . it's hard to find a job with my education . . . my experience has always been in retail . . . now there are only part-time jobs . . . I took evening courses in data processing because I thought I would need to know how to work with computers . . . but offices have changed a great deal since I was in school . . . it's hard to keep up . . .*
>
> *Divorced mother, mid-50s,*
> *unemployed and considering returning to community college,*
> *Ontario*

As well as affecting employment levels, technological change can affect skill levels and therefore wages. This has raised the spectre of the loss of many middle-level jobs as technology is substituted for skilled workers. The issue of the "declining middle" has been the subject of some controversy in Canada and the United States and is discussed in more detail in a subsequent section.

Norm Leckie's study published by the Economic Council of Canada indicated that technological change appears not to be eroding the number of middle-income jobs.[20] *Innovation and Jobs in Canada,* a 1987 report also by the Economic Council of Canada, reviewed a number of earlier studies on the effect of technological change on the declining middle and reports on new studies conducted. Although this 1987 report indicated that the studies often differed in their conclusions, it stated:

> While there is, thus far, no **strong** historical evidence of middle-class decline overall, there are enough signs pointing to the possibility of erosion that we feel compelled to sound a warning note.[21]

The effects of technological change and office automation on the **quality** of jobs are also not clear. Many jobs are being de-skilled as machines are performing tasks once performed by workers and the work itself becomes machine-paced. At the same time, machines allow employers to monitor more completely the pace of work, thus creating stress, strain, and health hazards. After surveying the evidence, the U.S. Panel on Technology and Women's Employment concluded:

> The panel has not been able to determine whether on balance, the technologies have thus far decreased the quality of clerical work by increased routinization, fragmentation, or abusive electronic monitoring, for example, or improved it by facilitating intellectual challenge and growth of competence . . . Several surveys show that workers are generally satisfied, and often happy, with the new capabilities because they have eliminated repetitive tasks, such as retyping manuscripts. But several surveys of health effects show that workers who use office equipment and respond that they have strict production quotas or are monitored closely are more likely to indicate stress-related psychological and physiological symptoms.[22]

RESTRUCTURING OF EMPLOYMENT

In large part because of increased competition and technological change, the Canadian economy has been undergoing dramatic industrial restructuring. The most important aspect is the shift from manufacturing employment to service employment. Some of this shift may be only a shift in the way that the work is organized and categorized for statistical purposes; for example, many jobs previously counted as manufacturing, such as cleaning and business services, have simply been subcontracted by manufacturers to the service sector.[23] Nevertheless, a substantial number of often well-paid, blue-collar jobs in manufacturing, especially the heavy, "smokestack" industries, have been lost. Virtually all new jobs are in the service sector, where wages tend to be more polarized.

Some of the new service jobs are at or near the top of the wage distribution scale, involving the development, financing, engineering, marketing, operating, and managing of new technology. Many of the jobs are in the financial and business service sector (the information economy), as well as in social services and public administration (the state sector). Many more, however, are lower-wage consumer service jobs and low-wage jobs in the wholesale and retail trade. The latter sector has also grown dramatically to meet the demands of the two-earner family for services traditionally provided by unpaid wives at home.

These changes in the structure of employment are another reason for concern about the "declining middle" and deskilling of the work force.[24] The job losses are occurring in the middle-income blue-collar jobs, and job gains are occurring either in higher-paid professional, technical, and managerial jobs or in lower-paid service jobs. Such changes are exacerbating the extent of working poverty among women, because the lower-wage service jobs are clearly associated with working poverty and women are segregated in these jobs.

For women, the concern is that they will continue to be excluded from higher-paid jobs and segregated in the growing number of low-wage personal service jobs. These low-wage jobs have the highest rates of female working poverty; they are often non-unionized and difficult to monitor for violations of employment standards, in part because many are located in small establishments.

In some cases, technological change creates opportunities for women by breaking down conventional job hierarchies. The new jobs may also provide opportunities for employers to meet employment equity objectives — if they have such objectives. Relying less on physical capacity and shiftwork, such jobs may be more conducive to the realities or stereotype of female employment. The more flexible modular factories, for example, using integrated systems and advanced communication, can be located so as to facilitate ties with the household. This may be a mixed blessing, however, since it will perpetuate and institutionalize women's double burden of household and labour market work.

Some empirical evidence for Canada suggests that deindustrialization and technological change have led to some increased polarization in wage and occupational structures. However, the patterns are rather complicated and do not clearly establish a vanishing middle or a de-skilling of the work force. The patterns are also difficult to disentangle from other demographic changes occurring in the composition of the work force.[25]

From a policy perspective, industrial restructuring does not have to be accepted passively with all its ramifications for low-wage jobs. Internationally, other countries have developed alternative patterns of postindustrial service economies. West Germany, for example, has followed a consistent policy of moving from a high-wage industrial economy to a high-wage information economy, based on technological change and computerization. Employers in Canada, by contrast, do not appear to be diffusing technology as fast or as effectively as their major international competitors.[26]

ANNA AND JACK
(British Columbia)

Anna and Jack are in their mid-40s, married and own their own home. Anna's youngest boy, aged 16, lives with them. She works part-time as a teaching assistant for children with learning disabilities; he works as a pipe fitter. Anna makes approximately $12 an hour for a 27 1/2-hour week but is laid off during holiday periods and the summer months. As a tradesman, Jack made approximately $25 an hour until he was laid off two years ago. Jack was unemployed for a year, relied on unemployment insurance benefits, and now works at another job for $6.90 an hour. Before Jack was laid off the combined income of the couple was more than adequate. Now, however, Anna has been taking on extra jobs, trying to make ends meet. In addition to meeting their current expenses, they also have to worry about the debt they incurred when Jack was receiving unemployment insurance. Their combined income placed them just at the poverty line last year, but with their debt load Anna is concerned that they may have to give up their house unless she is able to find extra work.

GROWTH OF PART-TIME EMPLOYMENT

One of the most pronounced recent changes in the Canadian labour market has been the growth of part-time employment.[27] As we saw in Chapter Three, this has important implications for the growth of working poverty, because the ranks of the working poor are made up increasingly of part-time workers, especially women.

By 1985, more than 26% of the female work force worked part-time (up from 20.3% in 1975), and 7.6% of the male work force worked part-time (up from 5.1% in 1975).[28] Of particular note is the dramatic growth in **involuntary** part-time employment (defined as workers who are seeking but unable to find full-time work). In 1985, 27.8% of the female and 33.5% of the male part-time work force worked part-time involuntarily; these proportions roughly tripled between 1975 and 1985. The large jump in involuntary part-time employment at the peak of the recession in 1982 provides additional evidence that the labour market **increasingly** is not providing adequate jobs for a substantial number of workers, especially women.

> "*. . . I'll probably work at two jobs again this summer . . . during the year my husband was without work we ran up a number of bills . . . when the Board lays me off in the summer time I need to apply for unemployment insurance . . . if I can't find work we need that money to live on . . .*
>
> *Married, part-time educational worker, British Columbia*"

Table 5.1 indicates the extent to which part-time and full-time jobs accounted for employment growth between 1966 and 1987. As the 1966-73 figures indicate, most of the employment growth was accounted for by full-time jobs. The percentage of full-time employment increased to 85.6% in 1973-79. However, in the period 1979-83, because of the recession of the early 1980s, all the employment growth was accounted for by part-time jobs. About half of these were filled by women aged 25 and over, and a further one-third were filled by men and women under 25 years of age. This predominance of women and young adults filling part-time jobs occurred throughout the period. As well, almost all the part-time employment was in the service sector. In 1983-87, the percentage of full-time employment fell to 86%, slightly above the 1973-79 level.

Part-time employment is associated with working poverty not only because of the smaller number of hours and low hourly wages, but also because of wage discrimination against part-time workers.[29] This means women are hit by double discrimination. As well, part-time employment is often associated with few or no fringe benefits, a lack of job security, and little protection under employment standards law or collective agreements.

TABLE 5.1: Part-time and Full-time Employment Growth as a Proportion of Overall Growth, Canada, 1966-1987

Category	1966-73	1973-79	1979-83	1983-87
Total employment	100.0	100.0	100.0	100.0
Full-time	74.0	85.6	0.0	86.0
Part-time	26.0	14.4	100.0	14.0
Part-time employment	100.0	100.0	100.0	100.0
Youth (under 25)	55.5	62.6	32.7	43.8
Adult women (over 25)	35.9	43.5	48.9	50.9
Adult men (over 25)	8.6	-6.4	18.4	5.3
Goods industries	10.2	1.0	7.7	-15.0
Service industries	89.9	99.0	92.3	115.0
Full-time employment	100.0	100.0	100.0	100.0
Youth (under 25)	26.2	23.9	--	1.1
Adult women (over 25)	37.1	43.0	--	53.6
Adult men (over 25)	36.7	33.0	--	45.3
Goods industries	10.0	25.1	--	28.1
Service industries	90.0	74.9	--	71.9

Source: Figures for 1966-83 from Stephan F. Kaliski, "Trends, Changes and Imbalances: A Survey of the Canadian Labour Market", in *Work and Pay: The Canadian Labour Market*, ed. W. Craig Riddell (Toronto: University of Toronto Press, 1985), p. 86; figures for 1983-1987 are computed from the annual issues of Statistics Canada, *The Labour Force* (Ottawa), cat. no. 71-001.

. . . I love this job but I can't afford to work for this money . . . It's a good hourly rate . . . but the kids and I are forced to do without in the summer months when they lay me off . . . How do they expect you to get by with two months off in the summer time? . . . During the school year I had to adjust my income tax deductions to try and get more take-home pay . . . And now the government is telling me that I don't qualify for unemployment insurance . . .

Single mother, teacher's aide,
Saskatchewan ”

Certainly part-time work is not inherently undesirable. For some people, it may provide the opportunity to combine household and labour market work or to bridge the transition between the labour market and education or retirement. The problem is that much part-time work is involuntary and is usually not afforded the protections and hourly pay associated with full-time jobs. As well, women are over-represented in the part-time job market for a variety of reasons, including their disproportionate responsibilities for child care and household work.

> " *. . . when I said 'no' to taking a part-time job, I really had to think about it . . . it's hard enough making ends meet when you're paid $7.00 an hour for a full-time job . . . who can live on 26 hours a week? . . . still I wonder if I'm doing the right thing . . . it's hard because I don't know what the future will bring . . .*
>
> *Unemployed retail clerk,*
> *Ontario* "

DEREGULATION, PRIVATIZATION, AND PUBLIC SECTOR RETRENCHMENT

In addition to pressure from technological change and international competition, changes in the demand side of the labour market are also emanating from deregulation, privatization, and public sector retrenchment, the latter occurring in the form of pressure to curb public expenditures including pay and employment.[30] Retrenchment has occurred in most elements of the public sector — health and welfare, education, and protective services, as well as in the public service. These changes subject labour more directly to market forces. This may be beneficial in terms of lowering government expenditures, but the changes will also likely result in lower wages, thereby contributing to working poverty.

Pressures for deregulation are most evident in transportation industries like trucking and airlines; as such, their most substantial effect will likely be to reduce the union wage premiums that tend to prevail for men in those industries. Privatization of Crown corporations, sub-contracting of government services to the private sector, and general retrenchment and cutbacks in the public sector are likely to be more broadly based and hence to affect women as well as men.

> " *. . . I worked for a Crown corporation for thirteen years as a secretary before they laid everyone off . . . we were shocked . . . it was just announced in the budget . . . there was no warning . . . I haven't been able to find a permanent job since then . . . it's unsettling . . . after thirteen years you thought you would just live and die at that job . . . for a year and a half I've been working on term contracts with different departments . . . my contract expires in four weeks and there is no indication that it will be extended . . . sometimes they wait until the last day to tell you . . .*
>
> *Divorced mother with three children,*
> *employed on term contract with federal government,*
> *Nova Scotia* "

Women will likely be affected disproportionately by cutbacks in the public sector for a variety of reasons. First, the public sector has been an important source of growth in female employment, especially in such areas as education, health, social services, and the public service. Second, while there certainly are low-wage jobs in the public sector, they tend not to be the extremely low-wage, dead-end jobs found in the private sector, especially in the service sector. Third, there tends to be less wage discrimination against women in the public sector than in the private sector, and women in the public sector tend to receive slightly higher wages relative to the private sector than do men.[31] Fourth, the promotion rate in the federal public service is slower for women than it is for men; therefore, while cutbacks are likely to retard all such advancement, women will be adversely affected to an even greater degree.[32] Finally, most of the current pay and employment equity initiatives affect the public sector or the federally regulated sector; hence, retrenchment in those sectors is likely to dampen those initiatives.

The effects of policies to reduce public sector employment or restrict public sector wages, therefore, are likely to fall disproportionately on women. As indicated in one study,

> At the policy level, our empirical findings highlight a basic dilemma that would be associated with the strenuous application of constraining influences on public sector earnings. Since the excesses are greatest for women and for low-wage workers in general, constrain-

ing them would have the most adverse impact on those already at a disadvantage in the labour market. While the inefficiencies of using public sector wages to redistribute income should be recognized, it must also be noted that a policy to curb excessive wages in the public sector could conflict with government objectives of equal pay for females and raising the wages of the working poor in general.[33]

CHANGES IN THE LABOUR FORCE

On the supply side, the Canadian labour market has been subject to a number of influences that have affected the wages and employment prospects of women. The dramatic increase in the labour force participation of women, especially married women with children, was discussed in Chapter One. This increase in female labour force participation has occurred in all industrialized countries, but has been particularly dramatic in Canada. For example, between 1961 and 1981, the female participation rate increased by an average of one-third in other industrialized nations while it almost doubled in Canada.[34] This partly reflects Canada's fairly low female labour force participation rate in 1960, compared to that of other industrialized nations.

The dramatic increase in female labour force participation has several implications for female labour market behaviour and working poverty. On the social side, the increased participation of women in the labour market creates demands on the labour market and on related institutions for child care and more flexible work arrangements; these are still not being adequately met. On the economic side, the influx of women continues to depress female wages as they compete for the available jobs, even the low-wage jobs that characterize the female labour market. The increase in women's labour force participation also has led to concern that women are "taking the jobs of male breadwinners" — a concern based on the fallacies that women do not have the same right to employment as do men and that the number of jobs in the economy is fixed.

The rise in women's labour force participation also occurred at the same time as a dramatic increase in youth participation rates as the baby boom entered the labour force, especially in the 1970s. Since both groups often competed for the same low-wage jobs, this tended to further depress already low wages. The substantial pool of unemployed youth and female household labour provided employers with a readily available supply of low-wage workers. Of course, young women were doubly burdened in this regard.

The declining youth cohort should provide some relief in the future by reducing the supply of youth labour at the lower end of the wage spectrum. In addition, the growth of female labour force participation will likely slow down, now that the majority of women are participating in the labour market. Whether reductions in the growth of the female and youth labour force will improve wages at the low end because of reduced competition is an open question.

Immigration has also been an important source of low-wage labour for Canada. Like the reserve of women at home and unemployed youth, the steady supply of immigrant labour helped depress wages that were already low. In addition, many immigrant women, even though often well-educated, tend to be working poor, occupying the lowest-wage jobs, for example, in the garment trades, cleaning, and domestic labour.

The low-wage position of many immigrant women likely reflects a variety of factors. As women, and often as members of racial minority communities, they face discrimination. Many may be spouses of men allowed into Canada under the point system to fill skill shortages; the women themselves may have qualifications acquired elsewhere which are not recognized here, or they may not have had labour market skills or skills easily transferable to the Canadian labour market, relegating them to jobs that are extensions of household work, such as cleaning and sewing. Barriers of language and culture also inhibit their integration in the labour market and participation in training programs.

. . . at first we moved to Winnipeg and I worked in a knitting factory . . . it was only for minimum wage but the manager spoke Spanish . . . I took English for six months later in Toronto . . . but it still didn't help . . . I could only find work as a cleaner . . . then in another factory where the people spoke Spanish . . . I never made more than $5.00 an hour . . . you need to speak English to find a better job . . . women like me need language and job training . . .

Single mother, Chilean immigrant, Ontario ”

Domestic workers are similarly disadvantaged.[35] They are invariably women and usually immigrants. Domestic workers often face a language barrier and discrimination because of their racial minority status, and they seldom enjoy the full protection of employment standards legislation. As well, domestic labour tends to have a low status, in part because of its association with unpaid household work.

> *. . . when I first came here I didn't know anything about the country . . . there were no jobs at home . . . and I needed to make a living . . . I left my children and moved here . . . it wasn't difficult getting a job working in someone's home . . . at first I lived in the family's home . . . I was always afraid that they would find out that I was working illegally . . . now that I am legally here it is a bit easier . . . but it's hard to find other work . . . but I've been lucky . . . I have friends who work for people who don't pay them enough and make them do all kinds of extra work . . .*
>
> *Jamaican immigrant, domestic worker, Ontario*

One group of domestic workers — visa domestics — is particularly vulnerable. Visa domestics are given temporary employment visas, which are arranged before they come to Canada. A formal agreement between the domestic and the household is arranged and is, in theory, enforced through provincial employment standards branches; however, in practice, little enforcement takes place. These workers are vulnerable to exploitation for various reasons:

- although domestic workers can change employers, they cannot accept employment other than domestic work for two years;
- they must live in with their domestic employer;
- they can apply for landed immigrant status but only after two years, making them particularly beholden to their employers from whom they need recommendations;
- they are unlikely to get recommendations if they search for new jobs; and
- because working arrangements are often informal, live-in domestics are especially vulnerable to exploitation if they are expected to be on-call or available at most times.

Clearly, this situation creates a captive pool of low-wage labour — akin to indentured servants — for employers.

Some domestic workers are covered by employment standards legislation, but the laws are notoriously difficult to enforce. Inspections of the workplace are not considered feasible, and domestic workers may be reluctant to complain (even if they know the procedures) for fear of reprisal.

Other closely related groups of low-paid workers — usually women, immigrants, and workers without the full protection of employment standards laws — include homemakers (employed by an organization or agency to work in a household, such as caring for an ill person) and homeworkers (employees of a company who do piecework, such as sewing or typing, in their own homes).[36] Such workers are very likely to fall into the category of working poor women.

UNIONIZATION

Any serious attempt to reduce working poverty must recognize the importance of unionization for a number of reasons.[37] First, unions broadly improve wages and working conditions for their members. As well, in general, unions tend to compress the wage structure and they bargain for fringe benefits, many of which involve the same cost per worker to the employer and hence benefit lower-wage workers disproportionately. Unions also provide a degree of due process through mechanisms such as grievance procedures, as well as monitoring and communication functions; these are likely to help workers who would otherwise have little individual bargaining power.

> “ *. . . I worked in a pizza place for a couple of months . . . but I wanted to find another job . . . there was lots of pressure and the manager was always looking at you kind of dirty . . . he never touched me but he would say things that would really make you feel uncomfortable . . . but I had to have a job . . . it was stressful . . . they made you nervous . . . I was always afraid I might lose my job . . . it's not like you have a union . . .*
>
> *Married, husband and wife are both working at non-unionized jobs, Saskatchewan* ”

Other aspects of unionization, however, can exacerbate wage inequality and deter the advancement of women. Unionization can increase the pay of many already well-paid workers, and, in fact, may depress pay levels in some lower-paying non-union jobs as persons who cannot get jobs in the union sector crowd into the non-union sector. Unions adhere to the seniority principle which often disadvantages women, given their intermittent patterns of employment. Also, unions have difficulty organizing low-wage workers and part-time workers — groups that are disproportionately female. There may be overt sexism within unions (as in all of society's institutions), and this may reduce the benefits of unions for women.

The wage premium for being unionized in Canada (after controlling for the effect of other wage-determining factors) is in the neighbourhood of 10% to 25%,[38] an amount broadly similar to that found in a range of U.S. studies. These studies also indicate that the union/non-union wage differential is fairly similar for women and men. (Systematic Canadian evidence on this point is not available.) However, women benefit less from unionization than men do, because women are less likely to be unionized. With respect to the overall degree of inequality, the evidence based on U.S. studies (no Canadian studies are available) indicates that unions in fact reduce wage inequality and thus are potentially important in the struggle to alleviate women's labour market-related poverty.

SUMMARY

Since 1977, real labour **income** has declined, although the decline in real **wages** was offset to some degree by increases in fringe benefits and transfer income. This highlights the problems of the labour market in providing an improved standard of living for working people.

Minimum wage increases are of particular relevance to the working poor because, since 1975, **real** minimum wages (adjusted for inflation) have fallen by more than 30% in Alberta, British Columbia, and Quebec, and by more than 20% in the other seven provinces. As a percentage of poverty lines, minimum wages have fallen dramatically. People cannot escape poverty by working at the minimum wage.

The state of the Canadian economy is the single most important determinant of change in levels of poverty, because poor economic conditions produce unemployment, and unemployment exerts downward pressure on wages.

Increased international competition in general, and the free trade agreement between Canada and the United States in particular, will create both positive and negative adjustment consequences for working poor women. While there is substantial disagreement on the net effects of economic change at the international level, the fact remains that significant adjustments will be required and that some workers will be adversely affected unless adequate adjustment mechanisms are put in place.

Technological change, including office automation, has likely had a neutral **overall** impact on employment growth; however, it has created adjustment problems in terms of job losses and skill adaptations that must be addressed through labour market policies.

The Canadian economy has undergone substantial restructuring in response to international competition and technological change. Some tentative evidence indicates that this has led to some deskilling of the work force, wage polarization, and a decline in the number of middle-income jobs, and that these have contributed to working poverty.

Growth in part-time employment has been substantial, especially for women in low-wage service jobs. Much of it is involuntary, as full-time jobs would be preferred. Part-time employment is associated with working poverty because of the low number of hours, low hourly pay, few fringe benefits, and lack of protection under labour law or collective agreements.

Deregulation, privatization, and public sector retrenchment are also occurring at a rapid pace. Public sector retrenchment, in particular, is likely to affect women adversely because this sector is an important source of reasonably well-paid jobs. It also provides greater opportunities for women through pay equity and employment equity initiatives.

On the supply side of the labour market, the growth of the female labour force, immigration, and the influx of young adults into the labour market have created considerable downward pressure on the already low wages of jobs held by working poor women. The rapid influx of women into the labour market has also created new demands for child care and alternative work time arrangements — demands that are still not being met adequately.

The labour market problems of immigrant women are acute for a variety of reasons — triple discrimination by virtue of being women, immigrants, and often members of racial minority communities; lack of recognition for qualifications acquired elsewhere; segregation into low-wage jobs; language barriers and inadequate training; and the lack of protection under employment standards laws or collective agreements. The problems of domestic workers, especially visa domestics, are notable in this regard.

Unionization is an important element in any strategy to improve the wages and working conditions of working poor women. However, because low-wage female-dominated sectors are traditionally difficult to organize, this will require extra effort. In addition, principles like seniority, which can disadvantage women, may have to be re-examined, and sexism within unions themselves will have to be eradicated.

NOTES (Chapter Five)

1. Canada, Statistics Canada, *Historical Labour Force Statistics 1988* (Ottawa: 1989), pp. 206, 212.
2. Stephan F. Kaliski, "Trends, Changes and Imbalances: A Survey of the Canadian Labour Market", in *Work and Pay: The Canadian Labour Market,* ed. W. Craig Riddell (Toronto: University of Toronto Press, 1985), p. 101.
3. *Ibid.,* p. 104.
4. R. Paul Shaw and Norman Paterson, "The Burden of Unemployment in Canada", *Canadian Public Policy,* vol. 11, no. 2 (1985), p. 143.
5. Robinson Hollister and John Palmer, "The Implicit Tax of Inflation and Unemployment: Some Policy Implications", in *Redistribution to the Rich and the Poor,* ed. K. Boulding and M. Pfaff (Belmont, Calif.: Wadsworth Publishing, 1972).
6. Rebecca Blank and Alan Blinder, "Macroeconomics, Income Distribution, and Poverty", in *Fighting Poverty: What Works and What Does Not,* ed. S. Danziger and D. Weinberg (Cambridge, Mass.: Harvard University Press, 1986), pp. 180-208.
7. See: Charles Beach, "Cyclical Sensitivity of Aggregate Income Inequality", *Review of Economics and Statistics,* vol. 59, no. 1 (February 1977), and "Cyclical Impacts on the Personal Distribution of Income", *Annals of Economic and Social Measurement,* vol. 5 (1976); McKinley Blackburn and David Bloom, "Family Income Inequality in the United States: 1967-1984", *Industrial Relations Research Association,* 39th Proceedings (1987); Alan Blinder and Howard Esaki, "Macroeconomic Activity and Income Distribution in the Postwar United States", *Review of Economics and Statistics,* vol. 60, no. 4 (1978); Edward Gramlich, "The Distributional Effects of Higher Unemployment", *Brookings Papers on Economic Activity,* vol. 2 (1974); Edward Gramlich and Deborah Laren, "How Widespread are Income Losses in a Recession?", in *The Social Contract Revisited,* ed. D. Lee Bawden (Washington, D.C.: Urban Institute, 1984); Charles Metcalf, "The Size Distribution of Personal Income During the Business Cycle", *American Economic Review,* vol. 59, no. 4 (1969); Thad Mirer, "The Effects of Macroeconomic Fluctuations on the Distribution of Income", *Review of Income and Wealth,* vol. 19, no. 4 (1973).
8. Isabel V. Sawhill, "Poverty in the U.S.: Why Is It So Persistent?", *Journal of Economic Literature,* vol. 27, no. 3 (September 1988), pp. 1073-1119.
9. Carol A.L. Prager, "Poverty in North America: Losing Ground", *Canadian Public Policy,* vol. 14, no. 1 (March 1988), pp. 52-65.

10. Pierre Perron and François Vaillancourt, *The Evolution of Poverty in Canada, 1970-1985* (Ottawa: Economic Council of Canada, 1988).
11. The subsequent empirical evidence is based on Fred Wong, in "Trends in Labour Income", *Employment, Earnings and Hours* (Ottawa: Statistics Canada, July 1988), cat. no. 72-002, pp. 219-248.
12. Information in this paragraph is from David Thornley, "Minimum Wages and Adequate Income", *Social Infopac* (Social Planning Council of Metropolitan Toronto), vol. 6, no. 1 (1987).
13. Kevin McQuillan, "Family Change and Family Income in Ontario: Some Recent Trends", *Discussion Paper* (Toronto: Child, Youth and Family Policy Research Centre, 1989).
14. Marjorie Cohen, *Free Trade and the Future of Women's Work: Manufacturing and Service Industries* (Ottawa: Garamond Press/Centre for Policy Alternatives, 1987); Ann Porter and Barbara Cameron, *The Impact of Free Trade on Women in Manufacturing* (Ottawa: Canadian Advisory Council on the Status of Women, 1987).
15. As stated in Sunder Magun et al., *Open Borders: An Assessment of the Canada-U.S. Free Trade Agreement* (Ottawa: Economic Council of Canada, 1988), p. 74: "Most of the net jobs created would be in the service sector occupations such as clerical, sales, service and managerial. The distribution of employment gains from free trade by sex is similar to the male-female distribution in current total employment."
16. As stated in Ronald Wonnacott and Roderick Hill, *Canadian and U.S. Adjustment Policies in a Bilateral Trade Agreement* (Toronto: C.D. Howe Institute, 1987), p. 4, a Canada-U.S. free trade arrangement "would allow the cost-cutting rationalization in Canada that would make many of its industries internationally competitive". However, there is some debate as to whether rationalization of Canadian industry could improve our competitive position with the Third World, especially given the low wages in those countries.
17. Katie Macmillan, *Free Trade and Canadian Women: An Opportunity for a Better Future* (Ottawa: Canadian Advisory Council on the Status of Women, 1987).
18. *Ibid.*, p. 28, cites a 1978 study by the Economic Council of Canada indicating that if all tariffs were removed in 1974, the price of food would drop by 10% and clothing by 20%. The overall incidence of poverty would have dropped by 25%, from roughly 1.4 million to 1.0 million people below the poverty line.
19. Leon Muszynski, "Manufacturing Matters! And So Does the Welfare State", in *Manufacturing Matters: Conference Proceedings and Research Papers* (Toronto: Industrial Development Institute, 1989), p. 62.

20. Norm Leckie, *The Declining Middle and Technological Change: Trends in the Distribution of Employment Income in Canada, 1971-84,* Discussion Paper, no. 342 (Ottawa: Economic Council of Canada, 1988), p. 86.
21. Economic Council of Canada, *Innovation and Jobs in Canada* (Ottawa: 1987), p. 68. [Also summarized in the Council's report, *Making Technology Work: Innovation and Jobs in Canada: A Statement* (Ottawa: Economic Council of Canada, 1987).]
22. Heidi I. Hartmann, Robert E. Kraut, and Louise A. Tilly, ed., *Computer Chips and Paper Clips: Technology and Women's Employment* (Washington, D.C.: National Academy Press, 1986), p. 168.
23. Muszynski, "Manufacturing Matters!", *supra,* note 19, p. 4.
24. In the sociology literature, these arguments have been advanced in Harry Braverman, *Labour and Monopoly Capital: The Degradation of Work in the Twentieth Century* (New York: Monthly Review Press, 1974); and Barry Bluestone and Bennett Harrison, *The Deindustrialization of America: Plant Closings, Community Abandonment, and the Dismantling of Basic Industry* (New York: Basic Books, 1982).
25. Competing factors that can affect the wage and occupational distribution of the work force are discussed in Charles Beach, *The Vanishing Middle Class? Evidence and Explanations* (Kingston: Queen's University Industrial Relations Centre, 1988). The factors include:
    - baby-boom effects;
    - the increase in single-person households (elderly and single-parent families);
    - more women in the paid work force;
    - labour's falling share of national income;
    - recessions;
    - deindustrialization;
    - trade-induced industrial shifts;
    - industrial relocations; and
    - increased part-time work.

    Based largely on reviewing the U.S. literature and other empirical evidence, Beach concludes that the most important factors in reducing the number of middle-income family units and increasing the number of low-income family units are:
    - the increase in single-parent families;
    - the recession of the 1980s;
    - the industrial relocation in the U.S. from the Northern and Midwest to the South and West; and
    - increased part-time work, especially among men.

Canadian studies on the wage polarization issue include: John Myles, G.W. Picot, and Ted Wannell, *Wages and Jobs in the 1980s: Changing Youth Wages and the Declining Middle* (Ottawa: Statistics Canada, 1988); and John Myles, *The Expanding Middle: Some Canadian Evidence on the Deskilling Debate* (Ottawa: Statistics Canada and Carleton University, 1987).

26. Economic Council of Canada, *The Bottom Line: Technology, Trade and Income Growth* (Ottawa: 1983).
27. Canada, Commission of Inquiry into Part-time Work (Joan Wallace, Commissioner), *Part-time Work in Canada: Report of the Commission of Inquiry into Part-time Work* (Ottawa: Labour Canada, 1983).
28. Figures in this paragraph are from a special survey from Canada, Statistics Canada, *The Labour Force* (Ottawa: December 1986), cat. no. 71-001.
29. Wayne Simpson, "Analysis of Part-time Pay in Canada", *Canadian Journal of Economics*, vol. 19, no. 4 (1986), pp. 798-807.
30. Mark Thompson and Gene Swimmer, ed., *Conflict or Compromise: The Future of Public Sector Industrial Relations* (Montreal: Institute for Research on Public Policy, 1984), including the article, Morley Gunderson, "The Public/Private Sector Compensation Controversy", pp. 1-44.
31. For a discussion of this evidence in the Canadian context, see: Gunderson, "The Public/Private Sector Compensation Controversy", in *Conflict or Compromise*, ed. Thompson and Swimmer, *ibid.*, pp. 1-44.
32. Nicole Morgan, *The Equality Game: Women in the Federal Public Service (1908-1987)* (Ottawa: Canadian Advisory Council on the Status of Women, 1988), p. 31. Also, in a grievance hearing reported by the *Ottawa Citizen* on July 13, 1989, the Public Service Alliance of Canada showed that, in all fields of the public service, women were more likely to lose their jobs than were men, as a result of the federal government's plan to cut 15,000 public service jobs.
33. Morley Gunderson, "Earnings Differentials Between the Public and Private Sectors", *Canadian Journal of Economics*, vol. 12, no. 2 (1979), p. 241.
34. Jacob Mincer, "Intercountry Comparisons of Labour Force Trends and Related Developments: An Overview", *Journal of Labour Economics*, vol. 3, no. 1 supplement (1985), p. 2.
35. Monica Townson, *Domestic Workers and the Employment Standards Act* (Toronto: Ontario Task Force on Hours of Work and Overtime, 1987).
36. Laura C. Johnson and Robert E. Johnson, *The Seam Allowance: Industrial Home Sewing in Canada* (Toronto: Women's Educational Press, 1982).

37. The empirical evidence in this section is from Morley Gunderson and W. Craig Riddell, *Labour Market Economics: Theory, Evidence and Policy in Canada* (Toronto: McGraw-Hill Ryerson Limited, 1988), chapter 16. A general discussion of women and unions in Canada is given in Julie White, *Women and Unions* (Ottawa: Canadian Advisory Council on the Status of Women, 1980).
38. Gunderson and Riddell, *Labour Market Economics, ibid.*, p. 313.

PART TWO: POLICY SOLUTIONS

Chapter 6: Labour Market Policies to Combat Working Poverty

THE IMPORTANCE OF FULL EMPLOYMENT

The importance of a full-employment, expansive economy to help alleviate working poverty among women cannot be overemphasized.[1] The previous chapter documented how unemployment and economic recession adversely affect the poor. For women working or seeking work in the labour market, the problems are particularly severe. In periods of high unemployment, they are often the first to be laid off, they may be discouraged from entering the labour market even to look for work, their opportunities to find full-time work are severely constrained, and their wage gains are severely limited.

As well, pay equity and employment equity policies are less likely to be implemented or enforced effectively when the economy is not healthy. It is easier to grant pay equity wage increases in female-dominated jobs when wages are increasing in general. It is also easier to achieve employment equity objectives by hiring and promoting designated employees when new jobs are being created and existing jobs are not threatened.

The Canadian unemployment rate was relatively high a decade ago and remains high by international standards (Table 6.1). Canada has not experienced rapid increases to high levels of unemployment as have France, West Germany, the United Kingdom, or the Netherlands. However, Canada's unemployment rate has not fallen off from high levels as has occurred in the United States. Nor does Canada's rate approach the low levels prevailing in countries like Japan, where many workers have a commitment to lifetime employment from their employers, or Sweden, where governments have invested heavily in active labour market policies such as public relief work, vocational training, and sheltered workshops for people who otherwise would be unemployed. The number of Swedes enrolled in these programs tends to be greater than the number who are unemployed.[2]

Some part of Canada's unemployment problem results from factors related to labour supply, such as the fact that the unemployed do not have the skills that are in demand or do not live in the area where jobs are available. But the recent Canadian picture is particularly disturbing because much of the continued high unemployment experienced since the recession reflects political decisions to use monetary and fiscal policy to curb inflation.[3] In 1988, the Canadian Labour Market and Productivity Centre noted that, throughout the 1980s, the number of unemployed people far exceeded the number of available jobs. More than half of all unemployment in 1987 was attributable to a simple job shortage, a factor that varied greatly by region.[4] But a large body of cross-national research indicates that the most important determinants of a low rate of unemployment are political rather than economic.[5] In commenting on the post-1983 recovery, Pierre Fortin, a noted Canadian economist, observes:

> . . . if Canadian macroeconomic policy does nothing serious to lift the economy out of the current stagnation of employment . . . then it will be proof that something is wrong not with the Canadian economy, but with our ideologies, our vested interests, and our political process.[6]

TABLE 6.1: Unemployment* in Selected Countries, Selected Years, 1975-1986

Country	1975	1980	1986	% change 1975-1986
Canada	6.9	7.5	9.6	39
United States	8.5	7.1	7.0	-21
Australia	4.9	6.1	8.1	65
Japan	1.9	2.0	2.8	47
France	4.2	6.4	10.7	155
West Germany	3.4	2.9	7.2	112
United Kingdom	4.5	7.0	11.2	149
Italy	3.0	4.4	6.3	110
Netherlands	5.2	6.2	9.7	87
Sweden	1.6	2.0	2.7	69

Note: * Unemployment rates approximating U.S. concepts of unemployment.
Source: Joyanna Moy, "An Analysis of Unemployment and Other Labour Market Indicators in 10 Countries", *Monthly Labor Review*, vol. III, no. 4 (1988), p. 41; Joyanna Moy, "Recent Trends in Unemployment and the Labour Force, 10 Countries", *Monthly Labor Review*, vol. 108, no. 8 (1985), p. 14.

Canada's current monetary and fiscal policies are geared to cooling down inflationary pressures in an overheated Ontario economy — at the cost of regional inequality and higher unemployment in areas like the Atlantic provinces. The use of restrictive monetary and fiscal policies to curb inflation worsens inequality and unemployment and increases poverty, especially labour market-related poverty. Much of the high unemployment in Canada throughout the 1970s and 1980s was induced by restrictive monetary and fiscal policies, exacerbating the already existing unemployment.[7] When decision-makers are faced with policy choices concerning inflation and unemployment, it should be borne in mind that the poor gain more from lower unemployment than they lose through higher inflation.

These observations suggest that the labour market position of women in general, and working poor women in particular, would be improved substantially by expansionary aggregate demand policies to reduce unemployment, even if that led to inflation. The consequences of restrictive aggregate demand policies in exacerbating inequality and the problems of the working poor do not seem to have been given adequate weight by Canadian policy-makers.

" *. . . I have worked and struggled for 25 years to try and get somewhere . . . two years ago my world fell apart when I lost my job and I can't seem to get it together again . . . I can't seem to find permanent work . . .*

Divorced single parent, children have left home,
working part-time,
Nova Scotia "

STRATEGIES FOR POSITIVE CHANGE

TRAINING AND EDUCATION

Training and education policies are critical to workers' ability to respond to labour market changes from any source. Even if there were no changes in the labour market, training and education could be an important avenue for working poor women to improve their labour market position. The likelihood of being working poor is much higher than average for women with less than grade 9 education in comparison with similarly situated men (Table 3.4, Chapter Three).

> *. . . when I was growing up it was not unusual for girls not to finish high school . . . we lived in a farming community . . . my father didn't think girls needed an education . . . now I have to look for a job with a grade 9 education . . . what work can I do? . . . my job ends after 20 years and now I have to think about going back to school . . . it isn't easy . . .*
>
> *Unemployed 55-year-old retail clerk, Ontario*

In the training area, women may be particularly disadvantaged because their pattern of more intermittent and part-time employment means that they do not accumulate on-the-job training. As well, they often occupy the low-wage jobs that offer few training opportunities. In many circumstances, employers are unwilling to pay for training because they do not believe that their organizations will benefit in the long term (primarily because of staff turnover). Some women question the value of investing time in training given the limited range of jobs generally open to women. Lack of access to language and skills training can be a form of systemic discrimination that can trap immigrant women in the lowest-paying job ghettoes.

CANADIAN JOBS STRATEGY

The federal government is responsible for most job-related training in Canada through the Canadian Jobs Strategy (CJS) program.[8] The CJS, instituted in 1985, replaced the previous array of federal training, job creation, and labour market adjustment programs with six programs:

- Skill Investment — assists workers to obtain new skills in response to technological and economic change (through subsidized training, help in setting up training funds, support for work sharing);
- Skill Shortages — provides training or relocation in designated occupations of regional or national importance;
- Job Development — assists long-term unemployed individuals to find a job (through on-the-job training, classroom training, and work experience);

- Job Entry — facilitates the transition of young people and women from school or home into the labour market, including students through summer work (through training, work experience, and counselling);
- Innovations — supports pilot projects and demonstration projects that can lead to employment development; and
- Community Futures — assistance to non-metropolitan communities facing severe economic conditions as a result of plant closures and layoffs (through small business development support, entrepreneurship support, training and relocation assistance).

The key differences between the CJS and previous labour market policies are its market orientation, its emphasis on training rather than job creation, and a shift in emphasis from public sector training to private sector training. In this market-oriented vein, it emphasizes "equality of access" for women and disadvantaged groups. By emphasizing access or opportunities rather than **results**, it seems to reject the possibility that training or job creation could be used to **compensate for** systemic differences that make equality of access insufficient for certain groups. By contrast, the thrust of employment equity is that equality of **access** is insufficient to compensate for the legacy of a cumulative history of discrimination and inequality, much of which may be systemic or hidden.

In fact, assisting the disadvantaged does not appear to be a general objective of the CJS. There is no clear expression of equity or distributional goals in the CJS, and "efficiency" goals take precedence over equity goals in the array of training, job creation, and adjustment programs. Women who are immigrants, or members of racial minority communities are not designated as specific target groups in CJS. They can, therefore, lose out in the scramble for scarce training spots, even though they face a multitude of barriers to employment in addition to the lack of adequate training. This entire approach is unfortunate, because labour market policies can play an important role in assisting disadvantaged groups out of poverty.

An implicit assumption of the CJS appears to be that training or assisting disadvantaged groups is not economically efficient — that is, it yields smaller benefits per unit of cost than training more advantaged groups. This is likely based on the perception that the advantaged groups seem more capable of absorbing the training or applying it on the job. The unspoken assumption is that members of disadvantaged groups may not emerge from the process highly trained and may still have problems finding well-paid jobs.

In fact, however, the benefits of training in terms of enhancing earnings prospects may well **be greater** for disadvantaged than for advantaged workers, even though disadvantaged workers may never achieve the earnings **level** of the more advantaged. The relevant measure of efficiency is **enhanced productivity** (for the employer), and it could well be that training **improves** productivity more for disadvantaged workers than for advantaged workers.

MARIA
(Ontario)

Maria is in her late 20s, a single mother with a 1-year-old child. She emigrated from Chile eight years ago with her family. She completed grade 12 in Chile but has had difficulty breaking out of low-paying jobs since she moved to this country. When she first arrived, she lived with her family and got a job in a knitting factory and later with a cleaning company. Both jobs paid minimum wage but the supervisors and other workers spoke Spanish. After she left home, Maria tried to secure higher-paying jobs but was unsuccessful because her English was considered inadequate. She attended a six-month language training program but was still unable to move from factory work. She tried a number of jobs to improve her English, including waitressing and cashier/counter clerk with a fast-food chain. She moved in briefly with her boyfriend but the relationship ended when she became pregnant. After the baby was born, Maria was forced to rely on social assistance before applying for a language and skill training program under the Canadian Jobs Strategy. Now she works with a large communications company at a starting wage of $8 an hour. The new position offers a wage considerably higher than her earlier jobs, but she is still having difficulty making ends meet. Maria's mother lives with her in a one-bedroom apartment and provides child care and help with expenses.

In essence, economic objectives of market efficiency need not conflict with social objectives of equity or fairness in decisions to direct training to the disadvantaged. Even if they did, legitimate social trade-offs should be considered. As well, the costs to governments and taxpayers are reduced if low-income people use training to improve their earnings or get off social assistance. In spite of these potential benefits from training the disadvantaged, the CJS is not fundamentally oriented toward that goal and therefore offers little opportunity for working poor women to escape labour market-related poverty.

> "*. . . I wanted to get off social assistance so I went back to vocational school for a data-processing course . . . it took two years and I had to take out a loan from the provincial government . . . the government paid the interest as long as I was on assistance . . . but when I finally found a job they started billing me $389 a month . . . how can I pay this out of my salary? . . . it's more than a week's wages . . .*
>
> *Single mother,*
> *employed on Canadian Jobs Strategy training project,*
> *Nova Scotia*"

The absence of equity objectives is reflected in the six CJS programs. Only the Job Development program, which assists the long-term unemployed, is geared specifically to equity goals. The extent to which other programs, like Community Futures, can help the disadvantaged depends upon the extent to which they are involved in plant closures and layoffs, as well as the extent to which the more disadvantaged would receive preferential treatment. This is unlikely, however, in the absence of specific objectives, despite recent efforts to integrate social assistance recipients, especially single-parent mothers, into the CJS and, hence, ultimately into the work force.

Working poor women are unlikely to be helped by any of the programs except perhaps Job Entry, which can assist the transition of women from the home into the labour market. However, this program is directed largely to women re-entering the labour force after an absence of at least three years. This approach has been criticized by women's groups, such as the Association for Community-Based Training and Education for Women, as favouring middle-class women who can afford a three-year absence from the work force.[9] Similarly, the Ontario Council of Agencies Serving Immigrants has pointed out that this requirement is particularly hard on immigrant women, as few can afford to stay out of the paid work force for that length of time.[10]

Women have also been hurt by the reduction of funding for orientation or "bridging" programs, which offered basic skills training and career counselling for people about to enter specific job-oriented training. Bridging training is particularly useful for women who have been outside the labour market for a considerable length of time or who are trying to enter non-traditional fields. As stated by the Community Coalition on the Canadian Jobs Strategy: "the reduction or elimination of orientation or 'bridging' programs for women . . . is a step backward."[11]

The reduction of funding for orientation and bridging programs occurred in the context of a general reduction in expenditures for training and labour adjustment under the CJS. This has been reflected in reduced federal funding for labour market programs as well as under-spending of existing budget allocations.[12] Under these circumstances, all groups are likely to suffer, not only working poor women. Evidence even indicates that the lack of commitment to an effective training policy for Canada is impairing productivity growth and therefore wage improvements.[13]

> "*. . . the problem with make-work or training projects is that they are too short or there is not enough money . . . then there are jobs if you are on welfare . . . and other jobs if you are on UIC . . . they all pay differently too . . . it's hard to keep track . . .*
>
> *Couple with one child,*
> *husband and wife both have combined part-time work*
> *with social assistance,*
> *have participated in federal CJS projects,*
> *trying to leave social assistance,*
> *British Columbia*"

The CJS has also been criticized because even when it does involve training for women, it tends to be in traditional low-paying, female-dominated clerical, service, and sales jobs. In these circumstances the CJS simply replicates the existing sex segregation of the work force. It provides little impetus for breaking down occupational stereotypes and encouraging women to enter non-traditional occupations.

This perpetuation of occupational segregation is particularly disturbing given its contribution to the overall male-female earnings gap. Although formal training could be a vehicle for breaking this vicious circle, the CJS has become part of the problem rather than the solution. The reality is especially harmful because women are not being encouraged to participate in training for skills identified as being in short supply in the labour market. This is particularly important for women because these skills are often necessary for well-paid jobs.

Concerns have also been expressed about CJS training being privatized, with the crucial decisions placed largely in the hands of employers. This makes it ". . . little more than a wage subsidy for employers. It is not real training for women, certainly not in the non-traditional areas."[14] The emphasis on employer-sponsored workplace-based training has also been criticized because it seldom reaches the unemployed or the working poor.[15]

For these reasons, poor women are unlikely to be helped much by the CJS. As it is, women are severely underrepresented in CJS programs (excluding the summer student program) compared to their representation in the labour force as a whole.[16]

LUCILLE
(Nova Scotia)

Lucille is a single parent in her mid-30s, separated, with three children. Her youngest child has required special medical attention since birth. Lucille has a diploma in social services from a community college. Before she was married, she worked full-time as a computer operator with the federal government; then she worked off and on after her first two children were born. After her third child was born it was difficult to continue working, and Lucille was forced to apply for social assistance after her marriage broke up. While on social assistance, she continued to work on a number of part-time projects, including leading groups of single parents and babysitting in her own home. Now she is working on a short-term Canadian Jobs Strategy project sponsored by a local community organization. The move to the labour market has placed Lucille at a great disadvantage. The youngest child requires regular medical attention, and Lucille needs flexible working arrangements to accommodate the trips to the doctor. She lives in public housing, but since she went off assistance, her rent has increased by $200 a month. She also lost her special medical benefit coverage, but medical expenses for the youngest child remain high. Lucille now takes home less than she would have on social assistance. She desperately wants to be free of welfare but is not sure that she will be able to afford to continue working.

TRAINING BEFORE THE CANADIAN JOBS STRATEGY

Women faced these same shortcomings in training under the *National Training Act*, which was replaced by the CJS. The CJS did not rectify those shortcomings, despite the increased role of women in the labour market, the advice of women's groups, and the increased recognition that their disadvantaged position is related to labour market irregularities.

" *. . . five months ago they told us that we would all have to take a course to upgrade our training . . . we would have to drive 30 miles to the classes . . . and we had to pay our own tuition . . . I couldn't afford to train to keep the job . . .*

Former home-care worker,
Ontario

Because CJS training programs perpetuated rather than rectified a number of inadequacies, training continues to be part of the problem, despite its potential to be part of the solution. The first inadequacy was that, relative to their representation in the labour force, women have been underrepresented in institutional training and, especially, industrial training. As well, over the period 1977 to 1984, not only did the total number of training spaces drop, but women's share of this declining number of spaces also dropped. For example, in 1977, women had 32% of the 179,000 institutional spaces; by 1984 their share had dropped to 27% of 163,000 spaces. In 1977, they had 28% of 70,000 industrial training spaces; by 1987 this had dropped to 24% of only 34,000 spaces. Second, the institutional training areas where representation of women was highest either had their funding cut dramatically (Basic Training for Skill Development) or there were few training spaces in any case (Language, Job Readiness Training, Occupational Orientation). Third, training programs under the *National Training Act* perpetuated the occupational segregation of women by training them for low-paying, female-dominated jobs. Fourth, these early training efforts were not as useful for women as for men. Women were often trained in occupations for which there was already a surplus of workers, such as hairdressing, and they were virtually absent from other non-traditional apprenticeship training, which was evaluated as most useful in terms of gains in employability and earnings. Fifth, while some efforts were made in the

1980s to improve training opportunities for women, especially in non-traditional occupations, the number of women involved was very small.[17]

EDUCATION

. . . it doesn't matter what kind of education you have here . . . there are only certain kinds of jobs and that's all there is to it . . . I have my grade 12 and secretarial skills from business college . . . do you think that makes a difference? . . . I have taken night courses in French, word processing, business entrepreneurship . . . and I still can't find a permanent job . . .

Public servant employed on temporary contract, Nova Scotia

Roughly the same proportion of women and men overall have low levels of education, a factor associated with working poverty.[18] For women, however, two notable differences are likely to affect the extent of their working poverty. First, about half as many women as men have trade certificates and diplomas. This highlights the fact that they are not receiving the **job-oriented** education that could help them get decent jobs. Second, women who are single heads of families (and who are overrepresented among low-income families) are about as well educated as other women of the same age group. As explained in a report published by the Canadian Congress for Learning Opportunities for Women,

> . . . it appears that these women are poor because they earn "women's" wages and support themselves and their children on this inadequate income . . . Since the education level of female heads of families is not substantially lower than that of other women in an equivalent age group, the wages they receive for performing "women's work" is clearly the cause of their low-income status. Thus, pay equity and job desegregation remain key issues to address in the years ahead in order to improve the status of these women.[19]

ADJUSTMENT TO CHANGES IN TRADE AND TECHNOLOGY

The free trade agreement between Canada and the United States is only one reason for improving adjustment assistance. Labour market adjustments are not unique to the free trade agreement but are part and parcel of broader adjustment consequences arising from technological change, international competition, industrial restructuring, and deregulation.

A Canada-U.S. free trade arrangement was recommended by the Macdonald Royal Commission on the Economic Union and Development Prospects for Canada. However, the Commission recommended that the free trade agreement be implemented together with (and not in isolation from) comprehensive income security in the form of a Universal Income Security Program (UISP) or guaranteed annual income. (The proposal is examined and assessed in Chapter Seven.) As well, the Commission recommended adjustment assistance policies in the form of a Transitional Adjustment Program (TAP) to deal with the adjustment consequences of free trade. Thus far, only the free trade component of the Macdonald Commission recommendations has been taken up by the federal government.

> “ *. . . when I was laid off I couldn't believe it . . . then they gave us severance packages and it screwed up our unemployment insurance . . . I needed the money . . . we had no savings . . . I didn't know where my next job was coming from . . . there I was left with three kids . . . money going out for rent . . . and nothing coming in . . .*
>
> *Single divorced mother with three children,*
> *federal public servant,*
> *Nova Scotia* ”

Assistance to those adversely affected by free trade is warranted not only on grounds of equity or fairness, but also for reasons of economic efficiency. The **equity** or fairness rationale for adjustment assistance is most obvious. If free trade provides efficiency gains and hence a growing economic pie, it seems only fair that some of those gains be used to compensate those injured by the agreement, especially if they are already disadvantaged in the labour market.

The **efficiency** rationale for compensating those who lose from free trade is more subtle but no less compelling. Ensuring the humane treatment of those affected adversely by change will reduce their resistance to other efficient changes. Knowing that they will be compensated or given adjustment assistance, people who may be adversely affected are less likely to try to block or resist change. If compensation or adjustment assistance is sufficient, they may even support change, thereby improving the chances that efficiency-enhancing changes will occur.

This is part of the more general proposition that a positive labour market adjustment strategy entails not only adjustment in the direction of (rather than against) market forces, but also compensation for those who lose as a result of otherwise efficient changes. Just as market forces need not **automatically** conflict with equity and fairness, so policies promoting equity and fairness need not automatically conflict with market forces. The challenge for policy-makers is to ensure that market forces provide a growing economic pie **and** that the pie is distributed equitably. Focusing on only one dimension may jeopardize the attainment of **both** efficiency and equity objectives.

If the decision is made to compensate those who lose from free trade, there remains the issue of whether adjustment assistance should be trade-related or part of a more general policy of adjustment assistance. In all likelihood, a trade-related adjustment assistance program would be difficult to administer, because it would be difficult if not impossible to identify whether adverse effects are resulting from free trade or from any of the other myriad changes (technology, industrial restructuring, deregulation) now occurring in labour markets. Even if it were possible, why should adjustment assistance be available only to those affected adversely by free trade, and not to those affected adversely by other types of changes? To ensure the equitable treatment of all groups so affected, it would be more sensible to include trade adjustment assistance in a more general adjustment assistance program. However, this requires putting into place a broad-based adjustment assistance strategy.

The Canadian Jobs Strategy is the main vehicle available for adjustment assistance. But it is extremely weak in this regard and is widely considered inadequate to deal with the adjustment consequences of Canada-U.S. free trade, let alone the other major adjustment challenges facing Canada.[20] Other measures will be necessary.

COMMUNITY ECONOMIC DEVELOPMENT

Given the failure of aggregate economic policies to achieve full employment in depressed regions, increased attention has been placed on local economic initiatives and community economic development.[21] These approaches often involve broader community goals rather than the profit-maximizing objectives of commercial enterprises. Community goals may pertain to the nature of the service provided (e.g., public parks, environmental goals) or the type of person involved (e.g., employing members of disadvantaged groups). As such, community economic development can be targeted to the needs of working poor women, both as **workers** in projects and as **consumers** of the services provided by projects.

Funds for community economic development usually come from government, through training, job creation, regional development or social service programs, as well as from community groups and, at times, the participants themselves. Support can take the form of start-up money, general advice and consultative services, or the full-fledged operation of the enterprise. What distinguishes community economic development projects from government services is that in addition to pursuing broad social goals of employment and development, they also operate on a full or partial cost-recovery basis. This is the economic part of the community economic development concept.

In contrast to conventional business enterprises, there is no typical structure for local economic initiative projects, and structure is constantly evolving. Examples include worker co-ops, community development corporations, business components of voluntary organizations, barter groups, and organized skills exchanges.

At the organizational level, community development projects involve grassroots participation, with worker-participants having a substantial say in the long-run objectives and short-run operation of the enterprise. Work arrangements are often more flexible to accommodate the varying needs of participants, and remuneration tends to be more egalitarian than in conventional profit-oriented firms.

While the output of private enterprise is dictated by profit opportunities associated with private needs, the output of community development initiatives is usually geared to local needs and may not yield a profit. This may be so, in part, because of the inability of many consumers of their services to pay normal commercial prices. In other cases, it simply may not have been profitable for the private sector to produce the service in the first place.

Although community development projects are not without their critics, these projects do have many positive characteristics. Such initiatives could be one avenue for employment or training of working poor women because they can be targeted to the needs of specific types of women, such as single mothers on welfare and Aboriginal women. Work arrangements could accommodate the household responsibilities of women in the labour market. For example, flexible working hours could be arranged and child care provided at the worksite — conditions that are seldom available in the private sector. Extra training could be given to those who have had long absences from the labour market because of child-care responsibilities, and fringe benefits could be provided that are of most use to working poor women. The workplace needs of some women with disabilities could be accommodated. Programs could also be targeted to specific groups of working poor women most in need, such as Aboriginal people, immigrants, racial minorities, and disabled persons. At the very least, experimentation in this kind of workplace is merited, and more information is needed on its advantages and disadvantages.[22] Special attention should also be placed on the ability of these initiatives to meet the needs of working poor women.

INCREASING WAGES THROUGH LEGISLATION

For people working full-time for the full year, low wages are a crucial factor contributing to their being poor. Policies to increase wages could go a long way to ameliorate low-income status.

Governments committed to a high-wage economy could attempt to achieve it in many ways. Most important are economic policies to encourage a high level of investment in productivity improvements. Training and education are also important. In addition, several legislative strategies could assist in the effort to raise wages, including:

- increased and indexed minimum wages;
- pay equity;
- wage extension by decree; and
- fair wages in government contracts.

The potential dangers of using wage augmentation to deal with working poverty are emphasized by some economists who argue that higher labour costs can reduce employment and ultimately make the poor even poorer. As well, they say that the adverse employment effects of strategies to increase wages are likely to be greater when:

- there are other good substitutes for the higher-priced labour;
- employers cannot easily pass on the cost increase to consumers in the form of higher prices without having to worry about reductions in the demand for their goods and services (and hence the derived demand for their labour); and
- labour costs are a substantial portion of total costs.

Unfortunately, these characteristics are often present in low-wage situations, suggesting that, if nothing else is done, there will be adverse employment effects from strategies to increase wages and that these will hurt the working poor most.

However, several factors emphasized especially by non-economists could reduce the adverse employment effects of wage-increasing policies. First, labour markets may not behave in the competitive fashion suggested by textbook economics, especially given the other non-competitive factors (monopoly, unionization, administered pricing) that permeate markets. In these circumstances, wage increases, at least over a reasonable range, may be absorbed without leading to adverse employment effects. Second, wage increases may "shock" management into more efficient practices and cost savings elsewhere. Third, wage increases could induce higher productivity (and hence partly pay for themselves) through improved morale, reduced absenteeism and turnover, and different job assignments. Fourth, even if these offsetting factors are insufficient and wage increases lead to job loss, it may be socially desirable not to support the low-wage industries where jobs are likely to be lost. This in turn could put increased pressure on governments and employers to encourage training and education, thus enabling workers to achieve higher-wage jobs rather than being unemployed.

Unfortunately, as is so often the case with public policy questions, the empirical evidence on the employment effect of wage-fixing legislation is scant and a clear consensus does not exist.[23] In the minimum wage area, where most of the empirical work has been conducted, there appears to be general agreement that raising the minimum wage does have an adverse employment effect, especially for teenagers. The magnitude of the effect varies considerably; however, typically, a 10% increase in the minimum wage is associated with a 1% to 3% reduction in employment for groups receiving the minimum wage increase. Such magnitudes appear neither immense nor inconsequential, suggesting that a legitimate trade-off is involved in the political decision to raise minimum wages.

. . . For two weeks' work and 64 hours I take home $289 . . . my rent is $300 a month . . . and I have to eat . . . I can't afford to work . . .

Telephone answering service operator, Nova Scotia ”

Raising wages through pay equity is another issue for which there is very little empirical evidence; what does exist comes from other countries. Some adverse employment effects were associated with the substantial equal pay increases awarded throughout the Australian economy since 1969; however, the magnitude of the effect was generally interpreted as small.[24] Similar results were found for British anti-discrimination initiatives, although here it is difficult to tell whether any adverse employment effect from equal pay initiatives was offset by employment-enhancing effects from equal employment opportunity initiatives introduced at the same time.[25] Simulations based on U.S. data have also indicated that pay equity wage increases of 10% to 20% would not likely lead to substantial employment reductions.[26]

MINIMUM WAGES

As we have seen, legislated minimum wages in Canada have not increased much in recent years. In fact, the substantial inflation of the past two decades has actually led to large declines (20% to 30%) in the **real** minimum wage. If there had been no inflation, it is extremely unlikely that policy-makers would have reduced the minimum wage. Because inflation has produced the same effect, policy-makers should be required to justify the decline in the real minimum wage that has been allowed to occur. Most transfer programs are now indexed for inflation; why not the minimum wage?

In the absence of a satisfactory argument to the contrary, it is reasonable to assume that the minimum wage should be adjusted more often to keep up with inflation. Any deviation from that level — either upward or downward — should require an explicit rationale and policy debate. It is likely (and appropriate) that any **increase** in the real minimum wage by 30% would have required an explicit rationale and policy debate. This should also apply to any decrease in the real minimum wage, even though the decrease occurred by default through inflation.

In many jurisdictions, low minimum wages are specified for youth, learners (trainees), domestics and nannies, and workers who receive substantial tips in service establishments. These two-tier minimum wage systems can affect women negatively, especially the immigrant women who tend to be concentrated in these service sector and domestic jobs.

. . . I just will not go back on welfare . . . I refuse to . . . But it's tough . . . I think the government should do something . . . minimum wage is garbage . . . you cannot live on $4.50 an hour . . . single or otherwise . . . if they just raised it to even $6.00 an hour . . . at least people would not be scraping to get by . . .

Single mother, formerly on social assistance,
now working as a sales clerk,
Saskatchewan ”

EQUAL PAY AND PAY EQUITY

Although all jurisdictions in Canada have some form of equal pay law, until the late 1970s and 1980s most had conventional equal pay for equal work legislation. The latter restricts comparisons for pay purposes to jobs within the same occupation and establishment; for example, it is not possible to compare the work and pay of a company's cleaning staff with that of its parking lot attendants. The restrictive scope of conventional equal pay legislation is highlighted by the fact that occupational segregation of females in lower-wage jobs is a more important factor in the overall male-female earnings gap than is unequal pay for the same job within an establishment. It is therefore not surprising that the limited empirical evidence available suggests that conventional equal pay initiatives have not narrowed the male-female earnings gap in Canada.[27]

Recognizing the limitations of conventional equal pay law, several Canadian jurisdictions have adopted equal pay for work of **equal value** — also termed pay equity in Canada or comparable worth in the United States. Such legislation allows pay comparisons of otherwise dissimilar occupations as long as they are of comparable value. Value is determined usually by a job evaluation procedure which typically involves comparisons of the skill, effort, responsibility, and working conditions of the job. Equal value legislation provides the potential to redress the pay inequity created by the fact that female-dominated jobs are often undervalued.

In Canada, equal pay for work of equal value legislation exists in Quebec (since 1977), the federal jurisdiction (since 1978), Manitoba (since 1985), the Yukon (since 1986), Ontario (passed in 1987, with wage adjustments begun in 1990), Newfoundland and Nova Scotia (since 1988), and Prince Edward Island and New Brunswick (since 1989). However, the implementation procedures are vastly different in the various jurisdictions; this has important implications for the effectiveness of the legislation.

Quebec follows a complaints-based approach; to date, almost all cases have been conventional equal pay, not equal value cases. The federal jurisdiction also uses a complaints-based approach and has had a small number of equal value cases. As well, although both the Quebec and the federal law can apply to the private sector, in practice application has been restricted to the public sector. In Manitoba, the legislation does not require a complaint; the system is administered largely through the collective bargaining process. However, so far it has been restricted to the public service. Legislation in Newfoundland, Prince Edward Island, New Brunswick, and the Yukon also applies only to the public sector. Only Ontario's legislation is based on a regulatory model that requires employers to implement pay equity whether or not a complaint has been laid. Also, Ontario is the only province where the pro-active legislation applies to both the private and the public sector.

Even the Ontario model, which is generally regarded as having the greatest potential to achieve pay equity, has severe limitations. Specifically, establishments with fewer than 10 employees are exempt, and establishments with fewer than 100 employees are not required to have a formal job evaluation requirement. Small establishments, especially in the service sector, are more likely to be lower-paying and to employ women. As well, the law requires that pay comparisons be made with male-dominated groups of the same value as the undervalued female-dominated jobs **in the same establishment**. This legislative restriction effectively exempts a large number of all-female establishments or female-dominated establishments where there are no male comparison groups. This is the case, for example, for many establishments in areas such as child care, social services, retail trade, and some manufacturing sectors. The problem is particularly acute for immigrant and racial minority women, who are heavily concentrated in small establishments and all-female job ghettoes.

> " *... It just isn't a question of work or assistance ... the problem is the type of jobs that women can get ... even with the level of education and experience that I have, I can't seem to make more than $4.50 an hour ... If I had two children and needed a baby-sitter I wouldn't be able to pay for it ...*
>
> *Single, mid-40s, business college diploma, Nova Scotia* "

Solutions to these problems exist. One is to allow proportionate pay for work of proportionate value within the same establishment. Thus, if a female-dominated job was found to have 80% of the value of a male-dominated job but received only 60% of the pay, the pay in the female-dominated job could be raised to 80% of the pay in the male-dominated job. Another solution would be to remove the restriction that comparisons be made only within the same establishment and allow comparisons across establishments. This could be done for a variety of jobs or only for key benchmark jobs, with the other jobs being adjusted to preserve their former positions relative to each other. Allowing comparisons across establishments could be very important, given empirical evidence suggesting that the scope of equal value legislation is severely limited by its inability to make such comparisons.[28]

An alternative, and administratively simpler, solution would be to impose a pay equity adjustment on establishments where there are no male-dominated comparison groups. For example, the adjustment could be the average pay equity adjustment introduced in other establishments, or the average increase in payroll costs resulting from pay equity.

WAGE EXTENSION BY DECREE

> *". . . if they don't pay high enough wages . . . I just can't work . . . I need to pay for food, clothes, and rent . . . work for low wages won't support my family . . . it's that simple . . .*
>
> *Single mother, unemployed, Saskatchewan"*

In addition to minimum wages and equal pay/equal value policies, wages can be set by legislative fiat through wage extension by decree. The decree system involves the relevant federal or provincial Minister of Labour extending by decree the wages and many of the terms and conditions of a collective agreement that have already been mutually agreed or followed by a significant portion of an industry. The decree could apply throughout the whole industry in a province or to separate economic zones.

While decree systems have been common in Europe where centralized bargaining prevails, they have never become firmly established in North America, given the prevailing decentralized, enterprise-level bargaining. However, they have existed to a minor degree in industries such as construction and the garment trades (e.g., under Ontario's little-known *Industrial Standards Act*) and they do prevail in the Quebec construction industry.

There is some renewed interest in the decree system in Canada. For example, the 1988 Ontario Federation of Labour Convention passed a resolution favouring wage extension by decree. This renewed interest arises partly from concern about growing non-union competition, including that associated with the marginalized work force (casual, part-time, and temporary workers and those working for subcontractors, especially in cleaning, food preparation, and security work). Interest in the decree system has also grown because of concern about the inability of unions to organize small, low-wage establishments, which tend to employ females. This could be an important initiative for immigrant and racial minority women, who tend to be heavily concentrated in these types of establishments.

FAIR WAGES IN GOVERNMENT CONTRACTS

The fourth type of law that could be used to raise wages is the requirement to pay "fair wages" in government contracts. Fair wages are usually taken to mean the "prevailing community rate", although the unionized rate is often used. This requirement could be part of more general contract compliance legislation whereby employers who bid on government contracts must meet certain requirements with respect to the pay and composition of their work force. Today we tend to think of contract compliance as the requirement to meet affirmative action or employment equity goals. However, it has also been used to impose such requirements as paying prevailing community wages for all workers. Because fair wage legislation currently applies only to government construction contracts, it is unlikely to be of great use in improving the wages of working poor women. However, women could benefit if fair wage legislation was extended to the full spectrum of companies receiving government contracts.

> " *. . . I worked for over a year as a homemaker . . . we visited older people in their homes . . . I liked the work but the company only paid $4.35 an hour for 7 to 25 hours a week . . . we were not paid for the travel time between houses . . . there just wasn't enough money to support myself . . . it was costing me money to work . . .*
>
> *Nursing home worker,*
> *previously employed with privately-owned home-care service*
> *under contract with provincial government,*
> *Ontario* "

POLICIES AFFECTING UNIONIZATION

As we have seen, unionization could have a positive impact on not only the wages but the working conditions of women. Policies to encourage unionization, especially in low-wage jobs that are disproportionately female, or to facilitate the effectiveness of existing unions include:

- restricting contracting out and subcontracting during the term of an existing collective agreement;
- ensuring that employers cannot de-unionize by moving a plant;
- discouraging low-cost non-union competition by enforcing minimum wage and employment standards legislation (e.g., health and safety, maximum hours of work) in the non-union sector;
- facilitating unionization in small units (bank branches, retail chains, franchise operations) and the extension of unionization to a regional or chain-wide level;
- allowing labour relations boards to impose a first contract on an intransigent employer who refuses to negotiate with a newly certified union;
- prohibiting the use of replacement workers during a strike;
- allowing a collective agreement to be reopened to deal with unforeseen circumstances such as technological change;
- imposing sanctions or penalties on employers who refuse to engage in meaningful collective bargaining with their unions;
- continuing the usual practice in most Canadian jurisdictions of allowing certification of new unions based on a majority of **signatures** rather than **votes**, the latter being the usual requirement in the United States; and
- opposing free trade because free trade will put more pressure on employers in Canada both to contain labour costs and resist unions so as to be competitive.

Obviously, most of these policies would help the development or retention of unionization in general, not just the unionization of low-wage women. In that sense, they are not focused only on assisting these women. However, facilitating unionization in small units would likely help low-wage women in bank branches, retail chains, and franchise operations. As well, since the public sector is disproportionately female, policies to sustain the high rate of unionization in that sector would benefit women.

> “ *. . . we're lucky to have a union . . . sure it's still part-time work . . . but last year they tried to cut back our hours even further . . . we refused to accept shorter hours as part of the bargaining package . . . what would have happened without the union?*
>
> *Part-time educational worker, British Columbia* ”

PUBLIC SECTOR EMPLOYMENT

The public sector, especially the public service, education, and health care, is disproportionately female. This means that policies aimed at improving public sector employment conditions tend to benefit women more than men.[29] Conversely, policies that restrict public sector growth will harm women. According to the April 1989 budget, federal direct spending as a proportion of Gross Domestic Product in Canada has declined significantly, from 19.5% in 1984 to 16.1% in 1989. This is having a dramatic impact on levels of public sector employment.

The effect of wage restraint in the public sector has already been shown to have its largest impact on low-wage women workers. Retrenchment in this sector is creating particular hardships now that employment equity policies are being instituted. Employment equity legislation is more effective when new jobs are being created and considerable job changing is happening, rather than in times of retrenchment.

The public sector has often been a model employer with regard to permanent jobs, setting an example for other employers to follow. This has been the case, for example, with respect to employment equity, maternity leave, and paid vacations. Obviously, retrenchment and restraint in the public sector make the leadership role more difficult; the increasing use of temporary contract work is evidence of this.

Privatization, subcontracting, and the increased use of casual, temporary, and part-time workers are all occurring in the public sector. While the newly employed workers are likely to be women, such as in privatized postal services, they will not have secure, public sector jobs that pay well and offer good benefits and advancement opportunities but rather will become part of a more marginalized, private sector work force.

> " *. . . this is no way to work . . . it's for three months at a time . . . I could be off next month and they will wait until the last day to let you know . . . when you have children it's pretty hard to live like this . . . you can't plan . . . you just try to put it out of your mind and go to work . . .*
>
> *Federal public servant working on temporary contract, Nova Scotia* "

RETIREMENT ISSUES

Mandatory retirement and homemakers pensions are measures which have been considered in order to combat poverty in the retirement years for working poor people. These measures may affect the poverty of women who left the labour force for a number of years to care for children and whose employment was part-time or seasonal.

MANDATORY RETIREMENT

The question of mandatory retirement is hotly debated and a key policy question in several Canadian jurisdictions. At issue is whether mandatory retirement should be banned or allowed as part of a collective agreement or company personnel policy. Opponents of mandatory retirement argue that it constitutes a form of age discrimination. Supporters argue that it is a mutually agreed arrangement (as evidenced by its prominence in situations of strong collective bargaining power and long-term employment relationships), usually in return for a pension. As well, requiring that workers retire at a certain age or after a given period of service may provide more job opportunities for younger workers and minimize the need to dismiss older workers. Whatever its pros and cons for all workers, a legislative ban on mandatory retirement could have complex implications, for women and the working poor, that are not immediately apparent.

A legislative ban could help older employed women by enabling them to continue working past what would otherwise be the mandatory retirement age, usually 65. While depriving them of what might be a full retirement period, working past age 65 could enable women to earn an adequate living wage, in contrast to what might be an inadequate pension income. It could also enable them to accrue additional service credits and seniority-based wage increases, both of which **could** augment their subsequent pension benefits. However, there is no guarantee that this would occur. Under most current pension plan arrangements, persons who postpone retirement past the normal retirement age are penalized.[30] Often they are not allowed to accrue further pension benefits and/or their previously accrued pension benefits are not increased to compensate for the fact that benefits are received later and for a shorter period of time. Of course, these penalties on postponed retirement could also be banned by legislation.[31]

While banning mandatory retirement might not augment pension benefits (unless also accompanied by a penalty ban), it could still enable people to continue working and earning wages for a longer period. For women with low wages or fewer years of pensionable service, this could be an important way of reducing poverty in old age.

What is not emphasized in the debate on mandatory retirement is that it tends to be associated with occupations having higher wages and occupational pension plans.[32] In fact, trade unionists are concerned that eliminating mandatory retirement may be a precursor to eliminating pensions; if people can continue to work, there may be less pressure to provide adequate pensions. The working poor tend not to be subject to mandatory retirement, nor are they members of occupational pension plans — the two usually go hand-in-hand. Because it is their low wages and not mandatory retirement that constrains the working poor, eliminating mandatory retirement will do little in the struggle against poverty and may make it worse.

It is possible that some working poor (e.g., those with a short labour force attachment) could be subject to mandatory retirement without the benefit of a pension, or with only a very small pension. The numbers may be small, but the consequences for these few people could be severe. As well, their situation may not be covered under human rights or employment standards laws (which tend not to apply to people 65 and older, largely to accommodate mandatory retirement).

One policy option would be to remove the age limit in human rights and employment standards laws. This would give older workers the normal protection against age discrimination and the protection of employment standards. Workers would be allowed to enter into contractual arrangements such as mandatory retirement only if they had strong bargaining power and a pension were part of the agreement. This could be accomplished, for example, by allowing mandatory retirement only in situations where there is a bona fide collective agreement and/or pension plan. This would protect older workers from age discrimination. It may also protect the few low-wage workers who may be subject to mandatory retirement but have no pension plan or collective agreement.

If mandatory retirement is banned outright, serious consideration should also be given to banning penalties for postponing retirement. This could be particularly beneficial to employed women given their greater longevity and the fact that, by working longer, they could augment their pension benefit accruals. It must be reiterated, however, that mandatory retirement is not a constraint usually faced by the working poor.

Women, especially working poor women, could be affected by any reduced employment opportunities that result from a ban on mandatory retirement, which is viewed as a form of worksharing, opening up employment and promotion opportunities for younger people and new recruits. This is one reason that trade unions often support mandatory retirement and early retirement policies, especially in industries that might otherwise be subject to employment reductions. New jobs vacated by people who retire could be filled by women, especially if employment equity policies assist them in getting a greater share of these jobs.

While mandatory retirement could open up more jobs for women, its effect is likely to be small. There is not a fixed number of jobs in the economy such that vacating a job means that it will be filled by someone else. It is certainly not obvious that there will be jobs available as a result of men retiring nor that working poor women (mainly in clerical, service, and sales work) would fill those jobs.

> “ *. . . I worry about the future . . . I used to say that I didn't want to be poor at the age of 60 . . . I realize now that I will never not be poor . . . what happens when I'm old enough to retire? . . . where will my pension come from? . . .*
>
> *Divorced mother, early 40s, university degree, working on federal training project and trying to leave social assistance, Nova Scotia* ”

HOMEMAKERS PENSIONS

Pensions for homemakers is another retirement issue that merits consideration. The subject has received considerable attention in the pension debate and from women's groups and anti-poverty groups. However, opinion is sharply divided.[33] At the heart of the debate is how best to provide adequate retirement income for homemakers and, specifically, whether allowing homemakers to contribute to the Canada/Quebec Pension Plans (C/QPP) is the best vehicle for doing so.

Numerous conceptual and practical problems are associated with using the C/QPP as the vehicle for providing adequate retirement income for homemakers. The C/QPP is designed to replace employment earnings that end upon retirement; however, the work of homemakers does not normally cease at the age of eligibility for these benefits. Does it then make sense to replace lost income (i.e., homemaker services) when the family is still receiving the services and they are still being provided by the homemaker? Would such support encourage women unduly to stay out of the labour market? In many cases, women who work in the paid labour market provide as much household work as homemakers without paid employment, yet the former would not be eligible for a homemaker pension. What about women who can afford to hire household help as compared with working poor couples who cannot afford such help?

In addition to these conceptual problems there are practical problems associated with calculating a value for household services to arrive at a figure upon which to base pension contributions and benefits. In all likelihood, a fixed figure would have to be used, although this could vary by the number of dependants or the extent of part-time employment.[34]

It must be emphasized, however, that comparable conceptual and practical problems are associated with most income support systems; the problems are real but not unsurmountable. While much better mechanisms for alleviating women's poverty in old age likely exist, the issue of pensions for homemakers merits more consideration.

SUMMARY

A full-employment, expansive economy is the first line of defence against poverty. In addition to providing essential job opportunities and jobs that are more likely to be full-time, it exerts upward pressure on wages. A full-employment economy also creates a favourable environment for pay equity and employment equity initiatives as well as training opportunities.

Working poor women can improve their labour market position through training and education, but these initiatives must be geared to their needs. The current Canadian Jobs Strategy is not oriented to meeting many of these needs which include:

- basic language and skill training and counselling;
- a fundamental commitment to equity objectives and training disadvantaged women;
- targeting of programs to specific groups such as immigrants and racial minorities;
- greater access to programs for women returning to the labour market after an absence for child-care or other household responsibilities; and
- training to break rather than perpetuate the entrapment of women in low-paying job ghettoes.

Although programs to help working poor women adjust to the consequences of free trade and technological change may not be the most effective use of training dollars on a strict cost-benefit basis, they may be merited on grounds of equity and efficiency. Such compensation may reduce the resistance of those adversely affected by change, thereby facilitating efficient change. Assistance should encourage adjustment of labour in the direction of (rather than against) market forces and should be general rather than tied to a single source of change such as free trade.

Local economic initiatives, as part of community development projects, also merit further consideration, in part because they could be geared to the needs of working poor women both as workers and as consumers of the services offered by community economic development projects.

Since 1975, the real value of minimum wages has fallen by between 20% and 30% in most Canadian jurisdictions. Considering the hardship that this imposes on the working poor, immediate attention should be given to restoring the real value of minimum wages.

Conventional equal pay legislation is unlikely to be effective in raising the wages of low-wage women. Equal value legislation has more potential because it allows comparisons of different occupations. However, its scope is also limited if restricted only to the public sector or to large establishments, if it relies on complaints-based compliance, or if it cannot deal with the problem of the lack of male comparison groups in predominantly female establishments.

Serious consideration should be given to using wage extension legislation to extend mutually agreed wages by decree throughout an industry. This could assist low-wage women in marginalized work forces, such as those working for subcontractors in food preparation and cleaning jobs.

The implementation of a wide variety of policies to encourage and sustain unionization in small businesses and the public sector would benefit working poor women.

Retrenchment in the public sector is likely to have adverse employment effects on women for a number of reasons. They are employed in disproportionately greater numbers in that sector, they receive higher wages in the public sector relative to the private sector than do males, and the public sector has initiated more and better programs beneficial to women, such as pay equity, employment equity, and paid maternity leave. Also, because women's progress in the public sector is already much slower than men's, retrenchment further retards their advancement.

Banning mandatory retirement is not likely to assist working poor women and, in fact, may harm them if their job opportunities are reduced by workers postponing retirement. The vast majority of the working poor are not covered by occupational pension plans and hence are not subject to mandatory retirement.

Allowing homemakers to contribute to and receive benefits from the Canada/Quebec Pension Plans is fraught with numerous conceptual and practical problems. Although a pension for homemakers merits further consideration, there are likely much better vehicles to deal with the inadequate retirement income of elderly women.

NOTES (Chapter Six)

1. For a review of the importance of full employment, see: *Policies for Full Employment,* ed. Duncan Cameron and Andrew Sharpe (Ottawa: Canadian Council on Social Development, 1988). For a discussion of the social importance of employment, see: Marie Jahoda, *Employment and Unemployment: A Socio-Psychological Analysis* (Cambridge: Cambridge University Press, 1982).
2. Joyanna Moy, "An Analysis of Unemployment and Other Labour Market Indicators in 10 Countries", *Monthly Labour Review,* vol. 111, no. 4 (1988), p. 40.
3. Stephan F. Kaliski, "Trends, Changes and Imbalances: A Survey of the Canadian Labour Market", in *Work and Pay: The Canadian Labour Market,* ed. W. Craig Riddell (Toronto: University of Toronto Press, 1985), pp. 121, 124.
4. Canadian Labour Market and Productivity Centre, "The Nature of Current Unemployment: Evidence from Job Vacancy Information", *Quarterly Labour Market and Productivity Review* (Spring 1988), p. 34.
5. See, for example: Goran Therborn, *Why Some People Are More Unemployed Than Others: The Strange Paradox of Growth and Unemployment* (London: Verso, 1986); and Andrew Martin, "The Politics of Employment and Welfare: National Policies and International Interdependence" in *The State and Economic Interests,* ed. Keith Banting (Toronto: University of Toronto Press, 1986).
6. Pierre Fortin, "Unemployment in Canada: Macroeconomic Disease, Macroeconomic Cure", in *Unemployment: International Perspectives,* ed. Morley Gunderson, Noah Meltz, and Sylvia Ostry (Toronto: University of Toronto Press, 1987), p. 82.
7. Empirical evidence on this point for Canada is provided in the articles by Pierre Fortin and by Morley Gunderson and Noah Meltz in *Unemployment,* ed. Gunderson, Meltz, and Ostry, *ibid.,* pp. 74-83, 164-175.
8. Canada, Employment and Immigration Canada, "The Canadian Jobs Strategy: A Review of the First Years", Ottawa, 1988, mimeo; Ontario, Ministry of Skills Development, *Discussion Paper on The Canadian Jobs Strategy: Policy and Implementation* (Toronto: 1987), pp. 1-2.
9. Ontario, Ministry of Skills Development, *Discussion Paper on The Canadian Jobs Strategy, ibid.,* p. 9.
10. Entrance requirements were made slightly more flexible in 1988, allowing program coordinators to accept a few women who had not been out of the labour force for three years, especially if they were immigrants.

11. Ontario, Ministry of Skills Development, *Discussion Paper on The Canadian Jobs Strategy, supra,* note 8, p. 9.
12. *Ibid.,* p. 3.
13. See: Leon Muszynski and David Wolfe, "New Technology and Training: Lessons from Abroad", *Canadian Public Policy* (September 1989).
14. Marjorie Cohen, "Current Economic Trends", in *Toward the Future: Proceedings of a Workshop on Women in Non-traditional Occupations,* ed. Pat Staton, Joyce Scane, and Dormer Ellis (Toronto: Centre for Women's Studies in Education, Ontario Institute for Studies in Education, 1987), p. 65.
15. Susan Wismer, *Women's Education and Training in Canada: A Policy Analysis* (Toronto: Canadian Congress for Learning Opportunities for Women, 1988), pp. 61-62.
16. Ontario, Ministry of Skills Development, *Discussion Paper on The Canadian Jobs Strategy, supra,* note 8, p. 8.
17. Daniel Boothby, *Women Reentering the Labour Force and Training Programs: Evidence from Canada* (Ottawa: Economic Council of Canada, 1986), pp. 15-19; Avebury Research and Consulting Limited, *Decade of Promise: An Assessment of Canadian Women's Status in Education, Training and Employment 1976-1985* (Toronto: Canadian Congress for Learning Opportunities for Women, 1986), p. 40-56; Patricia Dale, *Women and Jobs: The Impact of Federal Government Employment Strategies on Women* (Ottawa: Canadian Advisory Council on the Status of Women, 1980); Mary Pearson, *Women and Work: the Second Time Around: A Study of Women Returning to the Workforce* (Ottawa: Canadian Advisory Council on the Status of Women, 1979); Wismer, *Women's Education and Training in Canada, supra,* note 15.
18. Background information for this section is from Avebury Research and Consulting Limited, *Decade of Promise, ibid.,* pp. 19-23.
19. *Ibid.,* p. 23.
20. Ontario, Ministry of Skills Development, *Discussion Paper on The Canadian Jobs Strategy, supra,* note 8, p. 15.
21. David Ross, "Local Economic Initiatives", in *Policies for Full Employment,* ed. Cameron and Sharpe, *supra,* note 1, pp. 115-120; David Ross, Peter Usher, and George McRobie, *From the Roots Up: Economic Development as if the Community Mattered* (Croton-on-Hudson, N.Y./Ottawa: Bootstrap Press/Vanier Institute of the Family, 1986); Greg MacLeod, *New Age Business: Community Corporations that Work* (Ottawa: Canadian Council on Social Development, 1986).

22. Specific **practical** suggestions for the development of a community-based approach are outlined in: Canada, Employment and Immigration Canada, *Labour Market Development in the 1980s: Report of the Task Force on Labour Market Development* (Ottawa: 1981).
23. Recent surveys of the numerous studies include: Charles Brown, Curtis Gilroy, and Andrew Kohen, "The Effect of the Minimum Wage on Employment and Unemployment", *Journal of Economic Literature,* vol. 20, no. 2 (1982), pp. 487-528; Edwin West and Michael McKee, *Minimum Wages: The New Issues in Theory, Evidence, Policy and Politics* (Ottawa: Economic Council of Canada and Institute for Research on Public Policy, 1980). Recent Canadian studies include: Jacques Mercier, "Les effets du salaire minimum sur l'emploi des jeunes au Québec", *Relations Industrielles,* vol. 40, no. 3 (1985), pp. 431-457; Joseph Schaafsma and William Walsh, "Employment and Labour Supply Effects of the Minimum Wage", *Canadian Journal of Economics,* vol. 16, no. 1 (1983), pp. 86-97; Robert Swidinsky, "Minimum Wage and Teenage Unemployment", *Canadian Journal of Economics,* vol. 13, no. 1 (1980), pp. 158-170.
24. R. Gregory and R. Duncan, "Segmented Labor Market Theories and the Australian Experience of Equal Pay for Women", *Journal of Post-Keynesian Economics,* vol. 3, no. 3 (1981), pp. 403-428.
25. Anton Zabalza and Zafris Tzannatos, *Women and Equal Pay: The Effect of Legislation on Female Wages and Employment* (Cambridge: Cambridge University Press, 1985).
26. Ronald Ehrenberg and Robert Smith, "Comparable-Worth Wage Adjustments and Female Employment in the State and Local Sector", *Journal of Labor Economics,* vol. 5, no. 1 (1987), pp. 43-62; Mark Aldrich and Robert Buchele, *The Economics of Comparable Worth* (Cambridge, Mass.: Ballinger Publishing Co., 1986).
27. Morley Gunderson, "Male-Female Wage Differentials and the Impact of Equal Pay Legislation", *Review of Economics and Statistics,* vol. 57, no. 4 (November 1975), pp. 426-470; Morley Gunderson, "Spline Function Estimates of the Impact of Equal Pay Legislation: The Ontario Experience", *Relations Industrielles/Industrial Relations,* vol. 40, no. 4 (1985), pp. 775-791.
28. George Johnson and Gary Solon, "Estimates of the Direct Effect of Comparable Worth Policy", *American Economic Review,* vol. 76, no. 5 (1986), pp. 1117-1125.
29. Policies affecting women in the federal public service since 1908 are discussed in: Nicole Morgan, *The Equality Game: Women in the Federal Public Service (1908-1987)* (Ottawa: Canadian Advisory Council on the Status of Women, 1989).

30. James Pesando and Morley Gunderson, "Retirement Incentives Contained in Occupational Pension Plans and their Implications for the Mandatory Retirement Debate", *Canadian Journal of Economics*, vol. 21, no. 2 (1988), pp. 244-264.
31. At present, the jurisdictions in Canada that have banned mandatory retirement have also banned certain penalties for postponing retirement. Quebec requires that previously accrued benefits be actuarially increased to reflect the fact that they are received later and for a shorter period of time. Manitoba and the federal jurisdiction require the continued accrual of benefits.
32. Angela O'Rand and J. Henretta, "Delayed Career Entry, Industrial Pension Structure and Early Retirement in a Cohort of Unmarried Women", *American Sociological Review*, vol. 47, no. 3 (1982), pp. 365-373.
33. The pros and cons of pensions for homemakers are discussed in: National Council of Welfare, *Better Pensions for Homemakers* (Ottawa: 1984); Louise Dulude, *Pension Reform with Women in Mind* (Ottawa: Canadian Advisory Council on the Status of Women, 1981); and Canadian Advisory Council on the Status of Women, *Planning Our Future: Do we have to be poor?* (Ottawa: 1986).
34. The Canadian Advisory Council on the Status of Women (CACSW) recommended "that the homemaker pension be based on an income equal to half the average industrial wage . . ." See: Dolores Backman and Mary-Jane Lipkin, in collaboration with Louise Dulude, *Homemaker Pension: For Work That Deserves Concrete Recognition* (Ottawa: Canadian Advisory Council on the Status of Women, 1985), p. 20.

PART TWO: POLICY SOLUTIONS

Chapter 7: Income Security and Related Policies

CANADA'S SYSTEMS OF INCOME DISTRIBUTION

The labour market is the primary system of income distribution in Canada. As we have seen, however, the labour market does a poor job of keeping many people out of poverty. Distribution of income through the labour market is highly unequal, and has remained so for the past several decades in Canada. In 1985, the bottom 20% of families earned only 2.5% of total income (before receiving transfers from government and before income tax is deducted); the top 20% earned 42.9%.

A secondary form of income distribution (or redistribution) is the tax and expenditure systems of governments. Governments provide many explicit and implicit transfers to individuals and households through a variety of means: direct transfers through unemployment insurance, social assistance, and family allowances; indirect transfers through tax relief provided by tax credits or deductions; and transfers in-kind through services such as health, education, child care, and housing. Does the tax and expenditure system of government redistribute income effectively? Does it significantly reduce poverty? How effective is it in reducing working poverty, especially for women? Although transfers from government do tend to favour the poor much more than the well-off, even when transfers are taken into account, the bottom 20% of families still only earn 6.3% of total income, while the top 20% earn 39.4%.[1]

> "*. . . sure it's important to have a job you enjoy . . . but it's more important to have enough money . . . so you don't have to wonder whether or not you can get groceries . . . sometimes I feel bad . . . there isn't enough money and there is not enough food in the fridge . . . I think what am I going to feed my kids tonight . . .*
>
> *Married with two children,*
> *husband and wife both working,*
> *Saskatchewan*"

In addition to affecting the distribution of income, the transfer system reduces the incidence of working poverty significantly. Without government transfers the incidence of labour market-related poverty would have been 17.9% for all economic family units, rather than 12.3%, as it was in 1986 (Figure 7.1). The amount by which poverty rates were reduced was about equal for all family types despite much higher poverty rates for single-parent families and individuals.

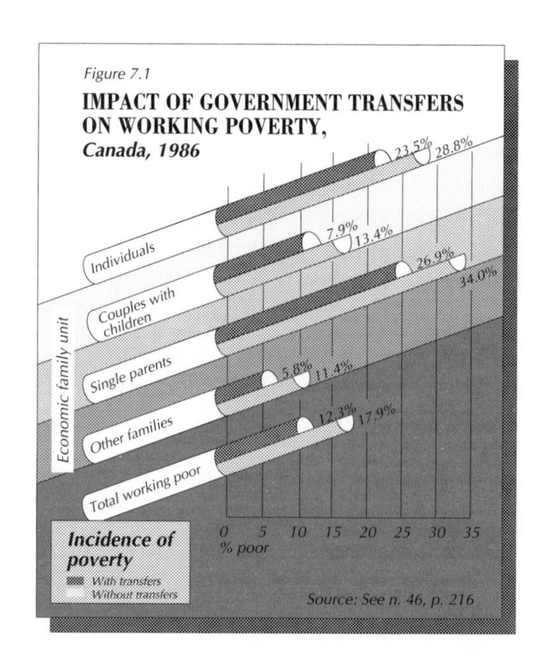

Figure 7.1
IMPACT OF GOVERNMENT TRANSFERS ON WORKING POVERTY,
Canada, 1986

Source: See n. 46, p. 216

The other side of the government expenditure coin is the tax system. The popular belief is that the tax system takes money from the rich much more than from the poor and therefore redistributes income. In fact, only the personal income tax part of the tax system, which generates only half of all government revenue, is progressive (i.e., the more one earns the more one pays as a percentage of income) — and only mildly so at that. Taking taxes and transfers into account, the bottom 20% of families had 7.2% of total income (up from 6.3% when transfers only were included), while the share of the top 20% fell from 39.4% to 37.3%.[2] The argument can be made that the tax system as a whole, however, including personal income tax, sales tax, and corporate tax, is regressive (i.e., the more one earns the less one pays as a proportion of total income).[3]

PRINCIPLES OF INCOME SECURITY POLICY

Canada's income security system is founded on three principles: the need for **income continuity**, the need for **income support**, and the need for **income supplementation**.

The need for income **continuity** arises because, even though income from employment is the first line of defence in income security, no modern economy can ensure that everyone will be employed sufficiently for their entire lives. Unemployment, ill health, and disability are contingencies that can befall anyone. Income continuity is also necessary to ensure that personal incomes are sufficient in periods of economic decline to sustain consumer demand and prevent economic instability.

Social insurance is the most common form of program to guarantee income continuity; it includes unemployment insurance (UI), worker's compensation, and the Canada/Quebec Pension Plans. These programs provide benefits to people who experience a loss or reduction of earnings because of unemployment, sickness, disability, or old age. Benefits are wage-related and based on contributions made while employed. They are considered insurance paid for by past contributions and are therefore widely regarded as a social right by recipients. This expression of "right to benefits", especially in relation to UI, was expressed by several working poor women in our interviews. It was contrasted with the "charity" aspects of programs such as welfare.

" *. . . I don't even want to be on UI . . . but compared to social assistance, UI gives me a little more prestige . . . it's fine to say I'm on UI . . . people don't look at you with the same stigma . . . it's no more dollars . . . but it means you have been working and you're trying to better yourself . . .*

Single mother, working on a short-term grant project,
trying to leave social assistance,
Nova Scotia "

The need for income **support** arises because there will always be people who cannot earn some or all of their living from paid employment even in the best of times. These include people with serious disabilities, people who do not qualify for some form of social insurance, and women who have been supported financially by their husbands but lose that support through divorce, separation, or widowhood. Income support programs such as welfare are considered public charity; recipients are subject to tests of entitlement based on their income and assets and in many cases are stigmatized (i.e., their need for support is regarded negatively by the rest of society and sometimes by program administrators). The number of people who have to depend on income support at any one time is related to a number of factors, including the availability of jobs for people who are disadvantaged in the labour market, the adequacy of social insurance or income continuity programs, and a range of social factors like divorce and disability.

The need for income **supplementation** arises from the recognition that wages are not always sufficient to ensure an adequate income. This was first recognized in Canada in 1945 with the adoption of the family allowance, which pays a benefit to families based on the number of children. Child-related income supplementation originated as a way of compensating families for the extra cost of raising children. In recent decades, interest in a more universal and generous form of income supplementation has arisen because of the failure of the wage system — due to low wages, part-time employment, and unemployment — to provide adequate incomes. The extension of income security to the working poor is often associated with the idea of a guaranteed annual income.

UNEMPLOYMENT INSURANCE

Unemployment insurance is the largest single income security program in Canada, covering approximately 90% of the labour force in Canada. Those excluded from coverage include the self-employed (except self-employed people in the fishing industry, who are covered by special arrangements), those 65 years old and over, and those who work less than 15 hours a week. Benefits equal to 60% of lost earnings up to a maximum are available to people who qualify on the basis of an interruption in earnings, and having worked for a minimum of 10 weeks or as much as 20 weeks, depending on the rate of unemployment in their region.[4] Benefit duration is determined by a complex formula that involves several phases and differs with the region and level of unemployment. A two-week waiting period is applied to those who lose their jobs, and up to an additional six-week period is applied to people who quit without just cause, are fired for misconduct, or who refuse suitable work. In addition to regular benefits, the UI program provides special benefits to people whose earnings are interrupted because of sickness or the birth or adoption of a child. The program is financed through a combination of employee and employer contributions and general tax revenue.

In 1985-86, $10 billion was spent on unemployment insurance benefits; this represented 22.3% of all income security expenditures in Canada.[5] Canada's high level of expenditure on UI is largely the result of its high rate of unemployment, particularly outside Ontario. In regions of high unemployment, UI plays a much more important role in overall income security protection. In Newfoundland, UI payments were 44.3% of all income security payments in 1983 and made up about 8.7% of all personal income, more than double the 3% of personal income in the rest of Canada.[6] Apart from its benefits for individuals, UI is an important contributor to the economies of many communities where unemployment is high.

. . . at least I was eligible for unemployment insurance . . . I was desperate not to go back on social assistance . . . and I'd rather be working . . . but I needed the money . . .

Single mother, after being laid off from a waitressing job, Ontario ”

UNEMPLOYMENT INSURANCE AND THE LABOUR MARKET

A great deal of controversy has surrounded the UI program since its major expansion in 1971. There has been a widespread perception that unemployment insurance is too easy to get and too generous and, as a result, has a negative effect on the labour market. Several government inquiries, most notably the Royal Commission on the Economic Union and Development Prospects for Canada (the Macdonald Commission) and the Commission of Inquiry on Unemployment Insurance (the Forget Commission), whose reports were published in 1985 and 1986 respectively, have recommended significant changes to UI. These would involve substantial cuts in the level of wage replacement and, more important, restrictions on eligibility and the length of the benefit period. More recently, the federal government has moved to reduce benefit levels and eligibility for UI substantially as part of its overall attempt at fiscal restraint.

The concerns raised by the critics generally have to do with the impact of UI on labour market behaviour. A number of studies concluded that the 1971 UI expansion resulted in a small but nevertheless significant increase in the measured rate of unemployment. According to the studies, UI encouraged people who would not otherwise have been in the labour market to enter or remain in the labour force long enough to qualify for UI benefits. As well, it was claimed, people remained unemployed (and collecting UI benefits) longer than they would have if benefits had been less generous.[7]

However, other research has challenged these conclusions.[8] One criticism was that most of the research was conducted in the early part of the 1970s, immediately after the 1971 changes, and did not take into account that amendments since 1971 have reduced eligibility criteria and benefit levels significantly. Administrative procedures to scrutinize claimants have also been tightened. These steps have strengthened the work incentive effects of UI. In addition, the employment-generating effects of UI spending, especially in regions with high unemployment, are not taken into account in most studies. This was particularly true in the 1980s; as the Macdonald Commission noted, unemployment insurance stabilized the incomes of unemployed people in Canada and helped prevent an even more severe decline in the overall level of employment by stimulating consumer purchasing and aggregate demand.[9]

The issues raised by those who advocate cutting UI or by those who support maintaining the status quo are primarily political; they represent different visions of the role of income security policies with respect to the labour market. It is not hard to understand why UI has always been a source of conflict between business and labour. Unemployment insurance is intended to provide income continuity for people who lose their jobs; as such, it removes the urgency of finding immediate alternative employment. One of the purposes of UI is to increase labour market stability by giving an unemployed person time to find suitable employment instead of accepting the first job that comes along. This exerts upward pressure on wages because employers have a smaller labour pool from which to draw. This reality of UI, and for that matter of all income security programs, is to shift the balance of labour market power in favour of labour and away from employers. Calls from business for "a more flexible labour market" have invariably been associated with reducing UI, based on employers' desire not to compete with the UI system in hiring labour. This fundamental difference in interests has meant that labour and business view the UI program in very different terms.

As we saw in Chapter Six, Canada continues to experience a high overall rate of unemployment by international standards. In some regions the problem of unemployment is so chronic that it seems misguided to worry that workers may be discouraged from taking the jobs. Increasing the incentive to work through UI or any other income security program makes sense only if jobs are available; it is jobs, not work incentives, that are lacking in these regions. If jobs were in plentiful supply, UI would undoubtedly discourage workers from taking low-wage jobs, particularly if they paid less than UI or were unstable. This may be the case in an area like southern Ontario where unemployment is considerably lower than anywhere else in the country. The benefit levels of Canada's UI program may create problems for individual employers in a few areas of the country, but its impact on raising the wage floor can be considered positive. As we have argued, creating a high-wage economy is an important step in the struggle to reduce labour market poverty. If stable jobs that paid well were widely available, it is unlikely that workers would chose UI over employment. There is no doubt that we spend too much on unemployment insurance, but this is because there aren't enough jobs for those who want to work in the paid labour force. Rather than reduce the relief paid to those who suffer the unemployment, the problem should be remedied by policies that improve the labour market prospects for secure and high-wage jobs.

This is not to say that UI is without its problems. Nor are the concerns of the UI critics totally invalid. Employers and communities as well as governments have adapted their employment practices and patterns to the certainty of UI after 10 weeks of paid employment. For example, in the Atlantic provinces the use of federal job creation projects is viewed as a "community resource" to be shared for 10-week periods in order to qualify as many people as possible for UI benefits.[10] Federal and provincial job creation projects clearly feed this problem because they are designed precisely to provide short-term employment to establish eligibility for UI. But this distortion in the labour market behaviour of individuals cannot be attributed to the ease of qualifying for UI so much as to the failure of the economy to provide an adequate supply of jobs. It also stems from the failure of government to direct its job creation efforts towards long-term employment.

> *... last winter we were only living on my husband's unemployment insurance and things were really tight ... we were pretty poor and we just managed to scrape by ... he was only making about $300 every two weeks ... we had some money saved because we knew it was going to be a hard winter and we got a credit overdraft at the bank ...*
>
> *Married, seasonal factory worker, British Columbia*

UNEMPLOYMENT INSURANCE AND LABOUR MARKET POVERTY

As a social insurance program, unemployment insurance was designed to provide short-term **income continuity** to people between jobs. Critics contend that it has become a major **income supplementation** program, providing regular top-ups to the wages of workers in seasonal industries, people in short-term job creation projects, and those who are laid off regularly. This income supplementation, which is achieved mostly, though not exclusively, through "regionally extended benefits", is thought to be an inappropriate function for an insurance program. As an insurance program, UI should provide protection only to people who are at **risk** of unemployment, not to those who are **certain** to experience it.

The income supplementation aspects of UI are large and important, and they play a significant role in protecting workers against the poverty that might result from unemployment. It is difficult to make clear distinctions between the income supplementation and the income continuity portions of all UI benefits paid out. But regionally extended benefits do account for 30% of all UI benefits, and in provinces like Newfoundland and Prince Edward Island they account for almost half of all benefits.[11] Without these benefits the number of working poor, which is already high in these provinces, would be much higher. The income supplementation aspects of UI in other parts of the country are much smaller but still important. The question remains: Are UI benefits an **appropriate** way to supplement the incomes of the working poor?

The Forget Commission argued that although supplementing the incomes of the working poor is necessary, particularly in regions where unemployment is high, earnings-related social insurance is not an effective means of doing so because it does not necessarily go to the people who need it most. The Commission claimed, as have many previous analysts, that a significant proportion of benefits actually goes to families with incomes well above the poverty line. Logic supports that claim: as a wage-related social insurance program, UI benefits go to people who are eligible because they have contributed and then become unemployed.

These concerns were shared by the Newfoundland Royal Commission on Employment and Unemployment (the House Commission)[12] and the Macdonald Commission. The reports of both commissions argued that the income supplementation aspects of unemployment insurance should be replaced by a new national supplementation program. The Macdonald Commission recommended sweeping reform of the income security system, including reductions in UI and other income security programs and their replacement with a Universal Income Security Program (UISP), a form of guaranteed annual income. As well, this commission recommended major transitional assistance programs, especially training, to help the unemployed. Although the Forget Commission recommended a reduction in the duration of UI benefits for people with short qualifying periods, it did so with an important **proviso**. The Commission linked the savings from these changes to the development of a new earnings supplementation program which would, in turn, be linked to economic and community development initiatives, education, literacy, and basic training programs, and policies and programs to promote flexibility in the labour market.[13]

As an income supplementation program for the working poor, the UI program does not work well; this should come as no surprise because it was not designed to supplement low incomes. However, it has taken on that role because of the erosion of labour market income and opportunities, and because the rest of Canada's income security system does very little to assist the working poor. Unemployment insurance provides income supplementation by default. This suggests that rather than reducing UI benefits, more attention should be paid to improving both the labour market earnings of workers as well as other aspects of the income security system to reduce working poverty and dependence on unemployment insurance.

LARISSA
(Nova Scotia)

Larissa is in her mid-40s, divorced, with two adult children. She has a long history of employment and has worked at a variety of secretarial and office jobs. She left school after grade 11 but has since completed business college training to upgrade her skills. After a brief period on social assistance when her children were younger, Larissa worked as a secretary for a private company for several years before being laid off two years ago. Since that time she has been off and on municipal social assistance (welfare) and unemployment insurance and has worked as a housekeeper and book-keeper, and at other jobs. She was living in public housing but was asked to leave when her two children left home and now lives alone in a one-bedroom apartment. Larissa currently works a 32-hour week but is considering re-applying for some form of social assistance. The hours and pay are inadequate and she cannot afford her rent and groceries. Her doctor has told her to improve her diet to lower her blood pressure, but she cannot afford the necessary expense. She is making less at her current wage than she would on provincial social assistance benefits. She cannot afford to work for these wages, but she also cannot afford to quit. The reduced income on unemployment insurance would be inadequate. Larissa considers herself too young to retire, but after a relatively steady employment history she has been unable to find work with wages high enough to support herself.

WOMEN AND UNEMPLOYMENT INSURANCE

Proposals to replace the income supplementation aspect of unemployment insurance with a program based on a test of family income would have dramatically negative effects on the income status of women living in a family unit. Women who become unemployed in high-unemployment regions, or because of low or unstable attachment to the labour market, would lose their right to an independent income under such a UI system. Wives of employed husbands earning above a predetermined income would be denied benefits previously available under the UI program if total household income was the major factor triggering transfer payments.

Under the Forget proposal, in contrast, these women would still be eligible for UI benefits although their right to a full year of benefits would be secured only if they had a high number of insured weeks. In many cases they would be eligible for far fewer weeks of UI benefits. For the reasons outlined in previous chapters, the patterns of women's work make it more likely they will have fewer qualifying weeks of employment. Women are therefore likely to exhaust their benefits much sooner than under the existing plan. If their husbands or other earners in the family had incomes that brought the family income above the poverty line (or whatever standard was established), these women would not have an independent income even though they were unemployed and wanting employment.

“ *. . . A percentage of low income means less income . . . Right now I am working a 32-hour week at $4.75 an hour . . . I can't afford to work for these wages, but I certainly can't afford to quit or get laid off . . . Imagine trying to live on even lower unemployment insurance benefits . . .*

Single, telephone operator,
Nova Scotia ”

Although the same conditions apply to men, the fact that women earn considerably less than men and tend to work part-time much more than men suggests that women will lose if the UI program is replaced by a targeted earnings or income supplementation plan. Such a plan would reinforce the traditional dependency relationship of women within families. It is not surprising that women's groups are adamantly opposed to the **replacement** of social insurance benefits by income-tested benefits.[14] Despite these concerns, income supplementation **in addition** to UI is not undesirable, either for the working poor in general or for women.

SOCIAL ASSISTANCE

. . . after five or six years of going off and on welfare . . . I know that the welfare office is there if we need money for us or the baby . . . sure, we would rather have jobs . . . but that isn't always possible . . .

Married mother with one child, unemployed,
British Columbia

Social assistance, or welfare, is the major provincial/territorial income security program. Although these programs are a provincial/territorial and, in some cases, a municipal responsibility, half of all welfare payments to individuals in Canada are paid for through transfers to the provinces/territories by the federal government under the Canada Assistance Plan. The cost of welfare programs amounts to approximately $6 billion nationally, accounting for about 13% of all government income security transfers. To be eligible for welfare under the terms of the Canada Assistance Plan, a person or family must be in need. Need is defined by applying a test of income, assets, employability, number of dependants, and special needs. Entitlement and benefit levels vary according to these needs. Eligibility and benefit levels are therefore open to some discretion on the part of program administrators and vary from province/territory to province/territory.

Welfare is designed to provide income support to people with no other means of support. The most common recipients are disabled people who have not qualified for benefits under social or private insurance protection (such as worker's compensation or private long-term disability insurance); single parents with children and few other means of support; and unemployed employable people who have not qualified for unemployment insurance or have exhausted their UI benefits.

“ *. . . things just got worse and worse . . . we used up our savings . . . then we just finally couldn't avoid it any more . . . my husband went in to apply [for welfare] . . . he didn't want me to go through it . . .*

Husband has disability,
family forced to apply for social assistance,
Saskatchewan ”

In no province/territory do welfare rates even approximate poverty level incomes. In most instances, welfare benefits, along with other supplements such as family allowances, provide incomes between 50% and 70% of the poverty line.[15] For example, a single parent on social assistance with a child two years old received a total income in 1986 of approximately $8,000 to $10,000, depending on the province of residence (Table 7.1). This was well below the Statistics Canada low income cut-offs of between $13,785 and $18,799 for single parents (Table 1.3, Chapter One).

TABLE 7.1: Incomes of Single Parents (one child, age 2) on Social Assistance, by Province, Canada, 1986

	Total Annual Income From All Sources*	Total Income as % of Poverty Line**
Newfoundland	$ 9,559	71.7
Prince Edward Island	9,739	84.3
Nova Scotia	9,074	68.0
New Brunswick	7,911	59.3
Quebec	9,101	64.8
Ontario	10,249	72.9
Manitoba	8,925	63.5
Saskatchewan	9,804	73.5
Alberta	9,860	70.2
British Columbia	8,861	63.0
Yukon	10,303	n/a
Northwest Territories	n/a	n/a

Notes: * Includes income from social assistance, family allowance, the child tax credit, provincial tax credits, and any additional social assistance benefits.
** Statistics Canada's low income cut-offs.
n/a means not available.
Source: National Council of Welfare, *Welfare in Canada: The Tangled Safety Net* (Ottawa: 1987).

People receiving social assistance have very little incentive to earn money through paid employment. Welfare programs allow recipients to exempt only a small portion (up to $300 a month depending on the province) of any earnings; everything earned above this level is taxed back, in most cases through a dollar-for-dollar reduction in benefits. This means that welfare recipients face implicit marginal tax rates of as much as 100% on earned income, far in excess of the income tax rate paid by even the highest income earner in Canada. Implicit tax rates can be even greater than 100% when one considers the loss of certain subsidies if the person goes off welfare and takes paid employment.

“ *. . . I guess you would class me as the working poor . . . we are totally ignored . . . we don't get any breaks . . . sometimes I think one of my biggest mistakes was getting off assistance . . . I no longer get drug coverage . . . and now there are all these extra costs that I didn't have on assistance . . . financially I'm further back than I was two years ago . . . but I work for the status . . . the independence . . . and I guess the pride . . .*

Single mother with two children, community worker, Nova Scotia ”

The loss of medical and housing subsidies if a person goes off assistance to take a job is a major barrier in moving from welfare to employment as is the lack of adequate support services such as child care, transportation for people with disabilities, and training. This makes it unattractive or even impossible for many people, especially those with dependants, to leave welfare for a job. This has been referred to as the "poverty trap" because it forces people into the difficult position of choosing welfare over paid work. Provincial governments have attempted to develop programs for employment support, especially for single parents, that incorporate several of these dimensions. Experience with these efforts varies widely across the country, making it difficult to generalize about their value.

WOMEN AND WELFARE

. . . it's almost as if the people who designed welfare tried to figure out a system that would keep these women poor and on the system for the rest of their lives . . . and they developed the perfect system . . .

Single mother, trying to leave social assistance, Nova Scotia

The social assistance system in Canada is rooted in the tradition of the British Poor Laws. Women, children, and elderly and disabled people traditionally have been considered the "worthy" poor, entitled to private or public charity. Able-bodied men seldom have been considered deserving of public or private support. Children are considered naturally dependent, and the assumption is that they need their mothers to take care of them. If a mother found herself alone, and in the past this was most often because of widowhood, she could turn to welfare because, in the absence of a husband, she could be dependent on the state. Women's dependency on men in marriage was assumed to be the natural state. This dependency has been reinforced by a welfare system that assumes (by way of means/needs testing, low benefit levels, and stigmatizing regulations and control of recipients) that the support of women by men is the preferred mode of dependency.[16] However, turning to welfare has never meant that a woman has had an **attractive** income alternative to support from her husband. Because women's dependency was assumed, single mothers were not expected to work, and benefit structures were, and still are, designed to provide an income without any earnings.

The reality of women's increasing economic independence, women's participation in the labour market, and concern about rising welfare costs has led most provinces/territories to redefine their work expectations for single mothers. Although single mothers are now more frequently considered employable, there is still some ambiguity about this expectation. Nevertheless, as one analyst of these changes notes, "the emergence of the work incentive for [single mothers], and their redefinition as employable, is one of the most significant developments to take place in social assistance policies in recent years".[17]

> " *. . . It was hard the first time I had to look for a job . . . I felt there was no way I could take a job for minimum wage . . . it was difficult to get off assistance . . . I was humiliated on it . . . I wanted no part of it . . . but I needed a high enough paying job to support my family . . .*
>
> *Single mother, transition-house worker employed on short-term training program, Ontario* "

Welfare is designed to provide **income maintenance** in the absence of any other income. Because the pattern of women's employment is considerably more intermittent than that of men, the likelihood of women having to choose welfare over work is much greater. However, women's use of welfare is, in fact, also intermittent despite the widespread perception that women are on welfare for overly long periods. There is considerable movement out of poverty and off welfare for most single mothers and the majority of them who use welfare do so for relatively short periods of time. A study for the Ontario Social Assistance Review Committee found that one-quarter of single mothers in Ontario were off welfare within one year, half were off welfare within two to three years, and only 15% were consistently on welfare for ten years.[18] The fact that women on welfare most often leave welfare within a few years, even though about 20% return to welfare at some point in the future, highlights the problems with any definition of working poverty that limits the analysis to people who are consistently in the labour market. Employment and welfare are two sides of the same coin of poverty for a large segment of women in Canada.

Improving work incentives by raising the limit on income that can be earned by social assistance recipients is an essential element of any effort to improve the income prospects of women on welfare. But, given the wages most women can earn in the labour market, doing so will likely do little more than make poor women who rely mostly on welfare into poor women who rely somewhat more on employment.

Nevertheless, there is growing concern that the limitations of the welfare system in promoting women's economic independence are inconsistent with the reality of women's lives in the 1990s and inconsistent with efforts to combat women's poverty. The majority of women, including single mothers with young children, are employed. Rather than promoting the continued dependence of women on what inevitably will be inadequate levels of social assistance, it makes more sense to assume that women want economic independence and to provide the supports required to achieve it.[19]

“ *. . . it's stressful when you end a marriage . . . especially when you have young kids . . . the first thing is you have to support them . . . without a job you have to go on welfare . . . if you have been out of the work force for some time . . . it's hard to get back in . . .*

Separated, retail clerk, recently left social assistance, Saskatchewan ”

In this context it is worth emphasizing that cross-national studies of single parents have found that in Canada, like in the United States, Great Britain, and Australia, a very high proportion of single parents are poor and on welfare; the proportion is lower in France, Sweden, and West Germany because of more generous support policies/programs.[20]

WELFARE REFORM

Widespread dissatisfaction with the welfare system in Canada has led to several recent examinations of the system and proposals for reform. *Transitions*, the 1988 report of the Ontario Social Assistance Review Committee (SARC), is the most comprehensive review of any welfare system in Canada.[21] The report provides a model for welfare reform for the rest of the country.

A basic premise of *Transitions* is that major changes to the employment system and to other aspects of the income security system need to be adopted if dependency on social assistance is to be reduced significantly. These include many of the objectives outlined in Chapter Six: the need for full employment, innovative economic development strategies, higher wages, pay equity, and training and education. On the income security front, *Transitions* proposed moving disabled people off welfare into a universal disability social insurance program, improving child-related benefits, and implementing a new income supplementation program.

On the question of welfare reform, SARC proposed major changes in the character of social assistance. Its proposals for significant increases in benefit levels, and therefore in overall welfare spending, signalled a rejection of the retrenchment mentality that has dominated other major income security reform proposals, including those of the Macdonald and Forget commissions. The Committee outlined a five-year strategy for reform that would cost Ontario in excess of $2 billion annually. In defending this expansion, SARC argued that because the financial and other costs of poverty are borne ultimately by society in general as well as by the poor, it is false economy for governments to believe that a massive anti-poverty strategy is not affordable and necessary.

According to *Transitions*, welfare should become a transitional program where people in distress are provided with income with the expectation that it will be needed for relatively short periods of time.

To make welfare truly transitional, the Committee proposed a program of "opportunity planning", with specialized opportunity planning staff separate from the administrative staff that determine welfare eligibility and need. Opportunity planning staff would assist recipients to develop individual plans for long-term financial independence.

There is legitimate scepticism about the ability of an employment support program, however well designed, to deal with the problems faced by welfare recipients. Research in the United States on employment supports for welfare recipients, including programs that require recipients to work for benefits (known as workfare), has found them to be of modest benefit at best.[22] And employment supports can be harmful if they are coercive within the context of a labour market that pays poorly and does not have enough jobs to go around. One of the most coercive aspects is pressure on single mothers to find employment without attention to the need for quality child care. Any effort to assist people into employment must be preceded by significant improvements in the labour market and in the support services, most notably child care, that make labour market work truly accessible.

. . . why is it that the poor do not have the right to stay home with their children? . . .

Single mother on social assistance, British Columbia ”

In this context, SARC argued that improvements to the welfare system, unless accompanied by specific assistance to the working poor, would prove self-defeating. Assistance proposed for the working poor included strategies to improve employment opportunities, wages, and programs that supplement their incomes. The key components of the Committee's strategy included a dramatic increase in child benefits, the expansion of the Ontario Work and Income (WIN) program for social assistance recipients, and an income supplementation program for the working poor.

INCOME SUPPLEMENTATION FOR THE WORKING POOR

On a federal level, the problem of the working poor in Canada was first highlighted in the early 1970s when the Senate Committee on Poverty (the Croll Committee) published *Poverty in Canada*.[23] It proposed the extension of the social assistance system to poor people in the labour market in the form of a guaranteed annual income (GAI). Although the term GAI was not used in subsequent policy discussions, the federal-provincial Social Security Review, which followed in 1973, embarked on a lengthy process to consider a new income support (welfare) program for those unable to work and a new income supplementation program for the working poor.

The Review ultimately failed. Economic stagnation, increasing federal deficits, and expenditure restraint in the latter part of the 1970s created a greater need for reform, but ironically also made government more reluctant to spend on new transfer programs. Economic conditions probably also precipitated a breakdown in the consensus between the federal government and the provinces/territories on a desirable reform option.[24] The legacy of the failure to develop a national income supplementation program was the adoption in 1978 of a federal refundable child tax credit and the establishment of several provincial income supplementation programs for the working poor. Three provinces (Manitoba, Saskatchewan, and Quebec) now have income supplementation programs for the working poor, and Ontario has an income supplementation program for recipients of social assistance to help them enter full-time employment.

“ *. . . it's that problem with the magic number [income above which applicants are ineligible for subsidy] . . . I work all day and have two kids to look after . . . the youngest should be in daycare but I can't afford it . . . instead I pay for a private sitter . . . she doesn't know her colours yet . . . I know she would be better off in a daycare centre with other kids . . . why can't I qualify for a subsidy? . . . or some other type of income program to make sure I have enough money . . .*

Divorced secretary,
Nova Scotia ”

CHILD BENEFITS

Income supplementation as a specific policy objective takes place mostly through child-related benefits — the family allowance program and the refundable child tax credit. These benefits for families vary with income and family size.

The monthly family allowance benefit was $32.74 per child under 18 years of age in early 1989 and cost the federal government approximately $2.6 billion a year. Benefits are universal in that they are paid to mothers in all families, regardless of income or family assets. This aspect is considered one of its major benefits because no stigma is attached to the receipt of benefits. Benefits are taxable; about one-quarter of the family allowance is recovered from high-income families through the tax system. The after-tax benefit of family allowance to a two-earner family with two children in 1988 was a maximum of $777 for families with annual earnings of $10,000; $566 for families with earnings of $15,000 to $40,000; $456 for families earning from $50,000 to $75,000; and $419 for families with incomes of $100,000. Quebec has a program to top up the federal family allowance with its own provincial family allowance; these are modest but important supplements for families, particularly low-income families with several children.[25]

In the 1980s, many deductions and exemptions were turned into credits. This is fairer, or more progressive, because deductions and exemptions reduce taxes more for people with higher incomes. In contrast, credits have the same value for everyone. In the case of refundable credits, any extra, above the amount of taxes, is refunded to the taxpayer. With other credits (the non-refundable sort), people with very small incomes may not have enough taxes to make use of all their credits. The more progressive the system, the better it is for most women.

The refundable child tax credit, introduced in 1978, provides a cash benefit to families with children under age 18 based on the total family income as determined by the tax return for the previous year. In this way it is a selective program as opposed to the universal family allowance. The maximum benefit was $659 per child 6 years of age or under for the 1988 taxation year; children between the ages of 7 and 17 entitled families to a maximum of $559. In 1988, families with incomes of up to $24,090 received maximum benefits; the tax credit is reduced by 5 cents for every dollar earned over this amount. This means that although benefits are income-tested, they carry little stigma because a majority of families with children receive some benefit. A family with two children and an income of $45,000 still had a $72 tax credit refund for 1988, while a family with four children and $65,000 in income was eligible for $119. The federal government spends approximately $1.5 billion a year on the refundable child tax credit.

An indirect income supplement is also provided to parents through the non-refundable child tax credit which was introduced recently to replace the tax deduction for dependent children. For the 1988 taxation year, the non-refundable tax credit was worth $65 for each of the first two children and $130 for the third and subsequent children. Benefits are of equal value to families at all income levels, except those with incomes so low that they pay no income tax. The non-refundable child tax credit therefore has the perverse effect of giving nothing at all to those most in need.[26]

The child-care expense deduction, which was expanded in the 1986 tax year from $2,000 to $4,000 for families with children 6 years of age and under, is another example of a supplementation program that operates through the tax system. The deduction allows families to deduct $4,000 per child from their taxable income if they provide payment receipts. Because it was part of the federal government's new child-care strategy, the child-care expense deduction is not intended to supplement incomes as much as compensate for the cost of child care.[27] Nevertheless, it plays a major supplementation role. Unfortunately, the deduction also provides the most supplement to those who need it least. Because the child-care expense deduction is a deduction rather than a credit, it is subtracted from income before taxes are calculated. This yields a higher tax saving for higher-income earners with higher marginal tax rates. In contrast, credits are subtracted from taxes owing. This yields a larger **proportionate** tax saving to lower-income people who pay income tax but not to people with incomes so low that they pay no tax. On the other hand, refundable tax credits go to everyone who files a tax return, even those with incomes so low that they pay no tax.

The refundable federal sales tax credit introduced in 1986 is not strictly a child benefit because it is also available to low-income families without children. However, its benefits do increase with the number of children in the family. In 1986 it was worth a maximum of $50 for every adult and $25 for every child for families with net incomes of $15,000 or less. Benefits are reduced by 5% per dollar earned over and above $15,000 and stopped for families earning $18,000.

> "*. . . we don't want to go on assistance . . . I'll take another job and so will he . . . the problem is that we would like to see our kids . . .*
>
> *Married mother with two children, Saskatchewan*"

THE IMPORTANCE OF CHILD BENEFITS AND PROPOSALS FOR REFORM

The impact of Canada's child benefit system on the incomes of the working poor is significant. Counting only the family allowance and the two child-related tax credits, a family of four with two children under age 7 and earnings of $10,000 would have had their incomes increased by approximately $2,200 in 1989. With earnings of between $15,000 and $25,000, the same family would have received a supplement of about $2,000. An employed single mother earning half the average wage would receive almost 15% of her income from these programs. More important, these benefits decline only slowly for any extra income the family earns. At $50,000 the family is still receiving a net (after tax) benefit of about $925. Thus, the child benefit system, unlike welfare, maintains a strong incentive to earn extra income and is non-stigmatizing.

Child benefits are particularly important to women. The family allowance is paid to mothers, and the refundable child tax credit is paid to the lowest earner in the family, most often the woman. For single mothers with very low incomes, these supplements can play an even bigger role in total family income, especially because single mothers who attempt to earn extra income are not penalized by any significant reduction of their child benefits.

Another reason to favour child-related income supplementation is child poverty. Child poverty is a major problem in Canada; more than one million children in this country are poor. As we have shown, having children is one of the factors related to an increased likelihood of poverty. The child benefit system by itself is inadequate to the task of alleviating poverty among families with children. But the fact of child poverty and the sympathy that this problem elicits make the child benefit system an attractive building block for creating a more effective system of supplementation for families with dependent children. For reasons we will explore, categorical child-related income supplementation may be politically more feasible and economically more desirable than more generalized forms of income supplementation.

A dramatic increase in child benefits was proposed by the Ontario Social Assistance Review Committee in the form of a new national child benefit system.[28] It would consolidate all existing child-related tax and transfer programs in an enriched refundable child tax credit. The program would provide a maximum benefit of $3,300 per child to families with incomes at or below $15,000 a year. Above that income the benefit would be reduced by an amount equivalent to 25% of additional earnings. A working poor family with two children and earnings of $15,000 would receive a benefit of $6,600, slightly more than three times what they now receive and about 45% of their total income. Because benefits would be reduced by only 25% for earnings in excess of $15,000, there would be a strong incentive to earn additional income. Like the refundable child tax credit, benefits would be received by most families with children. Benefits would end at incomes in excess of $50,000 for a two-earner, two-child family.

An expanded child benefit system, such as the one proposed by the Ontario Social Assistance Review Committee, appears attractive as an anti-poverty measure because it would be income-tested and would not use scarce transfer dollars to pay benefits to high-income individuals. The replacement of family allowance by a child benefit system that is targeted more effectively to low-income families has been the objective of several recent proposals for income security reform. But is it desirable? The family allowance is a popular program that provides benefits to mothers based, in part, on the belief that families without children should help to support families with children at the same income level because childrearing is socially necessary and valuable. Even though the family allowance is meagre (and is declining for reasons we explore later), because the payment goes to the mother of the child if she is present, it is in effect the only program in Canada that redistributes income from higher-income males to lower-income females within families.

“ *. . . when I was on social assistance I used the family allowance cheque immediately for groceries . . . it's hard to make social assistance last when you only get paid once a month . . . now I use it for gas for the car or clothes for the kids . . . it's not the same because I get paid every week . . . but I still need the money . . .*

Single mother, employed on short-term training project, trying to leave social assistance, Nova Scotia ”

CANADA'S COMMITMENT TO CHILD BENEFITS

Canada's system of income supplementation through child and other related benefits harbours several problems. The non-refundable child tax credit provides a benefit to families at all income levels except those without enough income to pay tax. The child-care expense deduction, like all tax deductions, provides its greatest benefit to high-income families and no benefit at all to families with extremely low incomes because they have no taxable income to reduce. For example, the child expense deduction provides a supplement of $3,286 to families with an income of $100,000 and two young children, but only $1,128 to a similar family earning $35,000. No benefit goes to families with incomes of $20,000, although the federal government did enrich the refundable child tax credit to make up for this inequity.[29] The failure to convert the child-care expense deduction, along with its recent enrichment, to a credit is a clear violation of the principles upon which federal tax reform is supposedly based.[30]

. . . the child tax credit is really only a boost . . . by the time you get it you need it for so many things . . . it comes in November and by that time you need a tank of oil . . . boots for the kids . . . or it's Christmas . . . I get $300 per child and another $150 later . . . maybe if they gave you that much every three months it might make a positive change . . .

Single mother with four children, employed on federal job training project, Nova Scotia ”

There is also a problem with the federal government's commitment to sustaining the real value of child-related benefits in the future. Although the federal government increased the refundable child tax credit several times between 1984 and 1988, in 1986 the child benefit package as a whole was partially deindexed. Under partial indexing, the three main programs — family allowance and the two child tax credits — are increased each year by an amount equivalent to the rate of inflation **in excess of 3%**. The fact that the first 3% of inflation is not compensated for means that each year child benefits will decline in real value by 3%. If nothing else is done, and if inflation continues to be at least 3%, in 10 years the amount the federal government pays out in child-related benefits will be 30% less than it is now.

This array of child-related benefits available to families can constitute a significant part of the total family income for working poor families. They could be further augmented by supplements such as housing allowances or subsidized housing, child care, and training allowances. Indeed, cross-national comparisons of the impact of these benefits on working poor families, particularly single mothers, has found that countries with generous child- and family-related benefits, such as France and Sweden, have been the most effective in keeping women and children out of poverty and off social assistance, and in promoting the employment of single mothers.[31]

PROVINCIAL INCOME SUPPLEMENTATION PROGRAMS FOR THE WORKING POOR

As previously mentioned, recognition of the problem of working poverty in the early 1970s led to the Social Security Review and discussions of a national income supplementation program which, for a variety of reasons, failed to materialize. The work incentive issue was one of the major stumbling blocks in achieving a national income supplementation program in the 1970s. The result was that several provinces went ahead and implemented their own programs specifically to supplement the incomes of the working poor.

The Saskatchewan Family Income Assistance Plan (FIP), the first of its kind in Canada, was established in 1974 in anticipation that a new federal plan would emerge from the ill-fated Social Security Review. FIP is designed to give benefits to families with dependent children where the head of the family is usually in full-time paid employment. In 1986, maximum benefits were $100 monthly per child for each of the first three children, and $90 per child for every child after that, to families with a maximum earnings of $8,200. For incomes above that level the maximum allowance is reduced by one dollar for every two dollars of income earned. The program provides substantial benefits to low-wage families. A family with one earner and three children can receive a supplement of up to $3,600 with a 50% reduction of the supplement for earnings over the net exemption level. It is also popular, non-intrusive (unlike welfare), and inexpensive to administer.

> " *. . . How can I make too much money to qualify for the income supplementation program? . . . right now, after I pay for my groceries, babysitter, and mortgage I still don't have enough money . . . my income is below the poverty line . . . there is so little incentive to encourage people to work . . .*
>
> *Divorced mother with three children, unemployed and trying to leave social assistance, Saskatchewan* "

Manitoba's Child-Related Income Supplementation Program (CRISP) is similar to the Saskatchewan plan. It differs, however, in that income, not just earnings, is counted in calculating the net income exemption level, the level of income under which maximum benefits are paid. In this way, it supplements the incomes of people who have low incomes and do not work, as well as the working poor. CRISP paid a maximum monthly benefit of $30 per child to families with incomes less than $10,025 in 1986. Any income above this amount reduced the supplement by one dollar for every four dollars of income (i.e., a 25% tax-back rate). The program is considerably less generous than the Saskatchewan plan, but it does have a better tax-back rate and it benefits more families.

The Manitoba and Saskatchewan Plans are geared to supplementing the income of families with children. Quebec's Work Income Supplement/Supplément au revenu de travail (WIS/SURRET), introduced in 1979, is more broadly based in that it provides support to families without children and to unmarried individuals. The program provided a maximum supplement of $2,193 for a family of four making a minimum of $8,772 in 1985. Different earnings ceilings are set for different family sizes and each dollar earned above the minimum reduces the allowance by 25 cents. The program is substantial; it paid out $2.2 billion in 1986-87. A number of problems with WIS and the social assistance program in Quebec in general have led to proposals for a massive restructuring of its social assistance system.

These Quebec proposals are based on a desire to create a two-tier social assistance system.[32] One tier, for unemployable recipients of social assistance such as people with long-term disabilities, would have a higher rate of assistance and would provide little financial incentive to earn. The other tier, for employable recipients, including single mothers, would have a lower basic level of benefits but a greater incentive to earn. Financial penalties would be imposed if those designated employable did not pursue employment or training in preparation for a job. A third part of the strategy involves a new income supplementation program for families with dependent children. The new Parental Wage Assistance Program (PWA) would encourage low-income parents to remain in or return to the labour market by giving them child-related assistance at a favourable tax-back rate. This program would be broadly similar to those already operating in Manitoba and Saskatchewan.

Although not strictly an income supplementation program for the working poor, Ontario's Work Incentive (WIN) Program provides special supplementation for people on social assistance to help them get into the labour market. WIN is available only to those who have been on Family Benefits (long-term assistance) for at least three months. It has several features in addition to cash benefits: it gives a $250 lump sum to help defray the costs of entering full-time employment; it guarantees rapid reinstatement of benefits if employment is terminated for any reason; and it continues coverage of health-related benefits (e.g., free health insurance premiums, dental assistance, drugs) for just over two years. Maximum benefits range from $145 a month to $275 depending on family size and type. Benefits are reduced by one dollar for every two dollars earned in excess of $675 a month.

The problem with these provincial income supplementation programs is that they are not designed to raise the incomes of the working poor to any pre-defined level of adequacy. Even when all the provincial income supplementation programs are taken into account, the income of low-wage workers is still significantly below the poverty level.[33] Most provinces do not have income supplementation programs, and only Quebec extends its income supplementation to working poor individuals. Our data indicate that there are 235,000 working poor unattached individuals in Canada; this is the fastest growing category among the poor.

One of the major constraints on adequacy and the expansion of income supplementation programs is that the provinces are not permitted to use Canada Assistance Plan (CAP) funds to develop cost-shared income supplementation schemes. Despite some recent flexibility in this regard, federal CAP support is provided only to people in need as defined by the application of a needs test. Because income supplementation programs use a less intrusive income test, they are not eligible for federal dollars; as a result, their development by provincial governments has been limited.

One of the main arguments for a national income supplementation program or guaranteed annual income is to allow the federal government, with its greater taxing and spending powers, to assist the working poor more adequately. As we have seen, income supplementation occurs by default in a number of ways through unemployment insurance and welfare. Should income supplementation be rationalized at the federal level through a major effort to combat working poverty? Should we adopt a guaranteed annual income?

A GUARANTEED ANNUAL INCOME FOR THE WORKING POOR?

The concept of a guaranteed annual income (GAI) has come to mean many things to many people. Some people consider it a panacea for all our income security problems and an adequate alternative to welfare, low wages, and poverty. But other visions of a GAI are much more miserly. Many GAI proponents believe it would be the best way to reduce government transfers overall, especially through the reduction or elimination of other programs such as unemployment insurance and family allowance. Still others view a GAI as a rationalization and integration of a complex tax and transfer system that could, depending on the ultimate design, be much fairer than the existing one.[34]

A key idea of all GAI concepts is the extension of income supplementation to the working poor through a more universal system than existing provincial income supplementation programs. The mechanism most often associated with a GAI is a negative income tax (NIT), although other mechanisms could achieve the same thing. There are many possible variations of a negative income tax. The current refundable child tax credit, for example, is a negative income tax that is restricted to families with children, but it does not guarantee a livable income. In any negative income tax scheme, benefit levels are determined using several elements: the **guarantee level**, which is the level of benefit provided to people with no other income, the **tax-back rate** which is the rate at which benefits are reduced as the recipient gains other income, and the **break-even point** which is the level of income at which benefits disappear. A high guarantee level is desirable because it gives people adequate incomes, while a low tax-back rate encourages people to work. But such a combination means that the level of income up to which benefits are provided (the break-even point) is very high, and so are the costs. Low guarantee levels simply perpetuate the existing problems of poverty while high tax-back rates create disincentives to work. These fundamental conflicts between costs, on the one hand, and work incentives and adequacy, on the other, have reduced the level of interest in a GAI in Canada or, for that matter, anywhere else.[35]

> “ *. . . I like to be out working rather than be home with the kids all the time . . . and I love my kids . . . but I like being independent of social assistance . . . I scramble to find jobs to keep off the welfare rosters . . . but we need more money . . .*
>
> *Single mother,*
> *employed as community worker on short-term contract,*
> *Nova Scotia* ”

One supposed benefit of a GAI is that it would get rid of categorical and objectionable distinctions between groups of beneficiaries, such as those based on age, family status, or employability. In practice, however, all significant proposals for a GAI in Canada have continued to use categorical distinctions to limit the payments to specific groups in order to contain costs. The Macdonald Commission proposal for a Universal Income Security Program (UISP) and the recent Quebec plan are simply reiterations of similar plans from earlier commissions and the Social Security Review in the 1970s. At least one of these plans was the basis for an experiment. The Manitoba Basic Annual Income Experiment, or "Mincome Manitoba", was a large-scale social experiment which began making income supplementation payments in January 1975. It was shelved in April 1976, leaving only a database for researchers.[36]

From the perspective of women, the first question is whether a GAI is based upon family or individual income. If it is the former, as was the case in the "Mincome" experiment, then women's traditional family dependency would be reinforced.[37]

Recent plans have adopted a two-tier approach distinguishing between employable and unemployable recipients. The first, or **support tier**, is intended for people who are not expected to work in the labour market. It has a higher guarantee level because they are not likely to have any other income. It also has a high tax-back rate and very low break-even level. The second, or **supplementation tier**, is intended for people who are expected to work in the labour market. It has a lower guarantee level but also a low tax-back rate.

One of the main difficulties is how "ability and expectation to work" are defined to determine whether a person or family belongs in the support or the supplementation tier. A great deal of subjectivity is involved; such judgements can be based on negative stereotypes and sexist assumptions. This is of particular relevance to women, given their changing status in the labour market. Single mothers, for example, have been variously considered unemployable and employable and, therefore, worthy or unworthy of support.

One of the major impediments to the development of any income security program is the fear that if people have adequate income security they will work less. But the preoccupation with the work disincentive effects of a negative income tax, or other income supplementation plans, is misplaced when one considers what they would replace and why they are being proposed. Advocates of income supplementation for the working poor believe that it has several advantages over the existing system. The first, and arguably the most important, is to provide the working poor with a decent standard of living by improving their incomes. A second major goal is to remove the poverty traps inherent in the welfare system by making it more attractive for people to leave welfare for paid employment. It does this by providing a basic guarantee that is taxed back at levels below the 100% plus now experienced by people on social assistance. The lower the rate of tax-back, the greater the incentive to earn extra income. In this sense, income supplementation is intended to change the either/or trade-off (work or welfare) faced by low-income workers. Income supplementation offers the opportunity of a third choice: welfare supplemented by labour market income, or vice versa, and in so doing would increase work incentives.[38]

The real concern about a GAI should not be about its work incentive effects, but about its possible impact on wages and the structure of employment. Recent work suggests that a GAI in the form proposed most often in Canada would have negative effects on the labour market by inducing downward pressure on wages, the growth of part-time work, the growth of low-productivity industries, and depressed aggregate demand.[39]

The danger is that in an economy with high levels of unemployment, a GAI/income supplementation policy will be seen by policy-makers as a simple solution to the complex problems of unemployment and poverty. Given the trade-offs between cost, work incentives, and adequacy, it is not likely that any GAI plan would be anywhere near generous enough, even if consensus could be achieved on adopting one. More important, without a broader policy framework in support of full employment and a high wage structure, a GAI might well increase labour market poverty, rather than reduce it.

PROGRAMS OF SPECIAL IMPORTANCE TO WORKING POOR WOMEN

The poverty of women is a complex phenomenon related not only to their inequality in the labour market, but also to their inequality in the home. Efforts to improve the income status of women require labour market equality, but this equality cannot be achieved without major changes in the relations between men and women, especially in terms of responsibility for children. Although these relationships can be reinforced or changed by social policies, the choice of policies is largely political.

We have concentrated on the main income security programs of relevance to the working poor — unemployment insurance, welfare, and income supplementation. These programs can and do benefit working poor women to varying degrees, although some major changes could have a dramatic impact on the income status of women. There is, however, a range of other income security and support programs that would be of particular benefit to working poor women.[40]

Labour market work offers the best road out of poverty for the majority of women, but the labour market work of women is constrained by the lack of policies in a number of areas. Foremost among these is the lack of a national child-care funding policy and the startling lack of fairness in what does exist in the form of tax breaks for child-care expenses.[41] The importance of child care to women has been stated in virtually every study of women in Canada, but it bears repeating here. **Without an adequate national child-care system, women will continue to face one of the most important barriers to full participation in the labour force.**

> “ *. . . I had to take a part-time job . . . my babysitter had gone . . . I couldn't afford another one for what they wanted me to pay . . . I asked around and I couldn't afford a daycare centre . . . besides I have to work nights when they aren't open . . .*
>
> *Married with two children, Saskatchewan* ”

In a similar vein, little significant improvement in the status of women in society can be made without a change in the relationship of both men and women to parenting and domestic work. Women now bear the bulk of the responsibility for child care, housekeeping, and emotional sustenance in the family. The fact that women — even though they may work full-time in the paid labour force — bear primary responsibility for the care of children, feeding the family, and ensuring that the house gets cleaned is a critical determinant of their ability to escape working poverty. One policy which would aid women in this regard is paid leave for either parent for the care of young, sick, and special needs children. Canada still lags behind several other nations in the types of supports which would encourage a more equitable sharing of parental roles.[42]

Much of women's poverty is associated with marriage breakdown and single parenthood. Changes are needed in family law to ensure adequate criteria for the disposition of family property and for spousal income maintenance after marriage.[43] Working poor women would also benefit by greatly improved enforcement of court-ordered child support and maintenance payments.[44] In addition, many women would be prevented from becoming poor by a program of advance maintenance payments, where government would ensure that women receive at least a minimum child support payment, even if a court-ordered payment did not exist. Where it did exist, government would collect from the estranged spouse on behalf of the woman. Such a system has proven successful in several European countries in keeping single mothers off welfare.[45]

> " *. . . they leave it all to the woman . . . the enforcement officer at family court told me to hire a private detective . . . I told him that if I could afford that I wouldn't be here looking for $50 a week . . .*
>
> *Single mother with two adolescents, Nova Scotia* "

In addition to training options, women — particularly single women on welfare — need adequate training allowances to enable them to make the transition from dependency on welfare or a man to independence in the labour market. Sex discrimination in training options reinforces the poverty of women, and the inadequacy of training allowances forecloses training as an option for women with dependants.

SUMMARY

Income security transfers reduced labour market poverty in Canada from 17.9% to 12.3% on a family unit basis in 1986.

The Canadian income security system does a particularly bad job of dealing with problems of working poverty, and too often it operates in ways that perpetuate poverty and keep women dependent.

Unemployment insurance is an important form of support for people who experience unemployment, but it has also become a major income supplementation program because of Canada's consistently high rate of unemployment and the failure or absence of other income security and labour market policies.

Efforts to restrict the availability of unemployment insurance benefits may have a particularly negative effect on women because the alternatives most often proposed are supplementation policies based on family income, which would deny women who lose their jobs the right to an independent income.

Welfare reinforces dependency and keeps women poor. Welfare reform to remove financial disincentives and to provide supports for employment are important ways to encourage the employment of women on welfare. But programs to move women off welfare and into the labour market can also be coercive and harmful if not accompanied by significant changes in the labour market.

Child benefits are an effective and well-targeted form of income supplementation for working poor mothers. The current federal commitment to the progressive erosion of child benefits through deindexation is a brutal long-term blow to women and poor families.

Existing income supplementation policies for the working poor are limited in impact.

There is little likelihood that a national guaranteed annual income or income supplementation plan would provide an adequate basic guarantee and an acceptable tax-back rate to encourage work without making categorical distinctions between employable and unemployable recipients. The problem of how to reconcile these competing objectives while keeping expenditures and tax levels within politically acceptable limits has never been resolved.

One danger is that income supplementation policies will be seen as an alternative to improving the labour market. As well, there is the possibility that in the absence of full employment and a high-wage policy, a guaranteed annual income could increase working poverty by contributing to an erosion of wage income.

Income security changes that would be of particular benefit to working poor women include child care, state-advanced and -collected child-support payments, paid parental leave, and adequate training allowances.

NOTES (Chapter Seven)

1. These figures are for economic family units made up of more than one individual; unattached individuals are not included. Figures are from National Council of Welfare, *Poverty Profile 1988* (Ottawa: 1988), p. 109.
2. *Ibid.*
3. François Vaillancourt, "Income Distribution and Economic Security in Canada: An Overview", in *Income Distribution and Economic Security in Canada*, ed. François Vaillancourt (Toronto: University of Toronto Press, 1985), p. 11.
4. At the time of writing the federal government had proposed a number of changes to unemployment insurance. Because they had not been enacted in legislation, the actual program may differ in some respects from the system described here.
5. Canada, Health and Welfare Canada, *Inventory of Income Security Programs in Canada* (Ottawa: 1988), p. 44.
6. David Ross, "Report on the Income Security System in Newfoundland", Background report for the Royal Commission on Employment and Unemployment (St. John's: September 1986), p. 21.
7. For a review of this literature, see a background report prepared for the Macdonald Commission by Jean-Michel Cousineau, "Unemployment Insurance and Labour Market Adjustments", in *Income Distribution and Economic Security in Canada*, ed. Vaillancourt, *supra*, note 3.
8. See: Lars Osberg, "Unemployment Insurance in Canada: A Review of Recent Amendments", *Canadian Public Policy*, vol. 5, no. 2 (Spring 1979); Derek Hum, *Unemployment Insurance and Work Effort: Issues, Evidence and Policy Directions* (Toronto: Ontario Economic Council, 1981); and Clarence L. Barber and John C.P. McCallum, *Unemployment and Inflation: The Canadian Experience* (Toronto: James Lorimer, 1980), p. 34.
9. Canada, Royal Commission on the Economic Union and Development Prospects for Canada, *Report*, vol. 2 (Ottawa: 1985), p. 610.
10. Canada, Commission of Inquiry on Unemployment Insurance, *Report* (Ottawa: 1986), p. 108.
11. *Ibid.*, p. 114.
12. Newfoundland, Royal Commission on Employment and Unemployment, *Building on Our Strengths. Report of the Royal Commission on Employment and Unemployment* (St. John's: 1986).

13. In this sense the changes to unemployment insurance proposed by the federal government (at the time of writing) are different from the thrust of the Forget Commission, because the government ignored the development of these other important policies.
14. See: Canadian Advisory Council on the Status of Women, *Brief Presented to the Commission of Inquiry on Unemployment Insurance*, prepared by Monica Townson (Ottawa: January 1986).
15. National Council of Welfare, *Welfare In Canada: The Tangled Safety Net* (Ottawa: 1987), pp. 66-69.
16. Dorothy C. Miller, "Feminist Theory and Social Policy or Why is Welfare So Hard To Reform?", *Journal of Sociology and Social Welfare*, vol. 12, no. 4 (1985), p. 672.
17. Patricia M. Evans, "Work Incentives and the Single Mother", *Canadian Public Policy*, vol. 14, no. 2 (June 1988), p. 126.
18. Patricia M. Evans, *A Decade of Change: The FBA Caseload, 1975-1986. A background paper prepared for the Social Assistance Review Committee* (Toronto: Ontario Social Assistance Review Committee, June 1987), p. 15. The degree of mobility for single parents on welfare is likely even higher because many single parents receive short-term assistance (General Welfare in Ontario) and go off before ever entering the longer-term welfare system (Family Benefits Assistance in Ontario).
19. Since the 1970s, most Canadian provinces have established programs to assist single mothers in their efforts to enter/re-enter the labour market. See: Patricia M. Evans and Eilene McIntyre, "Welfare, Work Incentives, and the Single Mother: An Interprovincial Comparison", in *The Canadian Welfare State: Evolution and Transition*, ed. Jacqueline Ismael (Edmonton: University of Alberta Press, 1987), pp. 101-125.
20. Sheila B. Kamerman, "Social Assistance: An Eight Country Overview", *The Journal* (Institute for Socioeconomic Studies), vol. 8, no. 4 (Winter 1983-84).
21. Ontario, Ministry of Community and Social Services, Social Assistance Review Committee, *Transitions* (Toronto: 1988).
22. Judith M. Gueron, "Reforming Work with Welfare", *Public Welfare* (Fall 1987).
23. Canada, Senate, Special Senate Committee on Poverty, *Poverty in Canada* (Ottawa: 1971).
24. Christopher Leman, *The Collapse of Welfare Reform: Political Institutions, Policy, and the Poor in Canada and the United States* (Cambridge, Mass.: MIT Press, 1980), especially Chapter Five.
25. The calculations for the family allowance and the child tax credit were prepared by Ken Battle of the National Council of Welfare.

26. An increase in the family allowance by the same amount as the tax credit would be more progressive because it would go to low-income families as well; moreover it would be taxable so that high-income individuals would lose some of the benefit.
27. This child-care strategy was largely abandoned in the April 1989 federal budget, although the tax break was not.
28. Ontario, Ministry of Community and Social Services, Social Assistance Review Committee, *Transitions, supra,* note 21, p. 117.
29. See: National Council of Welfare, *Child Care: A Better Alternative* (Ottawa: 1988).
30. See: Leon Muszynski, *Is It Fair? What Tax Reform Will Do To You* (Ottawa: Canadian Centre For Policy Alternatives and National Working Group on the Economy and Poverty, United Church of Canada, 1988), Chapter Five.
31. Alfred J. Kahn and Sheila B. Kamerman, "Income Supplementation and the Working Poor", Testimony prepared for presentation to the Employment and Housing Subcommittee of the Committee on Government Operations, U.S. House of Representatives, Hearing on the Problems of the Working Poor, December 12, 1985.
32. At the time of writing, these proposals had not been enacted in legislation.
33. Derek Hum, "The Working Poor, the Canada Assistance Plan, and Provincial Responses in Income Supplementation", in *Canadian Social Welfare Policy, Federal and Provincial Dimensions,* ed. Jacqueline Ismael (Montreal: Institute of Public Administration of Canada, 1985), p. 130.
34. Michael Wolfson, "A Guaranteed Income", *Policy Options,* vol. 7, no. 1 (January/February 1986).
35. Jonathan R. Kesselman, "Comprehensive Income Security for Canadian Workers", in *Income Distribution and Economic Security in Canada,* ed. Vaillancourt, *supra,* note 3, p. 289.
36. Sid Gilbert, "Poverty, Policy, and Politics: The Evolution of a Guaranteed Annual Income Experiment in Canada", in *Structured Inequality in Canada,* ed. John Harp and John R. Hofley (Scarborough, Ont.: Prentice Hall, 1980), pp. 444-495.
37. See the interview with Monica Townson on this subject in: Jennifer Dundas, "Economist Warns of Right Wing Support for Annual Income", *Herizons,* vol. 5, no. 1 (January/February 1987), p. 7. Olive Lumley Woodley uses a model based upon individual income in "The Case for a Guaranteed Annual Income", *Policy Options,* vol. 10, no. 2 (March 1989).

38. Mario Iacobacci and Mario Seccareccia, "Full Employment versus Income Maintenance: Some Reflections on the Macroeconomic and Structural Implications of a Guaranteed Income Program for Canada", *Studies in Political Economy*, vol. 28 (Spring 1989), p. 147.
39. *Ibid.*
40. For a review of policies of particular benefit to poor women, see: Harrell R. Rodgers, Jr., *Poor Women, Poor Families: The Economic Plight of America's Female-Headed Households* (Armonk/London: M.E. Sharpe, 1986), Chapter Five.
41. See: National Council of Welfare, *Child Care, supra*, note 29.
42. See: Monica Townson Associates, *Leave for Employees With Family Responsibilities* (Ottawa: Labour Canada, Women's Bureau, 1988); and Sheila B. Kamerman, "Women, Children, and Poverty: Public Policies and Female-headed Families in Industrialized Countries", in *Women and Poverty*, ed. Barbara C. Gelpi, Nancy C.M. Harsock, Clare C. Novak, and Myra H. Strober (Chicago: University of Chicago Press, 1984).
43. See: Canadian Advisory Council on the Status of Women, *Integration & Participation: Women's Work in the Home and in the Labour Force* (Ottawa: 1987), Chapter Two; Louise Dulude, *Love, Marriage and Money . . . An Analysis of Financial Relations Between the Spouses* (Ottawa: Canadian Advisory Council on the Status of Women, 1984).
44. See: Canadian Advisory Council on the Status of Women, *Council Recommendations: Enforcement of Maintenance Orders* (Ottawa: September 1984), listed under C4.1.
45. Kamerman, "Women, Children, and Poverty", in *Women and Poverty*, ed. Gelpi et al., *supra*, note 42, p. 57.
46. Tabulations by Analytical Services, Health and Welfare Canada on Statistics Canada, Survey of Consumer Finances, Public Use Micro-data Tape: Incomes of Individuals, 1986.

Summary and Conclusion

WOMEN, POVERTY, AND THE LABOUR MARKET

This book began with an examination of why women in Canada are much more likely than men to be poor. We saw that women's poverty is linked to their dual roles as unpaid workers in the home, and as low-paid workers in the labour market. In looking at different explanations for women's poverty, we saw that perspectives focusing on the individual "choices" of women to be mothers and wives, thereby constraining their ability to earn, are inadequate. Explanations focusing solely on the barriers faced by women in the labour market are also incomplete. The insights of political economy, and especially feminism, are essential in understanding the complex web of factors that condition women's choices and establish patterns of the economic domination of women both in the home and in the workplace. In this sense, the alleviation of women's poverty is constrained not primarily by the lack of adequate policies but by the structure of political relations between the rich and the poor, employers and employees, government and people, and perhaps most importantly, between men and women.

Many issues were raised in the interviews for this study, which yielded the numerous quotations throughout, but one theme stands out. Most of the women we talked to, no matter how hard they tried — and many tried very hard — could not earn enough through employment to support themselves and their families. This was true even though, in many cases, there was more than one earner in the family. We cannot help but feel the deep sense of frustration that working poor people experience in their struggle to make ends meet in a society that has not yet determined how to enable everyone to earn a decent living through their own efforts. This is the problem of working poverty in Canada.

While our statistical description of the problem cannot convey the experiences and feelings of working poor women, it does provide an indication of the magnitude of the problem. According to 1986 statistics, 9.3% of the Canadian labour force is poor. Women are slightly more likely to be working poor than are men, but a woman is much more likely than a man to be poor when neither is in the labour force. Moreover, women's working poverty has grown about five times as much as men's working poverty since the early 1970s. Both women and men are more likely to be working poor if they work part-time or less than a full year. But full-time employment does not guarantee that a person will have an adequate income. Roughly 383,000 persons in Canada work full-time for the full year but still live in poverty; they account for 30% of the working poor in Canada. Poverty among part-time workers is growing as a proportion of all working poverty.

Both men and women are more likely to be working poor if they are young, have low levels of education, or are recent immigrants. The ability to earn an adequate income from labour market work is also influenced by the number of earners in a family; unattached individuals, most of whom are young, are much more likely to be poor than people living in couple families. Similarly, single parents, most of whom are women, have very high rates of working poverty.

Working poverty in Newfoundland and Saskatchewan is much worse than it is in any other part of Canada. Only Ontario distinguishes itself by its relatively low rate of working poverty, at 6.6%. People are much more likely to be working poor if they work in service industries and occupations, where women are concentrated. Roughly $4.5 billion annually would be required to eliminate working poverty in Canada.

The late 1980s were characterized by economic growth, a significant decline in unemployment, and a reduction in poverty not related to the labour market. However, working poverty has not decreased and appears to be on the increase, highlighting the fact that something is fundamentally amiss in the labour market. The fruits of economic growth are not being shared evenly. The evidence of this is striking. Regional disparities in employment opportunities in Canada are glaring. The labour market is volatile with international competition, technological change, and deindustrialization leading to layoffs and plant closures, creating hardship and leaving many people out of work. The quality of the jobs now being created is in question, as part-time and low-wage service sector jobs have proliferated. These are the jobs that tend to be open to women, and they are the jobs that produce working poverty.

The main issue is that many people who work in paid employment, not only women, do not earn enough to escape from poverty, however defined. The reasons for labour market-related poverty are many and complex, the main sources lying in the labour market itself — instability and unemployment, the part-time nature of many jobs, growth in low-wage jobs, discrimination, and job segregation faced by women. The labour market as an institution is profoundly unfair to women. Progress in reducing female job segregation and discrimination against women has been limited. Women's poverty in old age or when they are disabled is also linked to inequalities in the labour market, because a large part of Canada's income security system is associated with labour market earnings, and the jobs women occupy tend not to have good pensions or fringe benefits — if they have them at all.

Although this study focused on the question of wage and income inequality, it is important to keep in mind that women confront many other dimensions of inequality in the labour market, such as job segregation, sexual harassment, and the lack of power. Resolving income inequalities alone would not likely resolve these equally serious inequalities.

Overlaid on this is the fact that women have always had the primary responsibility for child care. Many women face the dilemma of needing paid work but not being able to take jobs because they pay too little to cover the high cost of child care. Most jobs, especially those available to women, also lack flexibility to allow for integrating child and family responsibilities with paid work. The lack of both adequate training for women as well as family supports for labour market work contribute to women's poverty. As a result, women's opportunities to earn an adequate income from employment are severely limited. Despite these problems, full-time employment remains the best avenue out of poverty.

A POLICY FRAMEWORK

The labour market is the primary mechanism for distributing income in Canada. Secondary income distribution (or redistribution) through the tax and transfer system is an important but ultimately limited mechanism for alleviating labour market-related poverty. No significant progress can be made against working poverty unless labour market deficiencies — low wages, unemployment, involuntary part-time employment, discrimination, and segregation — are reduced. To achieve this, however, will require a political willingness to use public policy as an instrument to alter market outcomes. Unfortunately, this willingness to achieve a more equitable society does not currently exist in government and is fiercely resisted by business. The main problem is a critical lack of political will to tackle the problem of labour market-related poverty in any significant way.

We emphasize the need for policies that attempt to improve the number and quality of jobs as well as the wages attached to them. A national commitment to full and adequate employment is the minimum requirement for any effective policy framework to deal with labour market-related poverty. The call for full employment has become little more than a cliché. It is important to remember that Canada's high rate of unemployment is to a large extent policy-induced, that Canada has a poor record in keeping unemployment low, and that Canada could be doing much better in reducing unemployment, especially outside Ontario.

The current policy climate in Canada places a great deal of emphasis on the need for a flexible work force and to control wages in order to be internationally competitive. Downward pressure on wages is exerted through unemployment, reductions in unemployment insurance, privatization, deregulation, anti-union policies, government expenditure restraint, erosion of minimum wages, and the lack of effective policies to create wage equity in the labour market for women and other target groups. There is good reason to believe that the importance of comparative wage rates in securing our economic advantage, even in relation to the United States, is overstated. We could attempt to compete on the basis of wage reductions in Canada, or we could choose an alternative path where a high-wage, high-productivity economy becomes the goal of public policy. The key to such an achievement, however, is productivity growth.

Public policy strategies that could increase wages include the raising of minimum wages and the implementation of pay equity policies, wage extension by decree, a fair wage policy in government contracts, and policies to facilitate unionization, especially in sectors with large numbers of low-wage female employees. But the achievement of a high-wage economy requires much more than these specific policies. It needs to be part of a much larger social and economic strategy that sees social equity as being compatible with economic efficiency.

For women, Aboriginal people, disabled people, and members of racial minority communities, it is also critical to place emphasis on effective employment equity and pay equity policies to reduce and prevent further labour market inequalities.

Government tax and transfer policies, as well as training, supports for families, and government spending, are important parts of the solution to working poverty, especially if they are linked to labour market improvements. However, even if governments in Canada were willing to increase spending to create a more equitable society, measures to compensate for deficiencies in the labour market through income security policies, such as a national income supplementation program for the working poor or even a guaranteed annual income, are not likely to be successful. Attempts to hide unemployment, low wages, and other problems in the labour market through income supplements for the working poor have the potential to make those problems worse in the long run. A guaranteed annual income, therefore, would be a self-defeating strategy in the struggle to end working poverty. Without substantial labour market reform we also run the risk of creating a two-tier society, with one group earning substantial wages and another relying on transfer payments. This is unlikely to be politically stable or socially desirable in the long run.

Having said this, it is important to emphasize the critical importance of Canada's income security system in preventing much higher levels of working poverty; certain income security measures have the potential to decrease working poverty, especially for women. Many existing tax and transfer policies do little to improve the income status of working poor women while augmenting the incomes of already well-off people. The welfare system in particular frequently traps women in poverty. Income security reform is essential. Major reforms, particularly in the area of child benefits, welfare reform, spousal maintenance under family law, training allowances, and family support services such as child care and paid parental leave, are critical policy initiatives against working poverty. A large social policy agenda challenges governments genuinely interested in reducing working poverty.

The complete elimination of labour market-related poverty requires massive reform within the labour market and the creation of an income security system that supports employment rather than being an alternative to employment. The elimination of women's poverty requires, in addition, the restructuring of gender relations in Canadian society. Women cannot remain the **primary** providers of child care and homemaker services and hope to achieve equality in the labour market. We do not shy away from such an ambitious strategy, but we do believe that these major changes will take many years of political and social change. Reform will not come overnight, but it has to start somewhere.

As a starting point, we offer a constructive, affordable policy agenda for dealing with labour market-related poverty, especially the poverty of women. We believe this agenda has the potential to gain widespread support. It does not constitute the complete agenda, but rather the first steps in what should be a long-term strategy to improve employment opportunities, reduce labour market inequalities and discrimination, and provide adequate labour market supports through training, child care, and income security. We believe that these policy initiatives follow logically from our analysis and from the will to see the elimination of labour market-related poverty in Canada.

Overall, our policy recommendations (see: Authors' Proposals for Action: An Agenda for Reform) emphasize the importance of the labour market as a first line of defence in fighting the poverty of both women and men. Modified economic and labour market policies are crucial in enhancing the earnings capability of the working poor. These policies must be pursued to enable the Canadian labour market to provide better jobs. This in turn would enable women and men to earn a decent standard of living and to receive the individual gratification and social approval associated with employment. Any strategy that relies primarily on transfer spending to alleviate poverty is likely to be self-defeating in the long run. Income security developments in Canada should support, not supplant, the important goal of decent jobs at decent wages.

Authors' Proposals for Action: An Agenda for Reform

Governments in Canada, especially the federal government, through **aggregate demand policies** (i.e., monetary and fiscal policy) can dramatically affect the ability of the labour market to provide decent jobs at decent wages. There is considerable room for a more expansionary aggregate demand policy to move us closer to full employment. This is preferable to a more restrictive policy aimed at curbing inflationary pressures. The poor suffer more from unemployment than they do from inflation and, in any case, other strategies can be used to contain inflation without inducing high levels of unemployment.

Canada needs an explicit policy debate about the erosion of the **minimum wage**, which has occurred because the legal minimum wage in all provinces/territories has not kept up with inflation. In the absence of an explicit rationale for such a decline, the real value of the minimum wage should be restored to its former level of about 50% of the average industrial wage. Thereafter, increases in the minimum wage should at least match those of the average wage.

Where they exist, **pay equity initiatives** (equal pay for work of equal value) should encompass all jobs occupied by low-wage women. This means that systems must be developed to solve the problem of making comparisons for low-wage, female-dominated jobs when there are no male-dominated comparison groups, such as in child-care establishments.

The use of **employment equity initiatives** (affirmative action) should be expanded in the private and public sectors and should be directed at the needs of low-wage women, especially if they are also members of other groups that experience systemic discrimination, namely Aboriginal people, members of racial minority communities, and persons with disabilities.

The federal government should expand its **training programs** under the Canadian Jobs Strategy, particularly in areas that would benefit low-wage women. It should ensure that federal training resources do not reinforce the segregation of women in traditional low-wage occupations. It should also ensure that women receive at least their proportionate share of training dollars, as well as an additional share to compensate for other disadvantages they experience in the labour market. Training should be regarded as an important mechanism to achieve equity and fairness in the labour market, as well as efficiency and growth in a rapidly changing, high-skill, information-based economy.

Public sector job creation should be seen as an important component of any full employment strategy. The public sector often provides good jobs with opportunities for stable employment and advancement. Public sector retrenchment has led to a decline in the quality and availability of many necessary services. Many areas of service development offer opportunities for job expansion while meeting critical social needs such as child care and care for the aged. Public sector job creation could serve working poor women both by providing good jobs and by providing services that would be of particular benefit to them. Community economic development is a form of alternative job creation that merits experimentation and support from government.

Fair wage legislation requires companies/organizations that receive government contracts to pay their workers the prevailing community rate. Such legislation has the potential to benefit women working in these enterprises who often earn less than this rate. Governments should extend fair wage legislation to the full spectrum of enterprises that provide goods or services on a contract basis with governments.

Unionization can be an important mechanism for improving wages, especially if unionization is extended to jobs that tend to be held mostly by women. A positive climate for unionization could be created by governments. As well, specific changes in labour relations law (including but not limited to the following) could help in the unionization of low-wage workers:

- restrictions on contracting-out provisions;
- protection for workers against plant closures threatened/carried out to escape unionization;
- allowing labour relations boards to impose a first contract on intransigent employers who refuse to negotiate with a newly certified union;
- prohibiting the use of replacement workers during a strike; and
- sanctions against employers who refuse to engage in meaningful collective bargaining with their union.

Welfare reform is critical to any strategy to alleviate women's poverty. Federal law should be modified to allow for the cost-sharing of federal Canada Assistance Plan dollars to finance provincial welfare reform, especially to remove earnings disincentives and extend income-tested supplements to the working poor. The provinces should pursue welfare reform along the lines outlined by the Ontario Social Assistance Review Committee. This includes removing earnings disincentives, creating alternatives to welfare wherever possible, making welfare a transitional program, and providing considerable support for obtaining employment and other means to independence.

Child-related benefits are a major element in the fight against working poverty because they:

- are targeted to the people who need them most, i.e., families with children;
- are of particular benefit to women, especially single parents;
- are a good way to supplement incomes because they have a very low tax-back rate (and therefore an incentive to earn);
- are a non-stigmatizing alternative to welfare; and
- have broad political appeal.

The federal government should start by restoring full indexation of the family allowance and the refundable child tax credit. The next step should be to expand the child benefits package significantly through increases in family allowance and the refundable child tax credit.

Child care is an essential support for women and all parents who work in the labour market. Federal child-care policy consists of little more than the child-care expense deduction — a tax subsidy to parents which provides its greatest benefit to high-income earners. A strategy is required to expand the number of licensed child-care spaces dramatically, including a major investment in capital grants for child-care facility expansion. In addition, reducing the child-care deduction and converting it to a non-refundable tax credit would be in line with the federal government's own philosophy of tax reform. Converting the child-care deduction into a refundable tax credit would provide the most benefit to working poor mothers.

Improving child support and maintenance enforcement is essential, given the incidence of poverty among single mothers and the income loss for women who experience marriage breakdown. This should also entail an advance maintenance payment system that would forward to custodial single parents an amount equivalent to a court-ordered payment from a non-custodial parent, up to a maximum. In the absence of a court-ordered payment, a minimum payment should be provided on an income-tested basis.

Canada desperately needs a comprehensive policy of **support for working parents**. Such a package would be of particular benefit to single mothers, who experience the greatest difficulty in attempting to integrate paid work and family life. This would include expansion of paid parental leave for either parent, expansion of the right to unpaid parental leave, and various policies to ensure flexibility in jobs so that both parents can effectively fulfil both employment and parenting responsibilities.

Appendices

APPENDIX 1: NOTES ON THE METHODOLOGY OF INTERVIEWS WITH WORKING POOR WOMEN

The quotations and profiles appearing in this book were collected as part of the research for this study on women, poverty, and the labour market. The purpose of these interviews was to generate information about the real-life situation and attitudes of people with low incomes and some relation to the labour market.

Thirty women were interviewed between April and October 1988 in Nova Scotia, Quebec, Ontario, Saskatchewan, and British Columbia. This qualitative part of the study was never intended to be systematic or representative in any statistical sense. However, every effort was made to get a broad cross-section of people by age, industry, occupation, marital and parental status, geography, and experience with income security and labour market programs. Most important was that the interviewees fit the category of "the working poor" as we had broadly defined it. Individuals were selected through a lengthy process of talking with regional contacts about the best types of people to interview and through word-of-mouth suggestions. We believe that the interviewees provided a fair representation of the feelings, thoughts, and experiences of the people our statistics are attempting to count.

Interviews of one to two hours were conducted using a similar format that attempted to elicit four types of information:

- their experience with paid employment;
- their level of individual and family income;
- their use of and experience with government income security and labour market programs; and
- their family composition and family and community life experience.

All interviews were taped, profiles were constructed based on the information in the tapes, and quotations were selected from the taped interviews. Names have been changed to disguise the identities of the people interviewed.

APPENDIX 2: WOMEN AND THE MEASUREMENT OF POVERTY

The choice of one poverty line over another is essentially an arbitrary one, but it can have important consequences for the measurement of poverty.[1] In any study of women's poverty, a major concern is whether the use of Statistics Canada's low income cut-offs (LICOs) accurately reflects women's poverty or biases the analysis.

We wanted to understand what implications, if any, the choice of the LICO poverty line would have for the analysis of women and poverty. To this end, we investigated the effects, on the measurement of women's poverty, of creating two new poverty lines at levels one-third above and one-third below the LICO level. We refer to these three levels as severe hardship (LICO less one-third), hardship (LICO), and moderate hardship (LICO plus one-third). The results of this analysis are shown in Table A.1.

Using the **hardship** level, women were much more likely to be poor than were men in all family types.

The same pattern generally held based on the **severe hardship** level, albeit unattached women and men had about an equal probability of being poor. Women were almost three times more likely to be poor than were men if they were single parents. (At all three hardship levels, single mothers were much more likely to be poor than were single fathers.)

The **moderate hardship** level statistics also provided a fairly similar picture to that based on the hardship level. However, the proportions of females in poverty, relative to males in the same type of family unit, were diminished in the moderate hardship categories "Single parent" and "Other family units".

This general similarity of relative patterns justifies our choice of the hardship level as the most appropriate poverty line for this study of the three considered (although we make no judgement about the adequacy of the LICOs themselves).

TABLE A.1: Poverty Rates for Male and Female Heads of Economic Family Units, in Various Family Subgroups and Under Various Poverty Standards, Canada, 1986

Family Type and Sex of Head	Severe Hardship	Hardship	Moderate Hardship
	(LICO - 1/3)	(LICO)	(LICO + 1/3)
Unattached individual			
Total	15.3	34.3	49.8
Male	15.5	29.2	41.6
Female	15.2	38.5	56.5
Couple with single children			
Total	3.6	9.4	18.0
Single parent			
Total	21.8	39.7	52.8
Male	8.7	16.3	26.4
Female	24.2	44.1	57.8
Other family units			
Total	2.9	8.5	20.7
Male	2.6	7.9	20.1
Female	6.5	16.9	30.6
Total families units			
Total	8.2	18.7	30.6
Male heads	5.4	12.5	22.9
Female heads	17.0	38.6	55.1

Source: Tabulations by Analytical Services, Health and Welfare Canada on Statistics Canada, Survey of Consumer Finances, Public Use Microdata Tape: Incomes of Economic Families, 1986.

NOTES (Appendix 2)

1. Aldi Hagenaars and Klaas de Vos, "The Definition and Measurement of Poverty", *Journal of Human Resources*, vol. 23, no. 2 (Spring 1988), p. 211.

Bibliography

Abowitz, Deborah A. "Data Indicate the Feminization of Poverty in Canada, Too". *Sociology and Social Research*, vol. 70, no. 3, 1986.

Acker, Joan. "Women and Stratification: A Review of Recent Literature". *Contemporary Sociology*, vol. 9, 1980.

Aldrich, Mark and Robert Buchele. *The Economics of Comparable Worth*. Cambridge, Mass.: Ballinger Publishing Co., 1986.

Armstrong, Pat. *Labour Pains: Women's Work in Crisis*. Toronto: Women's Educational Press, 1984.

Armstrong, Pat and Hugh Armstrong. "Beyond Sexless Class and Classless Sex: Towards Feminist Marxism". *Studies in Political Economy*, vol. 10, 1983.

Armstrong, Pat and Hugh Armstrong. *The Double Ghetto: Canadian Women and Their Segregated Work*. Toronto: McClelland and Stewart, 1984.

Armstrong, Pat and Hugh Armstrong. *A Working Majority: What Women Must Do for Pay*. Ottawa: Canadian Advisory Council on the Status of Women, 1983.

Avebury Research and Consulting Limited. *Decade of Promise: An Assessment of Canadian Women's Status In Education, Training and Employment 1976-1985*. Toronto: Canadian Congress for Learning Opportunities for Women, 1986.

Backman, Dolores and Mary-Jane Lipkin, in collaboration with Louise Dulude. *Homemaker Pension: For Work That Deserves Concrete Recognition*. Ottawa: Canadian Advisory Council on the Status of Women, 1985.

Banting, Keith G. "The State and Economic Interests: An Introduction". In *The State and Economic Interests*. Ed. Keith Banting. Toronto: University of Toronto Press, 1986.

Barber, Clarence L. and John C.P. McCallum. *Unemployment and Inflation: The Canadian Experience*. Toronto: James Lorimer, 1980.

Battle, Ken. *1988 Poverty Lines*. Ottawa: National Council of Welfare, 1988.

Beach, Charles. "Cyclical Impacts on the Personal Distribution of Income". *Annals of Economic and Social Measurement*, vol. 5, 1976.

Beach, Charles. "Cyclical Sensitivity of Aggregate Income Inequality". *Review of Economics and Statistics*, vol. 59, no. 1, February 1977.

Beach, Charles. *The Vanishing Middle Class? Evidence and Explanations*. Kingston: Queen's University Industrial Relations Centre, 1988.

Becker, Gary. *Human Capital*. New York: Columbia University Press, 1964.

Bell-Lowther, Erica. "World Feminization of Poverty: A Conference Report". *The Social Worker*, vol. 53, no. 2, Summer 1985.

Benimadhu, Prem. *Hours of Work: Trends and Attitudes in Canada*. Ottawa: Conference Board of Canada, 1987.

Benston, Margaret. "The Political Economy of Women's Liberation". In *Roles Women Play: Readings Towards Women's Liberation*. Ed. Michele Hoffnung Garsoff. Belmont: Brook/Cole, 1971.

Bersharov, Douglas J. and Alison J. Quin. "Not all female-headed families are created equal". *The Public Interest*, no. 89, 1987.

Blackburn, McKinley and David Bloom. "Family Income Inequality in the United States: 1967-1984". *Industrial Relations Research Association*, 39th Proceedings, 1987.

Blank, Rebecca and Alan Blinder. "Macroeconomics, Income Distribution, and Poverty". In *Fighting Poverty: What Works and What Does Not*. Ed. S. Danziger and D. Weinberg. Cambridge, Mass.: Harvard University Press, 1986.

Blau, Francine and Marianne Ferber. *The Economics of Women, Men and Work*. Englewood Cliffs, N.J.: Prentice Hall, 1986.

Blinder, Alan and Howard Esaki. "Macroeconomic Activity and Income Distribution in the Postwar United States". *Review of Economics and Statistics*, vol. 60, no. 4, 1978.

Bluestone, Barry and Bennett Harrison. *The Deindustrialization of America: Plant Closings, Community Abandonment, and the Dismantling of Basic Industry*. New York: Basic Books, 1982.

Bluestone, Barry and Bennett Harrison. "The Growth of Low Wage Employment: 1963-86". *American Economic Review Papers and Proceedings*, vol. 78, no. 2, 1988.

Boothby, Daniel. *Women Reentering the Labour Force and Training Programs: Evidence from Canada*. Ottawa: Economic Council of Canada, 1986.

Braverman, Harry. *Labour and Monopoly Capital: The Degradation of Work in the Twentieth Century*. New York: Monthly Review Press, 1974.

Brown, Charles; Curtis Gilroy; and Andrew Kohen. "The Effect of the Minimum Wage on Employment and Unemployment". *Journal of Economic Literature*, vol. 20, no. 2, 1982.

Bruegel, Irene. "Women's Employment, Legislation and the Labour Market". In *Women's Welfare, Women's Rights*. Ed. Jane Lewis. London & Canberra: Croom Helm, 1983.

Cain, Glen G. "The Challenge of Segmented Labour Market Theories to Orthodox Theory: A Survey". *Journal of Economic Literature*, vol. 14, no. 4, 1976.

Cameron, Duncan and Andrew Sharpe, ed. *Policies for Full Employment.* Ottawa: Canadian Council on Social Development, 1988.

Canada. Commission of Inquiry into Part-time Work (Joan Wallace, Commissioner). *Part-time Work in Canada: Report of the Commission of Inquiry into Part-time Work.* Ottawa: Labour Canada, 1983.

Canada. Commission of Inquiry on Unemployment Insurance. *Report.* Ottawa: 1986.

Canada. Commission on Equality in Employment (Rosalie Silberman Abella, Commissioner). *Equality In Employment: Report of the Commission on Equality In Employment.* Ottawa: 1984.

Canada. Employment and Immigration Canada. "The Canadian Jobs Strategy: A Review of the First Years". Ottawa, 1988, mimeo.

Canada. Employment and Immigration Canada. *Employment Equity Availability Data Report on Designated Groups from the 1986 Census of Canada, for Employers under the Employment Equity Act and the Federal Contractors Program.* Ottawa: 1988.

Canada. Employment and Immigration Canada. *Labour Market Development in the 1980s: Report of the Task Force on Labour Market Development.* Ottawa: 1981.

Canada. Health and Welfare Canada, *Inventory of Income Security Programs In Canada.* Ottawa: 1988.

Canada. Royal Commission on the Economic Union and Development Prospects for Canada. *Report.* Ottawa: 1985.

Canada. Senate. Special Senate Committee on Poverty. *Poverty in Canada.* Ottawa: 1971.

Canada. Statistics Canada. *Historical Labour Force Statistics 1988.* Ottawa: 1989.

Canada. Statistics Canada. *The Labour Force.* Ottawa: December 1986, cat. no. 71-001.

Canada. Statistics Canada. *Pension Plans In Canada, 1984.* Ottawa: 1986, cat. no. 74-401.

Canada. Statistics Canada. *Women In Canada: A Statistical Report.* Ottawa: 1985.

Canada. Task Force on Child Care (Katie Cooke, Chairperson). *Report of the Task Force on Child Care* (Cooke Report). Ottawa: Status of Women Canada, 1986.

Canadian Advisory Council on the Status of Women. *Brief presented to the Commission of Inquiry on Unemployment Insurance,* prepared by Monica Townson. Ottawa: January 1986.

Canadian Advisory Council on the Status of Women. *Integration & Participation: Women's Work in the Home and in the Labour Force.* Ottawa: 1987.

Canadian Advisory Council on the Status of Women. *Planning Our Future: Do we have to be poor?* Ottawa: 1986.

Canadian Council on Social Development. *A CORE Income Security Plan for Canada.* Ottawa: 1987.

Canadian Labour Market and Productivity Centre. "The Nature of Current Unemployment: Evidence from Job Vacancy Information". *Quarterly Labour Market and Productivity Review,* Spring 1988.

Cohen, Cynthia. "The Impact on Women of Proposed Changes In the Private Pension System". *Industrial and Labor Relations Review,* vol. 36, no. 2, 1983.

Cohen, Marjorie. "Current Economic Trends". In *Toward the Future: Proceedings of a Workshop on Women In Non-traditional Occupations.* Ed. Pat Staton, Joyce Scane, and Dormer Ellis. Toronto: Centre for Women's Studies In Education, Ontario Institute for Studies In Education, 1987.

Cohen, Marjorie. *Free Trade and the Future of Women's Work: Manufacturing and Service Industries.* Ottawa: Garamond Press/Centre for Policy Alternatives, 1987.

Cohen, Marjorie. *Free Trade in Services: An Issue of Concern to Women.* Ottawa: Canadian Advisory Council on the Status of Women, 1987.

Courchene, Thomas J. *Social Policy in the 1990s: Agenda for Reform.* Policy Study No. 3. Toronto: C.D. Howe Institute, 1987.

Cousineau, Jean-Michel. "Unemployment Insurance and Labour Market Adjustments". In *Income Distribution and Economic Security In Canada.* Ed. François Vaillancourt. Toronto: University of Toronto Press, 1985.

Dahlby, B.G. "The Incidence of Government Expenditures and Taxes In Canada: A Survey". In *Income Distribution and Economic Security In Canada.* Ed. François Vaillancourt. Toronto: University of Toronto Press, 1985.

Dale, Patricia. *Women and Jobs: The Impact of Federal Government Employment Strategies on Women.* Ottawa: Canadian Advisory Council on the Status of Women, 1980.

Danziger, Sheldon H. and Peter Gottschalk. "Work, Poverty, and the Working Poor: A Multifaceted Problem". *Monthly Labor Review,* vol. 9, no. 9, 1986.

Danziger, Sheldon H. et al. "Work and Welfare as Determinants of Female Poverty and Household Headship". *Quarterly Journal of Economics*, vol. 97, no. 3, 1982.

Danziger, Sheldon H.; Robert H. Haveman; and Robert D. Plotnik. "How Income Transfer Programs Affect Work, Savings, and the Income Distribution: A Critical Review". *Journal of Economic Literature*, vol. 19, no. 3, 1981.

Dellaportas, George. "The Effectiveness of Public Assistance Payments (1970-80) in Reducing Poverty Reconsidered: The 'Safety Net' Was Still Very Leaky in 1980, but Less So and More Working Poor May Have Been Aided". *The American Journal of Economics and Sociology*, vol. 45, no. 1, 1986.

Doeringer, Peter B. and Michael J. Piore. *Internal Labour Markets and Manpower Analysis*. Lexington: D.C. Heath, 1971.

Drache, Daniel and Harry J. Glassbeek. "The New Fordism in Canada: Capital's Offensive, Labour's Opportunity". *Osgoode Hall Law Journal*, vol. 25, Winter 1987.

Dulude, Louise. *Love, Marriage, and Money . . . An Analysis of Financial Relations Between the Spouses*. Ottawa: Canadian Advisory Council on the Status of Women, 1984.

Dulude, Louise. *Pension Reform with Women in Mind*. Ottawa: Canadian Advisory Council on the Status of Women, 1981.

Dundas, Jennifer. "Economist Warns of Right Wing Support for Annual Income". *Herizons*, vol. 5, no. 1, January/February 1987.

Economic Council of Canada. *The Bottom Line: Technology, Trade and Income Growth*. Ottawa: 1983.

Economic Council of Canada. *Innovation and Jobs in Canada*. Ottawa: 1987.

Economic Council of Canada. *Making Technology Work: Innovation and Jobs in Canada: A Statement*. Ottawa: 1987.

Ehrenberg, Ronald and Robert Smith. "Comparable-Worth Wage Adjustments and Female Employment in the State and Local Sector". *Journal of Labor Economics*, vol. 5, no. 1, 1987.

Ehrenreich, Barbara and Frances Fox Piven. "The Feminization of Poverty: When the 'Family-Wage System' Breaks Down". *Dissent*, vol. 31, no. 2, 1984.

Eichler, Margrit. "The Connection Between Paid and Unpaid Labour". In *Women's Paid and Unpaid Work: Historical and Contemporary Perspectives*. Ed. Paula Bourne. Toronto: New Hogtown Press, 1985.

Eichler, Margrit. *Families In Canada Today*. 2nd edition. Toronto: Gage, 1988.

Ellwood, David. *Poor Support: Poverty in the American Family.* New York: Basic Books, 1988.

Evans, Patricia M. *A Decade of Change: The FBA Caseload, 1975-1986. A background paper prepared for the Social Assistance Review Committee.* Toronto: Ontario Social Assistance Review Committee, June 1987.

Evans, Patricia M. "Work Incentives and the Single Mother". *Canadian Public Policy,* vol. 14, no. 2, June 1988.

Evans, Patricia M. and Eilene McIntyre. "Welfare, Work Incentives, and the Single Mother: An Interprovincial Comparison". In *The Canadian Welfare State: Evolution and Transition.* Ed. Jacqueline Ismael. Edmonton: University of Alberta Press, 1987.

Fortin, Pierre. "Unemployment in Canada: Macroeconomic Disease, Macroeconomic Cure". In *Unemployment: International Perspectives.* Ed. Morley Gunderson, Noah Meltz, and Sylvia Ostry. Toronto: University of Toronto Press, 1987.

Garfinkle, Irwin. *Income-Tested Transfer Programs: The Case For and Against.* New York: Academic Press, 1982.

Gilbert, Sid. "Poverty, Policy, and Politics: The Evolution of a Guaranteed Annual Income Experiment in Canada". In *Structured Inequality in Canada.* Ed. John Harp and John R. Hofley. Scarborough, Ont.: Prentice Hall, 1980.

Goldberg, Gertrude S. and Eleanor Kremen. "The Feminization of Poverty: Only In America". *Social Policy,* vol. 17, no. 4, 1987.

Goodin, Robert E. and Julian Le Grand. *Not Only the Poor: The Middle Classes and the Welfare State.* London: Allen & Unwin, 1987.

Gower, D. *Labour Market Activity of Disabled Persons.* Ottawa: Statistics Canada, Labour and Household Surveys Analysis Division, 1988.

Gramlich, Edward. "The Distributional Effects of Higher Unemployment". *Brookings Papers on Economic Activity,* vol. 2, 1974.

Gramlich, Edward and Deborah Laren. "How Widespread are Income Losses in a Recession?". In *The Social Contract Revisited.* Ed. D. Lee Bawden. Washington, D.C.: Urban Institute, 1984.

Gregory R. and R. Duncan, "Segmented Labor Market Theories and the Australian Experience of Equal Pay for Women". *Journal of Post-Keynesian Economics,* vol. 3, no. 3, 1981.

Gueron, Judith M. "Reforming Work with Welfare". *Public Welfare,* Fall 1987.

Gunderson, Morley. "Discrimination, Equal Pay, and Equal Opportunities In the Labour Market". In *Work and Pay: The Canadian Labour Market.* Ed. W. Craig Riddell. Toronto: University of Toronto Press, 1985.

Gunderson, Morley. "Earnings Differentials Between the Public and Private Sectors". *Canadian Journal of Economics,* vol. 12, no. 2, 1979.

Gunderson, Morley. *Employment Income, 1986.* Focus on Canada Series. Ottawa: Statistics Canada, 1989, cat. no. 98-129.

Gunderson, Morley. "Male-Female Wage Differentials and Policy Responses". *Journal of Economic Literature,* vol. 27, no. 1, 1989.

Gunderson, Morley. "Male-Female Wage Differentials and the Impact of Equal Pay Legislation". *Review of Economics and Statistics,* vol. 57, no. 4, November 1975.

Gunderson, Morley. "The Public/Private Sector Compensation Controversy". In *Conflict or Compromise: The Future of Public Sector Industrial Relations.* Ed. Mark Thompson and Gene Swimmer. Montreal: Institute for Research on Public Policy, 1984.

Gunderson, Morley. "Spline Function Estimates of the Impact of Equal Pay Legislation: The Ontario Experience". *Relations Industrielles/Industrial Relations,* vol. 40, no. 4, 1985.

Gunderson, Morley, Noah Meltz, and Sylvia Ostry, ed. *Unemployment: International Perspectives.* Toronto: University of Toronto Press, 1987.

Gunderson, Morley and W. Craig Riddell. *Labour Market Economics: Theory, Evidence and Policy in Canada.* Toronto: McGraw-Hill Ryerson Limited, 1988.

Hagenaars, Aldi and Klaas de Vos. "The Definition and Measurement of Poverty". *Journal of Human Resources,* vol. 23, no. 2, Spring 1988.

Harrington, Michael. *The New American Poverty.* New York: Rinehart and Winston, 1984.

Hartmann, Heidi I.; Robert E. Kraut; and Louise A. Tilly, ed. *Computer Chips and Paper Clips: Technology and Women's Employment.* Washington, D.C.: National Academy Press, 1986.

Heineman, Ben W., Jr. et al. *Work and Welfare: The Case for New Directions in National Policy.* Washington, D.C.: Center for National Policy, 1987.

Hill, Martha S. "The Changing Nature of Poverty". *Annals of the American Academy of Political and Social Sciences,* vol. 479, May 1985.

Hird, H. Richard. "Poverty and the Minimum Wage: The Minimum Wage Helps Neither the Working Poor nor Industry". *Perception,* vol. 1, July-August 1978.

Hollister, Robinson and John Palmer. "The Implicit Tax of Inflation and Unemployment: Some Policy Implications". In *Redistribution to the Rich and the Poor.* Ed. K. Boulding and M. Pfaff. Belmont, Calif.: Wadsworth Publishing, 1972.

Hum, Derek. "Negative Income Tax Experiments: A Description with Special Reference to Work Incentives". In *Reflections on Canadian Incomes: a Collection of Papers presented to the Conference on Canadian Incomes, Winnipeg, Manitoba, May 10-12, 1979*. Ottawa: Economic Council of Canada, 1980.

Hum, Derek. *Unemployment Insurance and Work Effort: Issues, Evidence and Policy Directions*. Toronto: Ontario Economic Council, 1981.

Hum, Derek. "The Working Poor, the Canada Assistance Plan, and Provincial Responses in Income Supplementation". In *Canadian Social Welfare Policy, Federal and Provincial Dimensions*. Ed. Jacqueline Ismael. Montreal: Institute of Public Administration of Canada, 1985.

Iacobacci, Mario and Mario Seccareccia. "Full Employment versus Income Maintenance: Some Reflections on the Macroeconomic and Structural Implications of a Guaranteed Income Program for Canada". *Studies in Political Economy*, vol. 28, Spring 1989.

Income Insecurity: The Disability Income System in Canada. Downsview: G. Allan Roeher Institute, 1988.

INSTRAW News, no. 12, Summer 1989.

Jahoda, Marie. *Employment and Unemployment: A Socio-Psychological Analysis*. Cambridge: Cambridge University Press, 1982.

Johnson, Beverly L. and Elizabeth Waldman. "Most Women Who Maintain Families Receive Poor Labor Market Returns". *Monthly Labor Review*, vol. 6, no. 12, 1983.

Johnson, George and Gary Solon. "Estimates of the Direct Effect of Comparable Worth Policy". *American Economic Review*, vol. 76, no. 5, 1986.

Johnson, Harry G. "Some Micro-Economic Reflections on Inequality and Wealth Inequalities". *Annals of the American Academy of Political and Social Science* (special issue on "Income Inequality"), vol. 409, September 1973.

Johnson, Laura C. and Robert E. Johnson. *The Seam Allowance: Industrial Home Sewing in Canada*. Toronto: Women's Educational Press, 1982.

Kahn, Alfred J. and Sheila B. Kamerman. "Income Supplementation and the Working Poor". Testimony prepared for presentation to the Employment and Housing Subcommittee of the Committee on Government Operations, U.S. House of Representatives, Hearing on the Problems of the Working Poor, December 12, 1985.

Kaliski, Stephan F. "Trends, Changes and Imbalances: A Survey of the Canadian Labour Market". In *Work and Pay: The Canadian Labour Market*. Ed. W. Craig Riddell. Toronto: University of Toronto Press, 1985.

Kamerman, Sheila B. "Social Assistance: An Eight Country Overview". *The Journal* (Institute for Socioeconomic Studies), vol. 8, no. 4, Winter 1983-84.

Kamerman, Sheila B. "Women, Children, and Poverty: Public Policies and Female-headed Families in Industrialized Countries". In *Women and Poverty*. Ed. Barbara C. Gelpi, Nancy C.M. Harsock, Clare C. Novak, and Myra H. Strober. Chicago: University of Chicago Press, 1984.

Kamerman, Sheila B. and Alfred J. Kahn. *Child Care, Family Benefits, and Working Parents: A Study in Comparative Policy*. New York: Columbia University Press, 1981.

Kamerman, Sheila B. and Alfred J. Kahn. *Mothers Alone*. Dover, Mass.: Auburn House, 1988.

Kesselman, Jonathan. "Comprehensive Income Security for Canadian Workers". In *Income Distribution and Economic Security in Canada*. Ed. François Vaillancourt. Toronto: University of Toronto Press, 1985.

Kitchen, Brigitte. *Employment Strategies For Women and the Sexual Division of Labour*. Toronto: School of Social Work, Atkinson College, York University, 1988.

Leckie, Norm. *The Declining Middle and Technological Change: Trends in the Distribution of Employment Income in Canada, 1971-84*. Discussion Paper, no. 342. Ottawa: Economic Council of Canada, 1988.

Lefkowitz, Rochelle and Ann Withorn, ed. *For Crying Out Loud*. New York: Pilgrim Press, 1986.

Leman, Christopher. *The Collapse of Welfare Reform: Political Institutions, Policy, and the Poor in Canada and the United States*. Cambridge, Mass.: MIT Press, 1980.

Levitan, Sar A. and Isaac Shapiro. *Working But Poor*. Baltimore: Johns Hopkins University Press, 1987.

Levitan, Sar A. and Robert Taggart. "The Bitter Fruits of Labor: Hardship Among the Working Poor and the Unemployed is Worse Than the Jobless Statistics Suggest (United States)". *Challenge*, vol. 26, March-April 1983.

Love, Roger. "A Note on the Measurement of Poverty in Canada". *Canadian Statistical Review*, June 1984.

Luxton, Meg. *More Than a Labour of Love: Three Generations of Women's Work in the Home*. Toronto: Women's Educational Press, 1980.

MacLeod, Greg. *New Age Business: Community Corporations that Work*. Ottawa: Canadian Council on Social Development, 1986.

Macmillan, Katie. *Free Trade and Canadian Women: An Opportunity for a Better Future*. Ottawa: Canadian Advisory Council on the Status of Women, 1987.

Magun, Sunder et al. *Open Borders: An Assessment of the Canada-U.S. Free Trade Agreement.* Ottawa: Economic Council of Canada, 1988.

Marchak, Patricia. "Rational Capitalism and Women as Labour". In *Feminism and Political Economy: Women's Work and Women's Struggles.* Ed. Heather Jon Maroney and Meg Luxton. Toronto: Methuen, 1987.

Maroney, Heather Jon and Meg Luxton. "From Feminism and Political Economy to Feminist Political Economy". In *Feminism and Political Economy.* Ed. Heather Jon Maroney and Meg Luxton. Toronto: Methuen, 1987.

Martin, Andrew. "The Politics of Employment and Welfare: National Policies and International Interdependence". In *The State and Economic Interests.* Ed. Keith Banting. Toronto: University of Toronto Press, 1986.

McDowell, Ian and Ed Praught. *Report of the Canadian Health and Disability Survey, 1983-1984.* Ottawa: Statistics Canada, 1986.

McLanahan, Sara. "Family Structure and the Reproduction of Poverty". *American Journal of Sociology,* vol. 90, no. 4, 1985.

McQuillan, Kevin. "Family Change and Family Income in Ontario: Some Recent Trends". *Discussion Paper.* Toronto: Child, Youth and Family Policy Research Centre, 1989.

Meissner, M.; E. Humphreys; S. Meis; and W. Scheu. "No Exit for Wives: Serial Division of Labour and the Cumulation of Household Demands". *Canadian Review of Sociology and Anthropology,* vol. 12, no. 4, 1975.

Mellow, Wesley. "Determinants of Health Insurance and Pension Coverage". *Monthly Labor Review,* vol. 105, no. 2, 1982.

Mendelson, Michael. "Rationalization of Income Security in Canada". In *Ottawa and the Provinces: The Distribution of Money and Power.* Special Research Report, vol. 1. Ed. Thomas J. Courchene, David W. Conklin, and Gail C.A. Cook. Toronto: Ontario Economic Council, 1985.

Mercier, Jacques. "Les effets du salaire minimum sur l'emploi des jeunes au Québec". *Relations Industrielles,* vol. 40, no. 3, 1985.

Merrilees, William. "Labour Market Segmentation in Canada: An Econometric Approach". *Canadian Journal of Economics,* vol. 15, no. 3, 1982.

Metcalf, Charles. "The Size Distribution of Personal Income During the Business Cycle". *American Economic Review,* vol. 59, no. 4, 1969.

Miller, Dorothy C. "Feminist Theory and Social Policy or Why Is Welfare So Hard to Reform?". *Journal of Sociology and Social Welfare,* vol. 12, no. 4, 1985.

Mincer, Jacob. "Intercountry Comparisons of Labor Force Trends and Related Developments: An Overview". *Journal of Labor Economics*, vol. 3, no. 1 supplement, 1985.

Mincer, Jacob. *Schooling, Experience and Earnings*. New York: Columbia University Press, 1974.

Mirer, Thad. "The Effects of Macroeconomic Fluctuations on the Distribution of Income". *Review of Income and Wealth*, vol. 19, no. 4, 1973.

Monica Townson Associates. *Leave for Employees With Family Responsibilities*. Ottawa: Labour Canada, Women's Bureau, 1988.

Moore, Maureen. "Women Parenting Alone". *Canadian Social Trends*, Winter 1987.

Moore, Robert. "Are Male/Female Earnings Differentials Related to Life-Expectancy-Caused Pension Cost Differentials?". *Economic Inquiry*, vol. 25, no. 3, 1987.

Morgan, Nicole. *The Equality Game: Women in the Federal Public Service (1908-1987)*. Ottawa: Canadian Advisory Council on the Status of Women, 1988.

Mossman, Mary Jane and Morag MacLean. "Family Law and Social Welfare: Toward a New Equality". *Canadian Journal of Family Law*, vol. 5, no. 1, 1986.

Moy, Joyanna. "An Analysis of Unemployment and Other Labor Market Indicators in 10 Countries". *Monthly Labor Review*, vol. III, no. 4, 1988.

Moynihan, Daniel Patrick. *The Negro Family: The Case for National Action*. Washington, D.C.: U.S. Department of Labor, Office of Family Planning and Research, 1965.

Murray, Charles. "In Search of the Working Poor". *The Public Interest*, no. 89, 1987.

Muszynski, Leon. *Is It Fair? What Tax Reform Will Do To You*. Ottawa: Canadian Centre For Policy Alternatives and National Working Group on the Economy and Poverty, United Church of Canada, 1988.

Muszynski, Leon. "Manufacturing Matters! And So Does the Welfare State". In *Manufacturing Matters: Conference Proceedings and Research Papers*. Toronto: Industrial Development Institute, 1989.

Muszynski, Leon. "The Politics of Labour Market Policy". In *The Politics of Economic Policy*. Ed. Bruce Doern. Toronto: University of Toronto Press, 1985.

Muszynski, Leon and David Wolfe. "New Technology and Training: Lessons from Abroad", *Canadian Public Policy*, September 1989.

Myles, John. *The Expanding Middle: Some Canadian Evidence on the Deskilling Debate.* Ottawa: Statistics Canada and Carleton University, 1987.

Myles, John; G.W. Picot; and Ted Wannell. *Wages and Jobs in the 1980s: Changing Youth Wages and the Declining Middle.* Ottawa: Statistics Canada, 1988.

Nakamura, Alice and Masao Nakamura. "A Survey of Research on the Work Behaviour of Canadian Women". In *Work and Pay: The Canadian Labour Market.* Ed. W. Craig Riddell. Toronto: University of Toronto Press, 1985.

National Council of Welfare. *Better Pensions for Homemakers.* Ottawa: 1984.

National Council of Welfare. *Child Care: A Better Alternative.* Ottawa: 1988.

National Council of Welfare. *Jobs and Poverty: A Report by the National Council of Welfare on Canada's Working Poor.* Ottawa: 1977.

National Council of Welfare. *Poor Kids: A Report by the National Council of Welfare on Children in Poverty in Canada.* Ottawa: 1975.

National Council of Welfare. *Poverty Profile 1988.* Ottawa: 1988.

National Council of Welfare. *Welfare In Canada: The Tangled Safety Net.* Ottawa: 1987.

National Council of Welfare. *Women and Poverty.* Ottawa: 1979.

National Council of Welfare. *The Working Poor — A Statistical Profile.* Ottawa: 1977.

Newfoundland. Royal Commission on Employment and Unemployment. *Building on Our Strengths. Report of the Royal Commission on Employment and Unemployment.* St. John's: 1986.

Oakley, Ann. "For Love or Money — The Unspoken Deal". *New Society,* vol. 54, December 1980.

Ontario. Attorney General and Minister Responsible for Women's Issues. *Green Paper on Pay Equity.* Toronto: 1985.

Ontario. Ministry of Community and Social Services. Social Assistance Review Committee. *Transitions.* Toronto: 1988.

Ontario. Ministry of Skills Development. *Discussion Paper on The Canadian Jobs Strategy: Policy and Implementation.* Toronto: 1987.

O'Rand, Angela and J. Henretta. "Delayed Career Entry, Industrial Pension Structure and Early Retirement in a Cohort of Unmarried Women". *American Sociological Review,* vol. 47, no. 3, 1982.

Osberg, Lars. *The Future of Work in Canada: Trends, Issues and Forces for Change.* Ottawa: Canadian Council on Social Development, 1988.

Osberg, Lars. "Unemployment Insurance in Canada: A Review of Recent Amendments". *Canadian Public Policy*, vol. 5, no. 2, Spring 1979.

Osberg, Lars; R. Muzany; Richard Apostle; and Don Clairmont. "Job Mobility, Wage Determination and Market Segmentation in the Presence of Sample Selection Bias". *Canadian Journal of Economics*, vol. 19, no. 2, 1986.

Pahl, Jan. "The Allocation of Money and the Structuring of Inequality Within Marriage". *Sociological Review*, vol. 31, no. 2, 1983.

Pahl, Jan. "Patterns of Money Management within Marriage". *Journal of Social Policy*, vol. 9, no. 3, 1980.

Paltiel, Freda. "Women and Pensions In Canada". *International Social Security Review*, vol. 35, no. 3, 1980.

Panitch, Leo and Donald Swartz. *The Assault on Trade Union Freedoms: From Consent to Coercion Revisited.* Toronto: Garamond Press, 1988.

Pearce, Diana. "The Feminization of Poverty: Women, Work, and Welfare". *Urban and Social Change Review*, vol. 2, no. 1 & 2, 1978.

Pearson, Mary. *Women and Work: The Second Time Around: A Study of Women Returning to the Workforce.* Ottawa: Canadian Advisory Council on the Status of Women, 1979.

Perron, Pierre and François Vaillancourt. *The Evolution of Poverty in Canada, 1970-1985.* Ottawa: Economic Council of Canada, 1988.

Pesando, James and Morley Gunderson. "Retirement Incentives Contained in Occupational Pension Plans and their Implications for the Mandatory Retirement Debate". *Canadian Journal of Economics*, vol. 21, no. 2, 1988.

Pesando, James; Morley Gunderson; and John McLaren. "Pension Benefits and Male-Female Wage Differences: A Canadian Perspective". Toronto, University of Toronto, 1988, mimeo.

Peterson, Janice. "The Feminization of Poverty". *Journal of Economic Issues*, vol. 21, no. 1, 1987.

Piven, Frances Fox and Richard Cloward. "The Contemporary Relief Debate". In *The Mean Season: The Attack on the Welfare State.* New York: Pantheon, 1987.

Pleck, Joseph H. *Working Wives, Working Husbands.* Beverly Hills, Calif.: Sage, 1985.

Porter, Ann and Barbara Cameron. *The Impact of Free Trade on Women in Manufacturing.* Ottawa: Canadian Advisory Council on the Status of Women, 1987.

Prager, Carol A.L.. "Poverty in North America: Losing Ground". *Canadian Public Policy*, vol. 14, no. 1, March 1988.

Robb, Roberta Edgecombe and Morley Gunderson. *Women and Overtime.* Toronto: Ontario Task Force on Hours of Work and Overtime, 1987.

Robins, Philip K. "Child Support, Welfare Dependency, and Poverty". *The American Economic Review,* vol. 76, no. 4, September 1986.

Rodgers, Harrell R., Jr. *Poor Women, Poor Families: The Economic Plight of America's Female-Headed Households.* Armonk/London: M.E. Sharpe, 1986.

Ross, David. "Local Economic Initiatives: An Overview". In *Policies for Full Employment.* Ed. Duncan Cameron and Andrew Sharpe. Ottawa: Canadian Council on Social Development, 1988.

Ross, David. "Report on the Income Security System In Newfoundland". Background report for the Royal Commission on Employment and Unemployment. St. John's: September 1986.

Ross, David; Peter Usher; and George McRobie. *From the Roots Up: Economic Development as if the Community Mattered.* Croton-on-Hudson, N.Y./Ottawa: Bootstrap Press/Vanier Institute of the Family, 1986.

Rowley, Susannah. "Women, Pensions and Equality." In *CharterWatch: Reflections on Equality.* Ed. Christine Boyle et al. Toronto: Carswell, 1986.

Sarvasy, Wendy and Judith Van Allen. "Fighting the Feminization of Poverty: Socialist-Feminist Analysis and Strategy". *Review of Radical Political Economics,* vol. 16, no. 4, 1984.

Sawhill, Isabel V. "Poverty in the U.S.: Why Is It So Persistent?". *Journal of Economic Literature,* vol. 27, no. 3, September 1988.

Schaafsma, Joseph, and William Walsh. "Employment and Labour Supply Effects of the Minimum Wage". *Canadian Journal of Economics,* vol. 16, no. 1, 1983.

Schultz, Theodore, ed. "Investment In Human Beings". *Journal of Political Economy,* vol. 70, no. 5, part 2, 1962.

Scott, Hilda. *Working Your Way to the Bottom: The Feminization of Poverty.* London: Pandora Press, 1984.

Sharzer, Stephen. "Native People: Some Issues". In *Equality In Employment: Research Studies of the Commission on Equality In Employment.* Ottawa: Supply and Services Canada, 1985.

Shaw, R. Paul and Norman Paterson. "The Burden of Unemployment in Canada". *Canadian Public Policy,* vol. 11, no. 2, 1985.

Simpson, Wayne. "Analysis of Part-time Pay in Canada". *Canadian Journal of Economics,* vol. 19, no. 4 (1986).

Simpson, Wayne. "The Impact of Unions on the Structure of Canadian Wages: an Empirical Analysis with Microdata". *Canadian Journal of Economics*, vol. 18, no. 1, 1985.

Smith, Joan. "The Paradox of Women's Poverty: Wage-Earning Women and Economic Transformation". *Signs*, vol. 10, no. 2, 1984.

Strong-Boag, Veronica. "Discovering the Home: The Last 150 Years of Domestic Work in Canada". In *Women's Paid and Unpaid Work: Historical and Contemporary Perspectives*. Ed. Paula Bourne. Toronto: New Hogtown Press, 1985.

Swidinsky, Robert. "Minimum Wage and Teenage Unemployment". *Canadian Journal of Economics*, vol. 13, no. 1, 1980.

Swidinsky, Robert. "Working Wives, Income Distribution and Poverty". *Canadian Public Policy*, vol. 9, no. 1, March 1983.

Taggart, Robert. *Hardship: The Welfare Consequences of Labor Market Problems: A Policy Discussion Paper*. Kalamazoo, Michigan: W.E. Upjohn Institute For Employment Research, 1982.

Therborn, Goran. *Why Some People Are More Unemployed Than Others: The Strange Paradox of Growth and Unemployment*. London: Verso, 1986.

Thornley, David. "Minimum Wages and Adequate Income". *Social Infopac* (Social Planning Council of Metropolitan Toronto), vol. 6, no. 1, 1987.

Toronto. Social Planning Council of Metropolitan Toronto. *Living on the Margin*. Toronto: October 1986.

Toronto. Social Planning Council of Metropolitan Toronto. "Welfare Rates: An Inter-provincial Comparison". *Social Infopac*, vol. 5, no. 1, 1986.

Townson, Monica. *Domestic Workers and the Employment Standards Act*. Toronto: Ontario Task Force on Hours of Work and Overtime, 1987.

Townson, Monica. *Women's Labour Force Participation, Fertility Rates, and the Implications for Economic Development and Government Policy*. Ottawa: Institute for Research on Public Policy, 1987.

Treiman, Donald and Heidi Hartmann. *Women, Work and Wages*. Washington, D.C.: National Academy Press, 1981.

Vaillancourt, François. "Income Distribution and Economic Security In Canada: An Overview". In *Income Distribution and Economic Security In Canada*. Ed. François Vaillancourt. Toronto: University of Toronto Press, 1985.

Waring, Marilyn. *If Women Counted: A New Feminist Economics*. San Francisco: Harper & Row, 1988.

West, Edwin and Michael McKee. *Minimum Wages: The New Issues In Theory, Evidence, Policy and Politics.* Ottawa: Economic Council of Canada and Institute for Research on Public Policy, 1980.

White, Julie. *Women and Unions.* Ottawa: Canadian Advisory Council on the Status of Women, 1980.

White, Pamela. *Native Women: A Statistical Overview.* Ottawa: Department of the Secretary of State of Canada, 1985.

Wismer, Susan. *Women's Education and Training In Canada: A Policy Analysis.* Toronto: Canadian Congress for Learning Opportunities for Women, 1988.

Wolfson, Michael. "A Guaranteed Income". *Policy Options,* vol. 7, no. 1, January/February 1986.

Wong, Fred. "Trends in Labour Income". In *Employment, Earnings and Hours.* Ottawa: Statistics Canada, July 1988, cat. no. 72-002.

Wonnacott, Ronald and Roderick Hill. *Canadian and U.S. Adjustment Policies in a Bilateral Trade Agreement.* Toronto: C.D. Howe Institute, 1987.

Woodley, Olive Lumley. "The Case for a Guaranteed Annual Income". *Policy Options,* vol. 10, no. 2, March 1989.

Zabalza, Anton and Zafris Tzannatos. *Women and Equal Pay: The Effect of Legislation on Female Wages and Employment.* Cambridge: Cambridge University Press, 1985.

Zaretsky, Eli. "Rethinking the Welfare State: Dependence, Economic Individualism and the Family". In *Family, Economy and State.* Ed. James Dickinson and Bob Russell. Toronto: Garamond Press, 1986.

The Canadian Advisory Council on the Status of Women was established as an independent advisory body in 1973 in response to a recommendation by the Royal Commission on the Status of Women. Its mandate, "to bring before the government and the public matters of interest and concern to women" and "to advise the Minister on such matters relating to the status of women as the Minister may refer to the Council for its consideration or as the Council may deem appropriate", is wide and may be interpreted to cover all Council activities on behalf of women in Canada.

The following were members of the Canadian Advisory Council on the Status of Women at the time of publication: